SUPPER WITH THE CRIPPENS

SUPPER WITH
THE CRIPPENS

DAVID JAMES SMITH

ORION

First published in Great Britain in 2005
by Orion Books, a division of
the Orion Publishing Group Ltd
Orion House
5 Upper Saint Martin's Lane
London
WC2H 9EA

A CIP catalogue record for this book is available
from the British Library

ISBN 0 75286742 3

Typeset by Deltatype Ltd, Birkenhead, Merseyside
Printed in Great Britain by Clays Ltd, St Ives plc

www.orionbooks.co.uk

For my parents, celebrating fifty years of marriage

LIST OF ILLUSTRATIONS

39 Hilldrop Crescent (Public Record Office Image Library)
Basement of the house (PRO)
Remains of Belle Elmore (PRO)
Police team, led by Chief Inspector Walter Dew (PRO)
Wanted poster (National Archives Image Library)
Belle Elmore (Mirrorpix)
Dr Hawley Harvey Crippen (Mirrorpix)
Ethel Le Neve in disguise (Mirrorpix)
SS *Montrose* and Commander Harry Kendall (Topfoto)
Detective Sergeant Mitchell with two Holloway Prison
  wardresses (Mirrorpix)
Crippen arrives in Liverpool after his arrest (Mirrorpix)
Crippen and Le Neve (M. Tussaud's)
Old Bailey, first day of Crippen's trial (Getty Images)
Crippen in the dock (Mirrorpix)
Ethel Le Neve (Mirrorpix)

Ethel's parents (courtesy Author)
Ethel's sister Adine (courtesy Roger Palmer)
Ethel in *Lloyd's Weekly News*
Adine Brock (courtesy Roger Palmer)
Adine's children (courtesy Roger Palmer)
Ivy and Jack Palmer with their son (courtesy Roger Palmer)
Ethel Smith with friends Rex and Ada Manning (courtesy
  David Gainsborough Roberts)
Crippen's American Waltham pocket watch (courtesy David
  Gainsborough Roberts)
Nevé Family photograph, circa 1949 (courtesy Roger Palmer)
Prescription and letter (courtesy David Gainsborough
  Roberts)

ONE

On 29 December 1922, A.J. Wall, Secretary of the Prison Commission, Home Office, Whitehall, SW1 issued Circular No. 1027 to Pentonville Prison. The Commissioners had decided that the graves of persons who had been executed in prison should no longer be distinguished by names, initials, or any other marks on the walls. 'Such records are undesirable,' explained Secretary Wall, 'as they perpetuate the memory of the crime, cause unnecessary pain to the relatives and rouse a morbid interest in the prisoners.'

It had been decided to obliterate all existing marks, but before this could be done it was necessary to prepare records of existing graves. 'The Register of Graves will be kept on the enclosed form (forwarded in duplicate) and the enclosed plan, a duplicate of the latter having been retained in this office.'

Executions had been conducted at Pentonville since 1902, when it took over the role from Newgate Prison, which had been closed and demolished to make way for the construction of a new Central Criminal Court at the Old Bailey. The apparatus of the scaffold – beam, cantilevered trap-doors, lever – had been transported across to Pentonville from Newgate and installed in a purpose-built facility in the exercise yard just outside B wing, which promptly became known to all who worked or were imprisoned there as the topping shed.

In later years the scaffold would be taken into the main building of the prison and the site would be turned over to latrines, but this would not affect the small burial ground of eighteen graves which had been next to the topping shed and was separate from the main cemetery where all the executed were buried from 1911 onwards, sometimes three-deep in graves, one on top of the other on top of the other, all in strict accordance with another detailed, albeit unnumbered, circular:

INSTRUCTIONS TO BE OBSERVED IN BURYING THE BODIES OF EXECUTED PRISONERS

1 All the clothing, with the exception of the shirt or similar garment, will be removed from the body, which will be placed in a coffin made of $\frac{1}{2}$ inch wood, deal or pine.
2 The sides and ends of the coffin will be well perforated with large holes.
3 Lime will not be used.
4 The original size of the plot of ground will be 9 feet by 4 feet, and the grave will be from 8 to 10 feet in depth.
5 When the coffin has been covered with 1 foot of earth, charcoal to the depth of 3 inches will be thrown into the grave, which will then be filled in. The top coffin will not be less than 4 feet below the ground surface.
6 Arrangements will be made for the grave sites to be re-used in sequence, in such wise that no grave shall be used over again until 7 years have elapsed. When a grave is re-opened the charcoal and the foot of earth above the last coffin will not be disturbed.
7 A register of graves will be kept, containing the name of each convict buried, the date of burial, the site of the grave, and the position of the coffin in the grave.

The last execution in 1961, of Edwin Bush, aged twenty-one, would bring the total hanged at Pentonville to 120, comprising 112 convicted of murder and eight others (among them R.D. Casement, 03.08.16) convicted of assorted acts of treachery. They were registered in chronological order, so that the small burial ground simply became the last resting place of the first eighteen who were hanged in the topping shed, listed from number 1, J. McDonald, in 1902 through to number 18, M. Collins, in 1911.

Someone, perhaps a prisoner, later planted a single rose tree at this burial site and it was transformed into a more pleasing feature of the exercise yard between B wing and the prison hospital. The location of the rose tree became known as Crippen's Corner and not even Circular No. 1027 could prevent this enduring association with the occupant of plot 16. Even now, when the tree has long gone and the site has been covered with concrete for recent building works, there are old maps in the prison where Crippen's Corner is identified and the name continues to be remembered by long-serving staff.

Hawley Harvey Crippen has been buried there for ninety-five years and there, beneath the cement, he will now remain, but he also spent thirty-two nights alive in the prison, in the condemned cell on permanent 'execution watch', from late in the afternoon of Saturday, 22 October 1910, when he was transferred straight to Pentonville (he had previously been held on remand at Brixton) after being convicted and sentenced to death at the Old Bailey, until 9 am on 23 November 1910, when the sentence was carried out.

Crippen never spoke to his executioner, John Ellis, and only saw him fleetingly, at the last. Ellis, who was then in his mid-thirties, was every bit as meticulous in his attention to detail as those circular-writing civil servants at the Prison Commission. He was well known for his anxious fussing and this was often a source of irritation to his assistant executioners, such as William Willis, who was with Ellis when he arrived at Pentonville on the eve of Crippen's execution, in the late afternoon of 22 November, the pair having caught the first train down from Liverpool after hanging Henry Thompson, a sailor aged fifty-four, at Walton Prison.

Like Crippen, Thompson had killed his wife. Unlike Crippen, he had been too drunk to try and disguise the fact. Thompson had strangled Mary after coming home from a night's drinking. He had laid her out on the bed next to him, placed a handkerchief over her face and fallen asleep next to her; and that was how the couple were found next morning. On being asked by the judge after conviction if he had any words for the court, Thompson was reported to have replied, 'No, I've nothing to say. Sentence away and be done with it.'

He had apparently told friends that he had been miserable with his wife and was certain he could be no more miserable in the next world.

Just before he was hanged Thompson found out that Crippen – the more famous wife-killer – was next in line for the scaffold. Thompson said, 'I'll be waiting to sing for him.' Then, turning to the governor of Walton Prison, he added, 'And I'll sing for you too when your time comes.'

Ellis found a crowd outside Pentonville when he arrived at around 4 pm. Crowds had pursued the Crippen case from the beginning, gathering first outside his home, 39 Hilldrop Crescent in Camden, following the discovery there of human remains and later at every moment of drama or potential opportunity of glimpsing the man himself or his co-accused, Ethel Le Neve. Many hundreds of people had jostled on the quayside at Liverpool docks, and booed and jeered the couple's return to England after their arrest in Canada back in August. Hundreds more had been waiting for them at Euston when they arrived there a few hours later on the train and again had booed and jeered as the police steered them into waiting taxis. Another crowd had been waiting at Bow Street Police Station for a final boo and a jeer and a craning of necks when the taxis passed through the entrance.

Each court appearance since had been much the same and even now, outside Pentonville, with no prospect whatsoever of seeing what was going on, the crowd stood in a quiet vigil, in anticipation of tomorrow's execution. This was public theatre that had engaged a mass audience on an unprecedented scale.

Ellis was already fed up with the case. He would later say that it was the only time he ever regretted being a hangman. When he was not out on execution assignments he worked in the barber's shop he had opened on Oldham Road in Rochdale. Ever since he had been named as the man who would hang Crippen, the barber's had been crowded with customers who, it seemed to Ellis, didn't really want haircuts at all, but simply wanted to talk to him about the case, or point him out: 'There's the man who's going to hang Crippen!' Ellis resented being endowed, as he put it, with this unpleasant notoriety, which far exceeded anything else he would experience in his career tally of 203 executions.

Inside Pentonville he proceeded with what he would call the usual formalities. He discussed the hanging with prison officials and especially the under sheriff, who advised on a suitable length of rope for the drop. There was a formal Table of Drops, which calculated and set out the appropriate length according to the weight of the condemned prisoner. The scaffold was built over a pit that was twelve feet deep to allow for the longest of drops. The pit was a handy place to park a prison van when it was not in use.

The drop had to be just long enough so that Crippen's neck would be broken neatly and instantly at the bottom of the fall, but not so long that he would be decapitated and not so short that his neck would fail to fracture and instead he would choke slowly. Crippen had been weighed that day at 142 pounds (he had put on six pounds since he was first admitted). The under sheriff had recommended a drop of not less than seven feet six inches, but the final word was with Ellis and he liked to observe his subject before he made the decision.

Ellis peered in through a peephole in the door of the condemned cell and saw Crippen sitting at a table writing, stopping occasionally to chat pleasantly with his two warders. Ellis was struck by his calm demeanour. He noted too that Crippen's neck appeared normal and would not require any special adjustment to the noose. Ellis spoke of men as he found them and could only say, based on his, admittedly, extremely limited contact, that even in the hideous clothes of a convict Crippen had a natural amiability and innate gentlemanliness that endeared him even to his warders. He came across to Ellis as a most pleasant fellow.

Only yesterday, while alone in the toilet, Crippen had broken the frame of his gold-rimmed spectacles and removed the glass lens with the apparent intention of opening a vein to avoid being hanged. Preventing suicide and ensuring that Crippen would be subjected to the full majesty of the law had been uppermost in the authorities' minds since his arrest. The Home Secretary, Winston Churchill, had issued personal instructions that Crippen should be watched constantly and not given any opportunity to evade justice. The ruse with the glasses had quickly been discovered and there was nothing else, now, that Crippen could do, except continue to be calm and pleasant, as everyone who ever encountered him, almost without exception, always said he was.

He only cried once in the hours before his death, after being shown the final telegram from Ethel Le Neve: 'My living thoughts and prayers are with you. God bless you darling. Signed, wifey.' These had long been their affectionate names for each other: hub and wifey.

When he turned away from the peephole Ellis decided to go three inches further than the under sheriff and selected a drop of seven feet nine inches. He went to the scaffold and measured off the rope, then, as usual, attached a heavy sandbag to the rope, pulled the lever and dropped it, as if it were a body, where it remained hanging overnight to stretch the rope ahead of the execution and ensure that there would be no stretching at the actual execution which might cause a disastrous alteration of the calculations.

Both men – the murderer and his executioner – were up early on the morning of 23 November. Ellis woke at 6.30 and went to check that everything was in working order. He detached the sandbag and coiled the length of rope over the beam, leaving just the noose dangling over the trap-doors. He gave some thought to a change of procedure he was about to initiate, after discussing the hanging with the chief warder of Pentonville the night before.

Crippen was allowed to be executed in his own clothes. He dressed in his trademark grey frock coat and a shirt – albeit with no collar. He spent some time in the chapel, alone with the warders and the Roman Catholic Prison Chaplain, Thomas Carey, who was the Parish Priest of the nearby Church of the Sacred Heart of Jesus. Crippen had been converted to Catholicism by the wife he had killed, Belle

Elmore. Neighbours often used to see them setting off for church on Sunday mornings, all dressed up.

Belle had not been seen alive since the early hours of 1 February 1910, when she and Crippen said goodbye to their music-hall friends, Paul and Clara Martinetti, as they departed by taxi following supper at 39 Hilldrop Crescent. Crippen still maintained that she was in America, or somewhere. He couldn't say for sure, even though his life depended on it. Letters addressed to Churchill and others had been arriving at the Home Office in the last few days alleging recent sightings of Belle, or even claiming to have been written by Belle herself. The Home Office had not taken these very seriously.

After leaving the chapel Crippen sat down to breakfast but did not eat much. He sat in the corner of the condemned cell with his warders and the chaplain, talking quietly. At just before 9 o'clock the execution party gathered outside the cell door. The under sheriff nodded and it began, Ellis entering first with his assistant, Willis, just behind him. Ellis was momentarily thrown by the obstacle of some tables and chairs which he had to move to one side before he could reach Crippen.

Without speaking, Crippen stood and allowed his arms to be taken by Ellis and secured behind his back with the heavy leather strap and buckle designed for that purpose. Even without his linen collar, Ellis thought Crippen appeared smart and dapper. He hadn't shaved, but still looked fresher than many condemned men Ellis had seen. Now came Ellis's change of procedure. Instead of walking to the scaffold behind the condemned man, as he had always done in the past, Ellis hurried ahead so that he was there waiting when Crippen arrived. It cut down on the shuffling and confusion that sometimes occurred on the scaffold. No doubt the chief warder who had suggested it was trying to hasten the end of the ordeal and reduce the suffering of Crippen, and maybe that of everyone else in attendance too.

Ellis watched the procession come towards him from a short distance, just under forty feet. The priest led the way, praying.

Ellis saw a smile on Crippen's face then, and it was still there when Ellis placed the white hood over his head, while his assistant buckled Crippen's legs together with the other leather strap. They stepped back, Ellis threw the lever and the trap-doors fell open and Crippen dropped.

'Thud!' – as Ellis would describe it, exclamation mark and all, in his memoirs, under the chapter heading, 'Dr Crippen dies with a smile'. By Ellis's proud calculations, it was exactly one minute from the moment he first entered the cell until Crippen was killed. His constant aim was to try and smooth the process and reduce the time.

In accordance with the regulations for the conduct of executions, Crippen was left hanging for precisely one hour, after which he was lowered and a post-mortem carried out in the nearby prison mortuary. The doctor was unhappy with the extent of the damage to Crippen's neck and, blaming it on the excessive drop, complained to Ellis, who shrugged and said that so far as he was concerned it was a good thing as it confirmed that Crippen had died instantly.

The doctor made an oblique note of his displeasure in the logbook, *Record of an Execution*, which was kept at the prison in the governor's office. In the box headed 'Approximate statement of the character and amount of destruction to the soft and bony structures of the neck' he wrote: 'No destruction of soft parts. Cervical vertebrae about third was broken and distinct interval between bony structure.' His comments hinted at an excess of breaks and excessive stretching of the neck, a clear criticism of the executioner.

Ellis had no time to dwell on such details. Not right now, anyway. He said he was never troubled by the nature of his work. He had another train to catch, for an appointment the next morning at Reading Jail with William Broome, aged twenty-six, who had suffocated an elderly woman in Slough. He was pleased with the effectiveness of his new procedure and had already resolved to adopt it at all his future executions.

It must have been much later, following his retirement, that John Ellis stopped to reflect. He first attempted suicide (he tried to shoot himself, but missed and was slightly injured instead) in 1924 just a few months after his last execution. It was against the law to kill yourself in those days and Ellis was brought before Rochdale magistrates, where the chairman of the bench said, 'I am very sorry to see you here, Ellis. If your aim had been as straight as the drops you have given it would have been a bad job for you.'

The case was reported in the newspapers and seen by Tom Pierrepoint, of that well-known dynasty of executioners, who said to his nephew Albert, 'Bloody hell, Ellis has tried to commit suicide. He should have done it years ago, it was impossible to work with him.' Ellis evidently suffered from undiagnosed depression for most of the rest of his life, until early one Tuesday evening in September 1932 he chased his wife and daughter from his home with a cut-throat razor, shouting, 'I'll cut your heads off' and then stood at the front door and drew the razor across his own throat, twice, after which he collapsed and died.

As he left Pentonville en route to Reading, Ellis passed the bigger crowd which was now gathered, admiring their resilience on such a cold, foggy morning. He knew that they had even been denied the usual tolling of a bell to confirm that an execution had been carried out. The bell had been silenced as a courtesy to the three other men who were awaiting execution at the prison. In the event, two would be reprieved and only Noah Woolf would be hanged (by the Ellis/Willis team) on 21 December. He was fifty-eight and had stabbed another man at a home for the elderly in Upper Holloway.

Still, the crowd was satisfied eventually by the appearance of a notice of execution on the prison gates. Perhaps it was a copy of the notice which the Governor, Major Mytton-Davies, was obliged (under Standing Order No. 577) to forward to the Prison Commissioners, confirming that the execution had taken place: 'Gentlemen . . . I have the honour to submit . . .'

A short inquest was held at 2 pm the same day, before a jury, inside the prison's Visiting Committee rooms. The Coroner was Walter Schroder (who had some weeks earlier conducted the inquest into the death of Crippen's wife, in which that jury had returned a verdict of wilful murder against him). The sole witness was the doctor, the prison surgeon, Mr J.H.P. Wilson.

CORONER: There was no resistance?
DR: None at all, not the least.
CORONER: Nor any struggle?
DR: None. Nor was there any delay in carrying out the sentence. It took exactly sixty seconds from the time the executioners entered the condemned cell until the time of death.
CORONER: Was death instantaneous?
DR: Absolutely. There was a drop of seven feet nine inches. I have examined the body since the execution and find a fracture of the vertebrae. An absolute fracture right through.

The jury then found that the deceased was Hawley Harvey Crippen and that he had been executed properly according to law.

JURY FOREMAN: May I ask the governor of the prison if there has been a confession?
CORONER: That is not a question which concerns us.

It may not have concerned the inquest, but the question was the latest turn in public fascination with the story after publication the previous evening of an alleged full confession by Crippen in a new (and destined to be short-lived) London daily, the *Evening Times*. There would be another in that week's edition of the magazine *John Bull*, which would really incense the Home Office (its editor, after all, was a Member of Parliament) and get Crippen's solicitor, a flagrant oppor-tunist named Arthur Newton, into serious trouble with the Law Society. The Crippen case, as he had shrewdly seen from the start, had been rich pickings for Newton, in collusion with the press, but it would be his professional undoing too.

Even by today's standards of intrigue, deception and financial shenanigans in the print media, the conduct of the newspapers in pursuing Crippen and Le Neve had been rapacious. The wheelings and dealings continued unabated as his body was being stripped down to its shirt and the coffin vented and readied for plot 16. Lofty editorials in *The Times* could not loosen Crippen's grip on the imagination of post-Edwardian England – and the trail of mysteries was far from complete.

Much of the story would be hidden away in Home Office files and old police records for years to come and, given the dearth of reliable information, a number of myths and misrepresentations would arise and be perpetuated in a succession of studies of the case. It would, for example, become romantic 'fact' that Crippen had been buried with Le Neve's photograph and letters and that Le Neve herself – depicted everywhere, unbelievably, as an innocent young woman who always told the truth – had disappeared that very day, or the next, on a boat to the Americas, disguised as a Miss Allen and not returned to England for four, or even six, years. She would later supposedly turn up, in the 1930s, living in poverty in Perth, Australia.

Another 'fact', enshrined by the officer himself in repeated telling, maintained that it was Chief Inspector Dew, wielding a poker by his own hand, who first uncovered the loose bricks in the floor that led to the discovery of the remains in the coal cellar of Crippen's home.

None of these various 'facts', it turns out, and many more besides them, are quite true, and with some diligent research and access to papers now released into the public archive, it has been possible to create a completely new account of the Crippen case which bears close resemblance to what actually happened that year and afterwards.

One Tuesday, in July 1910, Mrs Clara Martinetti left the apartment she shared in the West End with her husband and took a familiar journey to their weekend home by the River

Thames at Penton Hook, Staines, which they called Clariscio Bungalow. The police had been asking more questions about that last meal at 39 Hilldrop Crescent. She had done her best to answer them but had realised afterwards that there was more to tell and decided to put something on paper, directly to Chief Inspector Dew.

Clara apologised for writing in longhand with a pencil and, although the original has not survived, it was dutifully typed up by the police and retained in their files and eventually passed, apparently unnoticed, into the public domain, in a box at the Public Records Office. 'I thought', she wrote, 'that I better write down to you the whole story from the beginning . . .' That was the the night of 31 January 1910, the night Belle disappeared, the story of *Supper with the Crippens*.

TWO

No one could later recall anything unusual about Crippen's behaviour the next day, Tuesday, 1 February 1910, even though it seems certain that he must have gone to work in the morning, more or less as usual, leaving his wife's corpse at home after killing her some hours earlier once the Martinettis had left.

The date had already acquired a significance for Crippen – possibly not unrelated to the crime – as the day he was to be replaced as the manager of Munyon's Homoeopathic Remedy Company for whom he had begun work fifteen years earlier, while still in the United States. He had come to England to launch the London office over a decade ago but his relationship with the firm had changed over the years as he had fallen in and out of favour with its founder, James Munroe Munyon – Professor Munyon, as he preferred to be known.

Crippen's business affairs and various medical endeavours were complex, and even though he had just finished at Munyon's he still went to the same suite of offices to work, having begun a partnership there with a young New Zealand dentist, Dr Gilbert Rylance, known as Crippen & Rylance, artificial teeth manufacturers, and also as Yale Tooth Specialists.

At about midday he must have left the offices, Rooms 57-61, on the third floor of Albion House, New Oxford Street, and walked the short distance to the Martinettis' mansion block at the top of Shaftesbury Avenue. Clara answered the door and welcomed him in. Crippen said he had come to see how Paul was. Clara's husband had an ongoing illness and had become unwell the night before, during supper. Clara told Crippen she had rubbed Paul's chest when they got home the previous night and had given him a hot drink.

That tenderness between a husband and wife was in sharp

contrast to what must have been going on at 39 Hilldrop Crescent.

'If you don't mind, Peter,' said Clara, 'Paul is fast asleep just now and I don't care to wake him up.' Crippen was known to his wife and all their mutual friends, for no obvious reason, as Peter. Perhaps his wife had taken against the name Hawley, and the name Harvey. He waved his hand and said, 'No, no, don't wake him up. I am glad he is not worse.' Crippen turned to leave the apartment and Clara opened the door to let him out.

'And how is Belle?' she asked as he was going.

'Oh, she is all right,' Crippen replied.

'Give her my love, will you?'

'Yes, I will.'

There was no mention of Belle going away.

Clara would have expected to see Belle the next day, at the regular Wednesday afternoon meetings of the Music Hall Ladies Guild. Both Clara and Belle were on the committee, and it was Belle who had introduced Clara to the Guild eighteen months before, soon after they had met. Belle had just become the Guild's honorary treasurer, and was already trusted and admired as a hard-working fund-raiser. The Guild had been formed to support the poorer women and children of the music-hall profession. It was still a relatively new organisation and keen to promote its activities in the trade papers, such as the *Music Hall and Theatre Review:* 'Friends of the charity are heartily welcome to tea and reception held every Wednesday four to five o'clock. Funds, boots and clothing are urgently needed . . . Secretary, Melinda May.' The receptions evidently followed the committee meetings at which the business of the week was conducted.

The Guild was based in room 63 at Albion House, right next door to Crippen's enterprises. Belle must have recommended the location. All the committee knew Peter anyway – they shared a social life together, his calm and quiet manner a foil to Belle's extravagant personality. They liked and respected him as the perfect, if not the most attractive, husband and could see no cracks in the surface of the

Crippens' marriage. Obviously, they had missed the fact that he was having an affair with his secretary.

According to Ethel Le Neve, she found the letters on her desk when she arrived for work on the morning of Wednesday, 2 February. Le Neve's role in Crippen's life was ambiguous, in all ways, at this stage. She would call herself his private secretary, that indispensible functionary who was fast becoming a symbol of the metropolitan age, amid the rise of the new secretarial class. In the chilly descriptions of others around them, who were less enamoured of her than Crippen, she was variously the typist, the little typist, the lady typist, or the typewriter, as she had been when she first met Crippen around 1901.

When Le Neve told – sold! – her story to the papers just before the execution she presented a self-serving narrative of her life with Crippen. There were many lies, but there is no reason to suppose this part of it is anything but true. In any case, it's all there is of her, other than a brief police statement. She never gave evidence in court and never talked or gave interviews other than this one serialisation in *Lloyd's Weekly News*, which was published soon afterwards as a short book. What she knew, and when she knew it, is the critical issue to be kept in mind as events progress.

There was, she said, a note with the letters, a note from Crippen that was addressed to her: 'Belle Elmore has gone to America. Will you kindly favour me by handing the enclosed packet and letters to Miss May as soon as she arrives at her office, with my compliments? Shall be in later when we can arrange a pleasant little evening.'

Of Crippen himself there was no sign. Le Neve says she assumed he had gone to his other business at Craven House on Kingsway, the new thoroughfare running south of Holborn, not far from Albion House. Maybe he was at Craven House. Or maybe, as the rest of the Guild committee gathered that Wednesday afternoon, he was at home working on the disposal of his wife's body.

Melinda May had no sooner arrived at the Guild's office,

just before one o'clock, than Le Neve appeared at the door. 'I think these are yours,' she said. The packet contained the Guild's pass-book and paying-in book, which Belle had held as treasurer. There was one letter addressed to the committee and one to Melinda May herself. Both letters were written in longhand by Crippen. Both were signed in Belle's name in Crippen's hand but the letter to Miss May at least acknowledged the deceit with a 'pp H.H.C'.

39 Hilldrop Crescent, N.
Feb. 2/10

Dear Miss May,

Illness of a near relative has called me to America on only a few hours notice, so I must ask you [sic] bring my resignation as treasurer before the meeting today so that a new treasurer can be elected at once. You will appreciate my haste when I tell you I have not been to bed all night packing and getting ready to go. I shall hope to see you again a few months later but cannot spare a moment to call on you before I go. I wish you everything nice until I return to London again.

And now goodbye – with love hastily,

Yours,
Belle Elmore
pp H.H.C.

Melinda May was not one of Belle's intimates, but they were friends and she had spent New Year's Eve at 39 Hilldrop Crescent only a few weeks earlier. It was a small gathering, just her and Lil Hawthorne and her husband, John Nash. Hawthorne, who was also on the Guild committee, was a celebrated music-hall performer with popular songs such as 'Rosie O'Grady' and 'I'll be your sweetheart' and her current favourite, 'Tell me if you love me'. Hawthorne's husband was also her manager and they may have been drawn to the

Crippens because they too were expatriate Americans. Like a number of other performers of the Crippens' acquaintance – the Martinettis among them – Lil had left American vaudeville to take advantage of the huge audience for music hall in Britain since the turn of the century, returning sometimes to undertake American tours.

There were forty-eight music halls in London alone with a total capacity for 70,000 people, which could be doubled by twice nightly performances at most venues. There were dozens more halls throughout the provinces, and hundreds of performers at work to fill the bills, since most turns only lasted for a maximum of ten or fifteen minutes, just long enough for two or three songs, a few well-rehearsed jokes or a sketch. The terms of appearance were strictly controlled by the hall owners and the overwhelming majority of performers earned very little. They did not travel around in chauffeured cars.

Melinda May had not planned to go out that night to see the Old Year out and the New Year in, and had excused herself to Belle on the grounds that she was untidy. But Belle had evidently ignored her. The Nashes called at Melinda May's on the way to Camden and made her come. So May had travelled there and back in style, in Lil Hawthorne's own car. The Crippens were certainly moving in exalted circles at this time.

Their three guests had arrived about eleven o'clock and Belle had gone downstairs to the kitchen to make American cocktails. At midnight the front door was opened and they gathered at the top of the stone steps listening to the hooting of sirens, the ringing of church bells, the hammering of trays and the rest of what May would call the 'strangely moving noises' that were made by those who marked the last new year of the Edwardian age. Belle handed round the cocktails and, true to May's impression of her large-hearted nature, offered a drink to Lil's chauffeur and a passing police constable, who both accepted.

They had then gone down to the basement parlour next to the kitchen for supper, and May and the Nashes had finally left at about half one in the morning, a time neighbours would often associate later with the noise of departure of the Crippens' supper guests.

May read the second letter from Belle, which was addressed to the committee. Crippen had obviously tried to cover all the angles.

39 Hilldrop Crescent,
London, N.
To the committee of
    The Music Hall Ladies Guild

Dear Friends,

Please forgive me a hasty letter and any inconvenience I may cause you but I have just had news of the illness of a near relative and at only a few hours notice I am obliged to go to America. Under the circumstances I cannot return for several months and therefore beg you to accept this as a formal letter resigning from this date my Hon. Treasurership of the MHLG.

I am enclosing the cheque book and deposit book for the immediate use of my successor and to save any delay I beg to suggest that you vote to suspend the usual rules of election and elect *today* a new Hon. Treasurer.

I hope some months later to be with you again and in [sic] meantime wish the Guild every success and ask my good friends and pals to accept my sincere and loving wishes for their own personal welfare

Believe me,
Yours faithfully,
Belle Elmore

The committee were puzzled – Belle was good at keeping in touch and it was unlike her not to have spoken to at least one of them directly – but they were not immediately suspicious.

They expected to hear from her soon and agreed under the guidance of the Guild President, Louise Smythson, to appoint a temporary treasurer – Lottie Albert, who would still be treasurer more than twenty years later – and write a letter to Belle saying they would keep the post open for her until she returned.

Lil Hawthorne was playing the Tottenham Empire that week and so missed the meeting and only got half the story, hearing that Belle had resigned but not that she had supposedly gone abroad. She asked her husband/manager to send a wire to Belle at home, saying they would visit her on Saturday. Lil hoped to persuade Belle to withdraw her resignation.

The Guild never received a reply to their letter and when the Nashes called round three days later the house was shut up and in darkness and there was no answer at the door.

Her resignation was a blow to the committee. The previous September Belle had been honoured during the Guild's second annual dinner, held at the Hotel du Boulogne restaurant on Gerrard Street in Fitzrovia. She must have been proud of the write-up afterwards in the trade paper *The Era*, which took up an entire column. Of the dozens who had been there – among them many of the best known performers on the halls – the name of Belle Elmore was listed first in *The Era* as among those present. *The Era* recorded the outgoing President, Mrs Fred Ginnett (she was really Isabel, but women were referred to by their husband's name in those days) as making a speech saying how subscriptions had doubled in the last year. She had gone on to thank the Guild's medical officers, Dr Burroughs and Dr Walker, who had, during the past five weeks, dealt with as many as seven maternity cases, all of which had been carried out successfully and comfortably.

Belle had read out the donations, from such elevated characters as Sir Herbert Beerbohm Tree the dramatic actor, one guinea, and Mr George Formby the ukulele player, ten shillings. There were many others, including six shillings from Mrs Doust of the Tally-Ho Trio.

After this there had been a special presentation to Belle, amid great enthusiasm, *The Era* reported, of 'a handsome illuminated address and a gold bangle' (Belle did love her jewellery) and a basket of flowers and a box of gloves. The bangle had been inscribed, 'To the Hustler'. Belle had spoken in reply and her speech was reported, apparently in full. They were almost her only recorded words, outside those conversations that people who had known her remembered later.

'I do not know how to thank you for this beautiful present. In fact, I don't think I really deserve it. I never anticipated anything of this sort. The work I have done for the Guild I have done because I really love doing it – and my reward was that we were always pretty successful.

'However, knowing this lovely compliment is paid me in appreciation of my work for the Guild, I can only say that as long as I am permitted I will do in the future as I have done in the past, and, as we all learn by experience, I hope to improve upon the work I have done, and further the interests of the Guild to the best of my ability.'

They did not sound like the words of a woman who was about to cut and run.

In Ethel's version of that Wednesday, 2 February, she saw Crippen for the first time at around 4 pm.

LE NEVE: I have had your note. Has Belle Elmore really gone away?

CRIPPEN: Yes. She has left me.

LE NEVE: Did you see her go?

CRIPPEN: No. I found her gone when I got home last night.

LE NEVE: Do you think she will come back?

CRIPPEN: No. I don't.

LE NEVE: Did she take any luggage with her?

CRIPPEN: I don't know what luggage she had because I did not see her go. I daresay she took what was wanted. She always said that the things I gave her were not good enough, so I suppose she thinks she can get better elsewhere.

Ethel wrote (or told the two ghosting journalists who wrote it for her – and, according to them, believed her every word): 'I was of course immensely excited at this disappearance of Dr Crippen's mysterious wife. But at the same time it did not altogether surprise me. I knew well enough that they had been on bad terms together. I knew she had often threatened to go away and leave him.'

This would be Crippen's version of his life with Belle, too, in his statement to the police and at his trial. He would say she was always threatening to leave him. Surprisingly, Crippen's account of Belle's character would take hold and become the basis for all the traducing of Belle that would occur later, in which the natural conclusion seemed to be that she deserved what she got and it was a wonder he hadn't killed her sooner.

In her desperate attempts to demonstrate her innocence, even after she had been acquitted at her own trial, Ethel wanted to show that Crippen was lying to her too and she knew nothing of what had really happened. Obviously, there was no luggage missing from the house and Crippen well knew that Belle had not gone away. It's possible, even probable that Ethel well knew that too. It's possible that the conversation was completely invented.

Next, said Ethel, Crippen produced a handful of jewels from his pocket.

CRIPPEN: Look here, you had better have these. At all events I wish you would please me by taking one or two. These are good and I should like to know you had some good jewellery.
LE NEVE: Well, if you really wish it, I will have one or two. Pick out which you like.

Crippen selected a couple of solitaire rings, a ring set with four diamonds and a ruby, and a small diamond brooch. That brooch was destined to become a famous emblem in the case. It was a sunburst design or, as the Lord Chief Justice would describe it to the jury at Crippen's trial: 'It is a sort of star, gentlemen, with apparent brilliants.' There was to be a second, alternative story of Ethel's acquisition of that brooch.

For now, Ethel said there was still a lot of jewellery left over from the handful. A very large brooch set with beautiful stones in the shape of a tiara, with many rows of diamonds arranged in a crescent, and half a dozen fine rings.

She wanted us – her readership – to know that Crippen was a real expert in diamonds and often used to show her how to tell their relative values by holding them up to the light and observing their colour. Here was Crippen the older, cultured tutor of the unworldly young woman: 'As a result I got to know the different fashions of setting and could distinguish between those set in London and New York.'

And finally we get to the point of the story, which is to explain how it was that Crippen came to pawn his wife's baubles, two days after her 'disappearance' – one of the more incriminating acts against him and which he would lie about to the police.

'I then asked what he would do with the remainder as it would not do to leave them about in the house and as we had no safe . . . [No safe? Not true, there was a safe] . . . it would surely be better either to sell them or to pawn them. Perhaps the latter course would be best as he could redeem them whenever he was disposed so to do.'

To which Crippen of course replied: 'That is a good idea. I will take your advice.'

Well, perhaps it really did happen like this, and it was this exchange with Le Neve that propelled Crippen to Attenborough's Pawnbrokers at 142 Oxford Street on Wednesday, 2 February. Though he must have been pushed for time if he went this late, since by now it would have been well after four o'clock and the shops usually closed around five.

In any event, it is a matter of record that Attenborough's paid £80 to Crippen for just two items, described as a brilliant marquise ring and a pair of single stone earrings. He was back there seven days later with 'a brilliant brooch and 6 brilliant rings', one with a stone defect, in return for which he was given a further £115. (£1.00 in 1910 would be worth approximately £63 today.)

He would say that he invested the money in his businesses, but there would be no trace of where it went. At his trial the crown would argue that he was short of funds, and that this was a motive in his killing of his wife. It is hard to divine the truth about his finances, even though all the records are available. There is evidence for and against him being broke. He was certainly £2 13s 11d overdrawn at the bank on the day his wife died, though funds were paid in later to bring it back to a credit balance. He applied for and was granted a £20 overdraft facility on 1 February. But of course he never needed it because he had the proceeds of the pawnings instead. And, there was £600 on deposit at the bank, albeit only redeemable after 12 months' notice.

For some reason, unfathomably, Crippen would blurt out at his trial that Ethel Le Neve had slept the night at 39 Hilldrop Crescent for the first time on Wednesday, 2 February. She would say that her first night came some days later. In court, and elsewhere, and this may be why he said it, the admission would be used as an argument against his having killed Belle. How could anyone be so callous as to bring their lover to the scene of the crime so soon after the crime?

But the real question is: how did she manage not to notice the corpse or traces of it, if she really was there? Remarkably, this statement of Crippen's was not used against Ethel at her trial. So many things – her frequent lies, especially – were not used against her. If she was there that night she must have known what had happened. She must have been in on the murder, either before or immediately after it happened.

By her own account, Ethel did not go into the house until three or four days later. Although she had called there occasionally on business during Belle's lifetime, she only went beyond the front door for the first time after Crippen had said he would like to take her to the theatre that evening but was worried about the animals at home, which he had forgotten to feed that morning.

There were various animals, which had mostly been Belle's. Sometimes, of course, domestic pets can be substitutes for children. Belle could not conceive, following an ovariotomy some years earlier. There were seven canaries in a cage, possibly some other birds, at least two cats – one a luscious white Persian – and a bull terrier, of which, said Ethel, Crippen was especially fond.

Ethel volunteered to go to Camden and feed the menagerie. Crippen gave her the key and she let herself in by the side door. Front doors were rarely used, then, by those fortunate enough to have an alternative means of entry, except on special occasions. She went into the kitchen and then down to the pantry to fetch some milk. The pantry was next to the coal cellar. As she did this, the Persian cat escaped from the kitchen and she had to chase it all round the house, she says, thus emphasising that she went in all the rooms. She was worried because there was a valuable bird in the front room which the cat might have eaten. And Crippen had told her to keep the cats in the kitchen in case they soiled the upstairs carpet.

She eventually caught the Persian and returned it to the kitchen. She had seen the whole house. If a murder had recently been committed there were certainly no traces of it, she wrote. We are not told what play, if any, she saw that evening.

Throughout February, Crippen was digging himself in deeper with the various members of the Guild who asked after Belle at every opportunity, apparently forcing him to invent or embellish his story on the hoof. He did not seem averse to drawing attention to it, either. 'Have you noticed how lonely I am?' he asked his dental partner, Dr Rylance, a day or two after Belle's disappearance. Evidently, Rylance had not noticed. Crippen said his wife was halfway to America, gone on legal business to settle estates after his mother's death (though his mother had died some time earlier).

When he next called at the Martinettis, on 7 February, Clara scolded him: 'Well, you're a nice one, Belle already gone to America and you don't let us know anything about it. Why did you not send us a wire? I would have liked to go to the station and bring some flowers.'

There had been no time, said Crippen, the cable had come late on Tuesday night (the night of 1 February), which meant that one of them had to go. As Belle had wanted to go, he let her. He then had to look out some papers and they spent the rest of the night packing.

CLARA: Packing and crying, I suppose?
CRIPPEN: Oh, we have got past that.
CLARA: Did she take all her clothes with her?
CRIPPEN: One basket.
CLARA: That won't be enough, one basket, to go all that way.
CRIPPEN: She can buy something more over there.
CLARA: Oh, she is sure to send me a postcard from the ship.

Crippen nodded.

Paul asked what it was that she had gone over for in such a hurry. Crippen said it was on important business for him, important legal business. In fact, there was a title attached to it, but he wouldn't use it. (This, I think, meant title deed to a property rather than title as in Duke or Lord.)

By the time they met again a week later, Crippen was already laying the foundations for his future story. He told the Martinettis he had heard that Belle had become rather ill and had something wrong with her lungs. Her lungs? Clara hadn't known there was a problem with Belle's lungs. She couldn't understand why Belle hadn't written. Crippen said he didn't know why. Clara said she thought Belle was going via New York and would see the old Guild President Mrs Ginnett, who was staying with relatives there while her husband, Fred Ginnett, was on tour. They too were Americans who had settled in London.

Fred Ginnett, a former circus owner, had transferred to the halls with an equestrian act and had become famous for his sketches, including his on-stage re-creation of 'Dick Turpin's Ride To York'. His wife, Isabel, had trained the horses he used. They were among the aristocracy of showbusiness. Fred had been King Rat of the Grand Order of Water Rats, the theatrical charity, in 1909. Paul Martinetti was a former King Rat too.

Oh no, said Crippen, Belle would not be seeing Mrs Ginnett, she wasn't touching New York, she was going straight on to California. Crippen's family, such as it was, now lived in California. New York was clearly tricky and had to be kept out of the story. Melinda May asked Crippen what she should do about Belle's Guild subscription, which was due. Could she write to her? No, said Crippen, she was up in the hills of California but he would forward a letter for her if she wished.

He again saw the Martinettis, and was asked and again had to say that he had still not heard from Belle. Clara asked him if he was going to the Ladies' Guild Ball which was coming up. He and Belle would have been certain guests. Crippen said, no, he didn't think so. Clara must have encouraged him. Paul could get him tickets from the club, she said, they were half a guinea each. All right, said Crippen, he would take two.

The ball was held on 20 February at the glamorous and ornate Criterion Restaurant on Piccadilly Circus. Crippen took Ethel Le Neve and joined the Martinettis' table, Crippen sitting with Clara on one side and Ethel on the other. Clara recalled that she merely nodded at Ethel but never spoke to her. Opposite them were Lil Hawthorne and John Nash. Louise Smythson was there too. They all saw the brooch Ethel was wearing, the sunburst brooch, which Clara described as a centre diamond with pearls radiating from it in a zigzag pattern, all the way around. It was, they all knew, Belle's brooch. Ethel was wearing a pink dress and there were those who thought it was Belle's dress she was wearing too. Crippen and his typist? Well, well, what was going on?

Mrs Smythson asked Crippen for Belle's address. Had he heard from her? Oh yes, he said, she was right up in the wilds of the mountains in California. Louise asked him to let her know when he got some news of her. Crippen said that he would tell her as soon as Belle had a settled address. John Nash could not help noticing that 'Crippen and the girl' were drinking freely of the wine. It was his wife who pointed out the brooch to him.

Ethel must have been stung by the remarks about her, when all this came out later. She took the opportunity of telling her life story to set the record straight. Neither she nor Crippen had been keen to go to the ball, she said. She had not danced in years and had nothing to wear. Belle's clothes would not have fitted her (they were different sizes, clearly). Ethel had gone to Swan & Edgar's, just across Piccadilly Circus from the Criterion, and they had made the pink dress for her.

Perhaps poignantly, the lie betraying a wish for a different kind of life (Belle's life, maybe) Ethel – who was still in lodgings at Hampstead at this stage – told her landlady Mrs Jackson that she would not be home, the night before the ball. She was going to stay at the Martinettis and Mrs Martinetti was going to do Ethel's hair for her, especially for the occasion.

THREE

Crippen married Belle Elmore on 1 September 1892 at St Paul's Church, Jersey City. She gave her age as nineteen. He was, it is stated, thirty years and two months. This is one of the few fixed dates in Crippen's past and there is limited information about his early history. Most of what is known is based on his own account in his statement to the police and in evidence at his trial, so must be treated with caution, except where there is corroboration. He seems to have had a terrible memory for dates. As does Belle – she was actually born on 3 September 1873, making her just eighteen at the time of her marriage.

Another fixed point is the death of Crippen's first wife, whose maiden name was Charlotte Jane Bell, on 24 January 1892 in Salt Lake City, Utah, so Crippen had returned to the east coast and met and married Belle in the space of a little over seven months. Not that Belle was going by that name in those days. Belle Elmore was an affectation she took to later, in England, perhaps styling herself after, or even blatantly stealing from Marie Lloyd, the greatest music-hall singer of the age, who began her career as Bella Delmere (or possibly Belle, or Delmore, Delamere or Delmare – different sources give different versions of the name). She might have hoped that some of Marie's stardust would fall on her. If so, she was out of luck.

According to Crippen, he met Belle in New York after going to work as an assistant to a Dr Jeffery in Brooklyn. Jeffery seems to have been a conventional general practitioner. Belle was a patient, though we do not know what her complaint was. Perhaps it was connected to the operation she had not long afterwards. Crippen said she had told him she was going by the name of Cora Turner. She had been living with a stove-manufacturer named C.C. Lincoln, but he had given up the house they were sharing and she was now living alone in a room Lincoln had rented for her, all expenses paid. As Crippen put it, she was living under the 'protection' of Lincoln.

Crippen and Cora started going around together. He took her to several places and became very fond of her. When Cora told Crippen that Lincoln wanted her to go away with him, Crippen said he could not stand that and would marry her right away, which he did a few days later, no doubt just as Cora had intended he would. Crippen says the wedding was held at a minister's house in Jersey City. The official record places it at the church, with Cora giving her name as 'Corinne Konny Turner, the daughter of Joseph Turner and Mary Wolff'.

It was only after they were married, said Crippen, that Cora told him the name Turner was a fiction. In fact, she was the daughter of Joseph Mackamotzki (this spelling is by no means certain – it is sometimes written as Makematski) and her given name was Kunigunde. Cora told Crippen that her father was a Russian Pole and her mother was German.

In London, some years later, during a conversation with a friend about actresses marrying titled men, Belle would produce a cutting from an American newspaper which she seemed to carry around, folded, in her bag. 'You won't believe I have a title,' she would say, showing the article which was about a woman with a name like Motzki, who was a baroness or maybe a countess, entitled to some property in Russia. Belle said the article was about her.

This must have been as fanciful as the name Turner. There was no real evidence of any title and Joe Mackamotzki seems to have been a typical poor Eastern European immigrant to the new world. There were two children, by the time of his death, Cora and a younger sister, Theresa. Their mother, Mary, then married a Brooklyn farmer (you won't find many of those in Brooklyn these days) called Frederick Mersinger, and there was a step-sister, Louise. Mary died before her daughter's murder.

Cora evidently did not invite her family to her wedding. Instead they met Crippen for the first time a day or two later, when he was presented to them in Brooklyn as her husband.

Not long after this, Crippen went to work in Philadelphia and settled there briefly with his wife. From Philadelphia, Cora, still barely twenty, wrote and told her mother she was to undergo an operation. Her mother visited her in hospital and later told Cora's sister Theresa that Cora's womb and her ovaries had been removed and she would never have children.

Later, when it was a matter of life and death for Crippen, Theresa would recall Cora showing her the scar from that operation, still fresh and livid. The aftermath of the operation was problematic and seems to have been a talking point with Belle for the rest of her life. Friends would recall being shown the scar or hearing about it, about the discharge that had resulted and about the 'pus bag' that had formed over it for a while.

In the old police files there is an anonymous letter from 1910 which seeks to confirm the details of the operation, that it took place at the Hahnemann Hospital at Broad and Vine Streets in Philadelphia in (so far as the anonymous writer can recall) 1893 or 1894. The letter-writer had visited Belle in the hospital where she was a private patient and Belle had said her ovaries had been removed and she would no longer menstruate. The wound had not healed well and had left a large scar on Belle's abdomen. Belle had talked about it constantly and once shown it to a group of women in the letter-writer's presence.

The writer recalled that Crippen had then seemed devoted to his wife.

Whatever the reason for the operation, and the messy aftermath, it seems reasonable to assume that it was a difficult adjustment for a young woman of those days – coming to terms with having your means of becoming pregnant, your womanhood taken away. Not an easy thing to embrace, either, in a young relationship.

According to Crippen, who probably had his dates wrong, he first went to live in St Louis after his marriage to Belle, where he was a consulting physician to an optician named Hirsch on Olive Street. He left there to go back to New York and start his long association with Munyon's. Although Belle's sister Theresa could remember her sister and her husband lodging at their family home for a while, Crippen recalled living at the offices of Munyon's on East 14th Street. Then he was transferred to Philadelphia. Then to Toronto. Then back to Philadelphia.

Travel featured as much in Crippen's life as it did in the events leading up to his death. He led an extraordinarily peripatetic existence. Was he keeping one step ahead of something or somebody, or was he always one step behind, chasing rainbows?

In many ways, he was reminiscent of a pioneer character: a singular figure in unfamiliar worlds, never still, always on the move, never quite fitting in, forming unlikely partnerships, always slightly tainted by the questionable nature of his work. With his horn-rimmed glasses and his frock coat he could have been Doc Crippen in a frontier town, or one of those eccentric patent medicine men, travelling around in a covered wagon with his name painted down the side, pausing on his way across the prairie to mop his brow beneath the sun, as those characters did in a hundred Hollywood westerns.

He was at 39 Hilldrop Crescent for nearly four and a half years, with Belle. Five years if you count the time he was there with what was left of her buried beneath the cellar floor. It was the only time from childhood that he was ever committed to one place. Though, of course, life at 39 Hilldrop must have been far from stable.

Crippen was born in Coldwater, Michigan in the mid-year of 1862. Thirty years earlier, Coldwater had been no more than a log cabin on the pioneer trail westwards, about halfway between Detroit and Chicago. There seems to have been a wholesale colonisation of the place by Crippens, who moved up there from New York state as Coldwater developed, and indeed played a role in its development. The name was English of origin, but there were Crippens in America from the seventeenth century, not far behind the pilgrim fathers. It could be written as Crippin, Grippen or Grippin, but they were old English varations and it was Crippen that became the recognised norm.

Crippen's grandfather, Philo, was born and married in Monroe, New York, but his two children were born and raised in Coldwater. Myron Augustus, Crippen's father, became a dry goods merchant. He married Andresse Skinner, who came from Pennsylvania and had a Welsh father. There is evidence of a child, Ella Sophia, who died in infancy in 1861, the year before Hawley Harvey Crippen was born. He was their only surviving child.

It appears that Myron and Andresse took the pioneer trail to California. It's possible that they became separated along the way, because only Andresse and her son appear at the same address on the 1880 US census for Santa Clara Street in San José. The spelling is all wrong but it must be them: Ardesse Crippin, aged forty-four, and her son Hawley Crippin aged seventeen (on his last birthday before 1 June 1880). Ardesse's occupation is listed as keeping house. Hawley is working in a canning factory. Hawley is said to have been born in Michigan and Ardesse in Pennsylvania. Myron, Crippen's father, resurfaces in Los Angeles with 'Ardessa' on the 1900 census. He does not appear anywhere on the 1880 census and there is no other record of where he was during this time.

Crippen himself said he was educated in Michigan, Indiana and California, first turning to medical studies at the University of Michigan School of Homoeopathic Medicine. He entered the Homoeopathic Hospital College in Cleveland but first left without completing his studies, only returning to graduate in 1884. In the meantime he had made a trip to London where, he said, he attended various hospitals to see operations and attended lectures at, among other places, the Bethlehem Royal Hospital in the City of London. The hospital specialised in the treatment of the insane and had given the word bedlam (an asylum for lunatics, a madhouse, a place of uproar), a corruption of its name, to the world. It was here, Crippen would claim, that he first heard of the use of the poison hyoscine, which could be used in modest doses to calm the symptoms of madness.

Chief Inspector Dew would find Crippen's Cleveland medical diploma during the search of 39 Hilldrop Crescent. The police would translate it into English, from Latin, just to be sure it was what it appeared to be. There was no doubt that he was entitled to call himself Doctor, or, as his various business letter headings would proclaim: H.H. Crippen, MD.

Crippen was of course entering a profession which was not subject to anything like the controls and standards that are in place today. Britain was forty years away from a national health service. Like America, it was still in the realms of unregulated private practice and inexact science.

Perhaps it was in the absence of established medicine that the vogue for homoeopathy first arose. It was very popular and highly fashionable on both sides of the Atlantic in the latter years of the nineteenth century and the early years of the twentieth century. Strictly speaking, homoeopathy was the method of treating illnesses with small doses of drugs that reproduced the very symptoms they were intended to cure. Somehow, this became enmeshed with the patent medicine business – or racket, as it was sometimes described.

Patent medicines would have been great, if they were genuine and if they matched the often outlandish claims made for their beneficial effects. They were often based, or alleged to be based, on ancient herbal cures or remedies from traditional communities. They were easily available, not being subject to the usual rules of prescriptions, and so probably cheaper too. They were certainly heavily promoted through advertising. The common practice was to assess illnesses and provide treatments by mail order and this no doubt suited many patients, too – not having to look a doctor in the eye. It must often have outweighed any concerns about someone unseen in an office diagnosing what was wrong with you from a letter.

Patent medicines were, and still are, essentially medicines developed out of secret formulas known only to their creators, who protected them by means of patents. Sadly, they came to be associated with quackery and nostrums, as such dubious remedies were also known.

Quite why Crippen pursued this branch of medicine was never recorded. Maybe he was no good at being a real doctor. Maybe there wasn't enough money in it; maybe he was lured by the promise of the riches to be earned from these formulas. Maybe, at the time, it seemed like the exciting future of medicine, the pioneers' end of the profession. Or maybe he was corrupt at heart. Most probably he was motivated by a combination of these factors.

He says he worked for a few months in Detroit, Michigan as an assistant to a Dr Porter. Then he was back in New York where he took a degree in 'specialist eye and ear work' at the 'Ophthalmic hospital' (there was no supporting certificate for this, though his later letter headings for 'The Aural Remedies Coy.' would state beneath his name: Oculi Et Auris Chirurgis, NY Ophthalmic Hospital College, 1887. The Latin translates as 'eye and ear surgeon'). He went back to Detroit with Dr Porter, then went on to California, to practise as an eye and ear specialist, taking with him his new wife. It was by now about 1887 or 1888.

There is almost no information on the first Mrs Crippen and she did not live to tell the tale. There is some evidence that she was working as a nurse in New York and this was where he met and married her. Their only child – and the only acknowledged child of Crippen's – was born on 19 August 1889 and named Hawley Otto Crippen. Later he seemed to prefer the usage Otto Hawley, or Otto H.

They moved on to Salt Lake City – Crippen does not tell us what he was practising while he was there – and Charlotte was in the ninth month of pregnancy when she died of 'apoplexy' on 24 January 1892. The sexton's record of her death at Salt Lake City cemetery records her birth year as 1859, in Ireland, making her three years older than Crippen.

Of course, it is tempting to think he could have killed her. But there is no way of knowing that and there does not seem to have been any suspicion at the time. The poison, hyoscine, which Crippen said he had seen used at Bedlam, and which he was to deploy in London in 1910, could produce symptoms similar to apoplexy. But that's all speculative. Charlotte died, Crippen moved on. In months he had a new wife. And she would die too.

He left behind his son Hawley Otto Crippen, who would have been two years old when his mother died. Hawley Otto was sent by his father to live with his grandparents in California. There is no evidence that he ever saw his father again. Imagine the lifelong effect of your mother's death, followed in short order by your father's exit. His grandmother too was dead by 1910. I have been unable to find a record of Andresse/Ardesse/Ardessa's death. There is a suggestion that it was 1909. It may have been earlier.

Hawley Otto was recorded on the 1900 census, where he is ten years old, living with Myron A. Crippen, aged sixty-five and Ardessa Crippen, aged sixty-four, his grandparents, at 296 Howard Street, Pasadena, Los Angeles. Myron is listed as a merchant, renting his home. The census tells us they have been married for forty-four years and that Ardessa is the mother of two children, but only one is living.

We have only Crippen's word for the story of Cora's ambitions to train for the opera. The grand opera, as he called it. According to him, she returned to New York, leaving him in Philadelphia, and began singing lessons, for which he paid all her expenses. He visited her there but was then sent by Munyon to London, to manage the new branch on Shaftesbury Avenue, opposite the Palace Theatre. It was Munyon's first overseas venture, and the premises were described as palatial.

Crippen initially said he came over in 1900 but at his trial he put it earlier, at April 1898. He lodged first at Queen's Road, St John's Wood, but when Cora, soon to be known as Belle, joined him in the August they moved into South Crescent on the edge of Bloomsbury, the area that was to be their home until they moved to Hilldrop Crescent. (South Crescent, on Store Street, immediately to the east of Tottenham Court Road is now the site of the offices of the advertising and promotion group, Imagination.)

Contradictions begin to creep into Crippen's narrative from this point. He told Chief Inspector Dew that from the time of her arrival in England, Belle's manner towards him had changed. She had developed an ungovernable temper and seemed to think he was not good enough for her. She boasted of men of good position she had met on the boat during the Atlantic crossing who made a fuss of her, and some had visited her at South Crescent.

That was one version.

Then, giving evidence at his trial, Crippen said that the change in her manner came later and they had always been on friendly terms beforehand, except for a 'previous trouble' he had had with her and men before they moved away from South Crescent. Maybe this was a reference to male visitors from the boat.

Belle's ambitions had changed, along with her temper. She no longer harboured a passion for the opera, but had set her sights on the music hall instead and needed some material – a vehicle for her voice, an operetta. She was introduced to a woman of about her own age, Adelene Votieri, a writer and actress of French origins who was soon to be married to a prolific popular song-writer, Denham Harrison.

Adelene Harrison would become a journalist and find herself with a scoop on her hands, having been intimately acquainted with the principals in the North London Cellar Murder of 1910. She would reach back and recall meeting

Belle for the first time at Munyon's: Adelene standing waiting in the reception area until the green draperies parted and there was a striking woman, 'a brilliant chattering bird of gorgeous plumage'.

This was Belle, as Adelene first saw her: filling the room with her personality, dark eyes twinkling with the joy of life, teeth betraying a gleam of gold, hair in dark curls, her plump, voluptuous figure encased in a tight-fitting pair of corsets beneath a gown of black and emerald green silk gauze, mounted over glacé silk, with voluminous underskirts that rustled as she moved. She wore very high heels and a smart black hat with 'a panache of magnificent plumes'. She spoke in a very high key with a strong American accent.

'Come, sit down here,' said Belle, pointing to a green sofa. 'I guess we'll have a little chat right away. You know, I'm going to make my debut at the Empire, Leicester Square.'

They became friends, and Belle gave Adelene an outline of an operetta she had drafted, for Adelene to develop. Belle would never make it to the Empire, Leicester Square but would begin – and end – lower down the ranks at the Old Marylebone Music Hall and other venues of similar stature.

Belle was first billed as Macka Motzki. According to Crippen, she had wanted to try out the name Belle Elmore but he had advised against it. 'Fun, music & variety', promised the playbill for Macka Motzki. Her acting manager was listed as H.H. Crippen. If Adelene is to be believed, this playbill, or a description of it, travelled back to America and was reported to Munyon, who was upset that Crippen was conducting his own business on Munyon's salary and fired him. It is certainly true, confirmed by Crippen, that Munyon recalled him to Philadelphia and that he did not go back to Munyon's on his return to England.

Before he left, Crippen moved Belle into lodgings in Guilford Street in Bloomsbury. He sent funds home regularly while he was away, money drafts via Munyon's, from where the office clerk, William Long, took the cash round to Mrs Crippen.

The year was either 1899 or 1900 and, after her husband had gone, Belle went to dinner at the home of a music teacher in Torrington Square and was introduced to a fellow performer from Chicago, Bruce Miller, who was on his way to the 1900 Paris Exposition with his one-man-band automatic orchestra. Miller said they merely shook hands, at that stage, and he went on his way.

Miller and Belle soon began a relationship of unknown description. When he was squirming on the hook of a hostile cross-examination during Crippen's trial, Miller would repeatedly deny that he had ever overstepped the mark. He would admit to kissing Belle and sending her letters signed 'love and kisses to brown eyes' but he would insist that he only ever behaved like a gentleman. He had been an 'affectionate friend' and there had never been 'improper relations'.

In a statement to Chief Inspector Dew he would disclose the existence of a string of champagne corks which, he claimed, did no more than commemorate a succession of dates. He would say they had always celebrated the date 5 January as their first meeting, even though he had already said they met in December 1899. Perhaps it was another anniversary, celebrating the start of their sexual relationship, and maybe the string of champagne corks commemorated their subsequent sexual encounters.

Miller had been married for nearly fifteen years, and had a son, when he came to London. He said he was separated from his wife at that time and remained in England until 1904, when he returned to Chicago and left showbusiness. It is worth bearing in mind that he was reconciled with his wife by the time of the trial and so had a vested interest in maintaining an innocent account of his friendship with Belle. The story of Crippen had been almost as big in Chicago, and everywhere else in America, as it was in London. If there was anything to keep secret, Miller had nowhere to hide, except behind lies.

He said his friendship with Belle continued even after Crippen's return to London, when the couple moved back to Store Street, living first in lodgings at number 34 and later at number 37. They are registered there in the 1901 census as Hawley Crippen, aged thirty-eight, physician retired (is what it says) and Corinne Crippen, aged twenty (she was actually twenty-six). The American couple are sharing the house with a German hotel waiter, a sixty-year-old Indian from Bombay living on his own means, a Kilburn accountant and a taxi-driver from Suffolk. Perhaps this is the London described by Arthur Conan Doyle as 'that great cesspool into which all the loungers and idlers of the Empire are irresistibly drained'.

Bruce Miller is registered ominously nearby, a thirty-four-year-old American musician living at 18 Colville Street, just west of Tottenham Court Road, no more than a cork's throw from Store Street.

Even though Miller never met Crippen, he visited his home and never tried to hide or time his visits during Crippen's absence. He even had the feeling that Crippen was there in the flat, on one or more occasions. Belle had sent Miller six photographs of herself in the census year, telling him that Crippen had taken the pictures on his Kodak. Miller inferred from Belle's letter that Crippen knew she had sent them to Miller.

Miller had sent Belle pictures of himself and knew for a fact that they had gone on show, one on the piano and others elsewhere. (Indeed, they were still there, at Hilldrop, after Belle had been killed.) Belle used to tell him that anything they did together was always satisfactory to her husband.

On one occasion Miller became unwell while on tour in the provinces. He caught bronchitis in Sheffield and wrote to Belle describing what was wrong. She told her husband, who recommended a course of treatment, and Belle wrote back to Miller explaining what Crippen had prescribed. Miller said he too was a qualified doctor in the United States and so he recognised the remedies Crippen had suggested and had them made up and soon felt better.

Going to dine at Store Street on one of the last occasions, Miller had found the table set for three. Belle had delayed the dinner and eventually said, 'I am getting quite uneasy. I expect another party to dinner. I am often disappointed that way.' Miller assumed she was waiting for the doctor. She had always spoken of her husband in the highest terms, Miller said. When he showed Belle the letters his wife was writing him, pleading with him to return, Belle had told Miller to go back to his wife and, eventually, he did.

There was plenty of speculation later – when people realised how much she had – that Belle must have been showered with presents by male admirers, but Miller said he never gave Belle any gifts or money, other than small tokens. There was no evidence that anyone else, apart from her husband, had ever given her anything. Miller used to write to her at Christmas and birthdays and send her two dollars for a bouquet.

At his trial, Crippen would suggest that her friendship with Miller had been responsible for the change in his wife's behaviour towards him. He said that after his return from America she was always finding fault with him, and every night she took the opportunity to quarrel so that they went to bed in rather a temper with each other. Crippen said he eventually found that Belle did not wish to be familiar with him. She said she had met Bruce Miller and he had been taking her out while Crippen was away and she had got very fond of him and did not care for Crippen any more.

'I told my wife I thought it was very strange,' Crippen would say at the trial, 'though I had seen this coming for a long time, for a previous trouble I had had before we moved away from South Crescent.'

He said they continued to live together and occupy the same bed, but not as man and wife. That was one of the reasons they eventually moved to a house: there was only one bedroom in Store Street but at Hilldrop Crescent they could each have their own room.

They had made an agreement, said Crippen, that they would always treat each other in front of friends as if there was no trouble between them. Crippen had hoped she would give up her ideas. If others knew about any of this they never mentioned it, not to the press, not to the police and not in evidence at the trial.

It is clear from the tone of Adelene Harrison's commentaries that some disapproval creeps into her view of Belle, and mutual friends describe a falling-out between Belle and Adelene not long before Belle's death, without saying what caused it. One or two others who saw the Crippens together concede that Belle could sometimes be 'hasty' or even 'ill-tempered' towards her husband.

So perhaps they really did present that united face to the world and save the reality for the privacy of their home. Or maybe, just as everyone else saw it, they were genuinely happy together, or at least not miserable all the time, and still took pleasure in each other and, as the evidence suggests, tried to please each other too, in those early years in London before Crippen became involved with Ethel Le Neve.

Adelene Harrison says they were like a couple of children in their love for excitement when she first knew them. It was as if the wheel of fortune had suddenly turned, bringing for them the money to acquire the good things of life. Dinners, supper parties and theatres were the order of the day, and every form of novelty and excitement appealed to them.

In Harrison's eyes, Crippen was the typical quiet unassuming American who gave his wife all the running socially and whose one aim and object appeared to be to earn money for her to spend and have a good time. His devotion for her was remarkable. Idolised wife! Why, nothing was too good for her. Her craze for diamonds and the acquisition of gorgeous gowns knew no limit, nor was it restricted by him. Never a week passed but he gave her some handsome jewel. Daily she visited well-known West End shops and purchased endless yards of silks, laces, satins, embroideries etc. She accumulated a large stock of stage gowns and furs.

Belle liked to babble to her diamonds and kiss them, according to her friend. Sometimes she could show the petulance of a spoilt child who needed controlling. She had an absorbing passion for stage life and a fascination for the society of everyone connected with the profession. She had visions of fame – was possessed of the soul-hunger of the modern woman for notoriety, and developed that prevalent disease 'selfitis', which if not checked becomes chronic.

Her desire for appreciation, admiration, flattery was pitiful at times. Harrison said Belle had a pretty mezzo-soprano voice, and she did play at a few suburban halls, but the managers thought her performances were too weak. Still, she went around town night after night visiting the various halls in the town and her one and only topic of conversation was the stage. She imagined, said Harrison, that she was Marie Lloyd.

Though Harrison wrote quite a lot of material for Belle, a play called *The Unknown Quantity* and several other plays or sketches, she clearly did not consider herself to blame for Belle's failings as a performer. It must have been a soul-destroying experience, trudging your act around those provincial and suburban halls, knowing you would never be better than second-rate, at best. All those slow journeys by train, the waiting around on station platforms and dingy dressing-rooms at the venues, going back to grim digs.

There was a landlady in Bath, with whom Belle stayed a couple of times while performing at the Lyric Music Hall in the town. She signed the landlady's guest book, 'Belle Elmore, La Belle American', and paid sixteen shillings a week for the room. She took the landlady with her every night to the hall – perhaps as a chaperone – and naturally told her all her business, especially the bit about the operation. As the landlady remembered it, Belle told her she had had her womb removed and scraped out and then put back in.

There were similar shows, as Crippen recalled, in Oxford, Camberwell and Balham, at the Town Hall, Teddington and the Empire, Northampton. Then there was the Palace Theatre of Varieties, Swansea where Miss B. Elmore appeared in November 1902 low down the order beneath a long forgotten headlining act, The Original Ross Combination.

Crippen told Chief Inspector Dew that when he returned from America he discovered not only that Belle had been seeing another man, but also that she had been performing at 'smoking concerts' – and being paid for it. He made it sound as if she had stooped low, though smoking concerts, so named because they were all-male events, were common enough at the time and, though maybe inclined to be a little bawdy or ribald, were not exactly indecent.

The Era, in a later account of the case, gave a brief account of Belle's career, saying she had begun at the Old Marylebone Music Hall, appearing in a small operetta wearing an embroidered gypsy gown. She had appeared at the Grand, Clapham and the Holborn, and had toured the provinces. She had last appeared at the Bedford Music Hall early in 1907 when she had sung 'Down Lovers Walk' and also a coon song, wearing a short spangled dress. She sang 'Sister Mary Ann' and a costume song, 'The Major', wearing full military regalia. She performed a duologue, 'The Unknown Quantity', with a Mr Douglas whose sharp eyes, so *The Era* reported, had saved Belle from disaster after she had held a sheaf of genuine £5 bank notes for a scene and accidentally left them on the stage, where they were spotted by Mr Douglas. Another of her songs had been called 'She Never Went Further Than That'.

No wonder she gave it up. Or it gave her up. There was certainly evidence of lingering professional disappointment and frustration.

Adelene Harrison said that, after he left Munyon's, Crippen invested heavily in a new enterprise in which he lost a lot of money. This must have been the Sovereign Remedy Company which had offices at 13 Newman Street, just north of Oxford Street and near Tottenham Court Road, in that same neighbourhood where it seems much of Crippen's London life was being played out. The company failed after a few months, leading Crippen to the Drouet Institute for the Deaf which was further afield, near Regent's Park initially and later at Marble Arch.

Crippen was followed to Drouet's by William Long, his assistant from Munyon's who would become a loyal associate.

He could recall some of the enterprises Crippen neglected to mention to the police, such as the sign on the door at Store Street, promoting 'Belle Elmore, Miniature Artist'. So far as Long knew, Belle was no artist and the miniatures were painted by a man from the Sovereign Remedy Company and another man from Drouet's.

Then there was the nerve tonic, Amorette, which Crippen marketed himself, also from Store Street, where letters would arrive and he would package and send out the drugs himself. A little later, when Crippen had again moved on (back to Munyon's) and Long was temporarily left behind at Drouet's, Long was helping Crippen out by packing tubes of his own ointment cure for deafness, which he named Ohrsorb (Ohr is ear in German; sorb is absorb). There was also the Aural Clinic Company at 102 New Oxford Street, which Crippen ran for a few months (this was not the Aural Remedies Company of Craven House, Kingsway, which he began later).

As Long remembered it, Ethel Le Neve was already working at Drouet's as a typist when Crippen arrived. She had followed her sister Nina into the business, but Nina left a little while later to get married. When the Drouet Institute was taken over by a new owner in 1905 it was a three-man band: Crippen, Long and Le Neve.

The new owner was a character called Eddie Marr, probably the leading patent medicine huckster in the country. He was also trading as the Sanalak Syndicate, specialising in rheumatism, from its offices in Vine Street, Clerkenwell. He was G.K. Harvey at 117 Holborn, selling a deaf cure which was only advertised in Russia; the Elmer Shirley Catarrh Cure at 6 Great James Street; and he later had a hand in the Aural Remedies Company too. He probably picked up Drouet's for a song, the previous owner, a Frenchman called Monsieur Carre, having fled attacks in the press from a crusading publication known as *Truth*. There had also been at least one death attributable to the cures of Drouet's, a Staffordshire locksmith named Johnson. An earlier physician, a Dr Simon, had been stripped of his diploma for his involvement with the firm.

In 1907 Crippen was cited during a much publicised libel trial, in which a Dr Dakhyl, who was properly qualified and had worked alongside Crippen at Drouet's, sued *Truth* for describing him as a 'quack of the highest species'. The same article called Carre a rascal. One of the presiding judges called for a definition of a 'quack'. A lawyer explained that it was normally accepted as 'a boastful pretender to medical skill', but the definition could be extended as follows: 'A man might have all the medical skill in the world and yet he might be a quack if he pretended to cure people of diseases by remedies which he knew had no efficacy at all, and he might be a trickster in that he represented that the bread pills he gave contained ingredients which would deal with serious illness.'

Ironically, Drouet's had once advertised in *Truth*. Indeed it was part of Dakhyl's allegation that *Truth* only attacked Drouet's when it took its business elsewhere and started advertising in the *People's Friend* and the *Daily Telegraph* instead. It emerged during the trial that Drouet's cures were all prepared in Paris and included sticking plasters. It was one of *Truth*'s criticisms of Drouet's that sticking plasters could not properly be considered a treatment for deafness.

There was also unease at the idea of being treated by correspondence. A gardener named Binnie from North Berwick had been told by post that he was suffering from, among other things, otorrhea, otitis media, tinnitus and eruptive eustachitis. Binnie had spent several pounds on treatments and had even said he was making progress. But did he really know what was wrong with him from these arcane diagnoses?

Dr Dakhyl said during evidence that he had complained to his colleague Dr Crippen and the office manager, after discovering that they were sending out letters promising cures. He had not known of Drouet's notoriety and would not have joined if he had. Dakhyl claimed that he was being paid £32 a month plus percentages, which must have upset Crippen, who had started on £6 a week but had his salary halved when the business was struggling. Marr closed it down after nine months because it didn't pay.

Unsurprisingly, when a genuine GP called Dr John Burroughs set up a surgery beneath the Crippens' flat at 37 Store Street, Crippen never mentioned his own branch of doctoring. Burroughs heard from others that Dr Crippen was an ear, eye and nose specialist. He and his wife Maud became friends of the Crippens and Dr Burroughs took on the role of medical officer to the Music Hall Ladies Guild. It was he who would later say that Belle could at times be somewhat hasty in her manner towards her husband. But even though they lived above them, the Burroughs never heard the Crippens quarrelling. They seemed to live comfortably together.

It was to Maud that Belle said one day, 'I don't like the girl typist Peter has in his office.'

'Why don't you ask him to get rid of her then?'

'I have but he said she was indispensable to his business.'

Belle asked Maud if she would like to see her scar. Maud declined.

Following their marriage, Adelene Harrison and her husband rented a house on Hilldrop Road in Lower Holloway. Belle was visiting one evening and, according to Adelene, was so charmed with the old-world garden and bower of roses that she came up the next day and began to search for a house of her own in the neighbourhood. In the end, the Crippens could not find a house with a large garden and so rented 39 Hilldrop Crescent and, wrote Adelene, 'set to work to transform the ugly back garden into a flowery bower'.

The house was set in the middle of a row of semi-detached Victorian villas somewhat grey in appearance, on the outer ring of the crescent, the houses only on one side of the street so that, unusually for London, the house numbers ran consecutively, rather than odds on one side and evens on the other. Number 39 had previously been occupied by a forty-two-year-old mechanic, his wife, their four children and a lodger.

Peter and Belle moved in on a three-year lease on 21 September 1905, at a cost of £52 10s, which was later reduced to £50 after the Crippens said they would have to leave because they couldn't afford it.

FOUR

At the beginning of March 1910 Crippen appeared to be making plans for his future. After the second pawning of his wife's jewellery, he entered into a new business arrangement with his dental colleague, Dr Rylance, that apparently put their partnership on a surer footing. Crippen invested £200 and Rylance contributed his professional experience and expertise as a properly qualified dentist. They now had an equal share of the enterprise.

He gave Marion Curnow, who was formerly his book-keeper at Munyon's but had now replaced him as office manager, two sealed envelopes which he asked her to place in the office safe (you see, there *was* a safe – and Ethel said there wasn't ...) along with some fire insurance papers. One envelope was marked Dr Crippen and the other, which he gave her a day or two later, was marked Dr Crippen, Personal.

CURNOW: Well, doctor, you are a bachelor now, seeing that Mrs Crippen is away.
CRIPPEN: Oh yes, she has gone away for a little while to transact some business for me. I don't know when she will be back. You know she went away about six years ago for a holiday without me.

One morning around this time a horse and van pulled up at 39 Hilldrop Crescent, driven by a 'greengrocer and cartage contractor' (his own description) named Fred Simmonds, who had been asked the day before by William Long to move some property from the house. Long had said he was an assistant to a dentist. He met Simmonds at the house and, while Long and Crippen brought the furniture downstairs into the front passage – the hallway – Simmonds loaded it on to the van. Then Simmonds and Long went down together to Albion House – a modern building near a chapel, as Simmonds recalled it – and took the property round the back and into the lift. They repeated the exercise a few days later, and this time Simmonds was asked to take some more boxes to a second-hand shop on Shaftesbury Avenue, where Crippen was waiting, no doubt to complete a financial transaction.

When the police heard about this later they must have thought they might find some of Belle in the boxes Simmonds had transported. But no, there were no body parts, just two or three occasional tables, a suite of cloth-covered furniture, a pair of elephants' feet, several plants in pots, a two-foot square packing-case, nailed down – very heavy, Simmonds said (he too must have thought it might be a body when he came forward to the police) – and more boxes. Simmonds was paid six shillings for each trip.

A few weeks later, Crippen invited Long to clear some more stuff, a lot of clothing this time. He was shown into the kitchen, where there was a pile of things on the table, and told to help himself to what he wanted and dispose of the rest. There were women's clothes – stockings, underwear, shoes, theatrical costumes, some blouses – as well as old curtains, tablecloths, rugs and various odds and ends, including the seven canaries in a cage.

Crippen told Long that he was going to leave the house and take a flat in the West End. He saw his landlord and gave him three months' notice, explaining that he had been left some property in the United States and his wife had gone to attend to it. The landlord asked for a letter of notice, which came a couple of days later. Crippen volunteered to try and find a new tenant. When the landlord's clerk next called at Hilldrop to collect the rent, Crippen complained of damp in the breakfast-room and said the cause was a cracked pipe.

The Martinettis bumped into Crippen and his typist at the Aldwych Theatre, and when the play was finished Paul invited

them to join him and Clara at the Gaiety for some refresh-
ments. When they parted, Crippen and Ethel went off in a
cab, while the Martinettis walked home.

Paul Martinetti was just about retired by now, nearly sixty
years old and with failing health (though he would live on until
1924), after a lifetime on the stage, beginning at the age of six.
His father, grandfather, even his great-grandfather were said
to have been stage mimics and, though the family were of
French origin, Paul had been born in the States and had been
in a theatrical management partnership with his father before
forming his own troupe of pantomimists, which included his
wife Clara, and coming to London.

Here is a review from the Christmas season of 1877 in
London: 'The most genuinely amusing pantomime fooling
takes place at the Adelphi, where ... a number of pantomimists, styling themselves the Martinetti troupe, give an
admirable performance. Anyone desirous of knowing of what
pantomime is capable should see this representation, the
whole of which occupies little more than half an hour.'

Paul and his brother Alfred made a number of individual
appearances in shows in addition to their appearances in the
troupe. When he became King Rat for the year 1899, the
Grand Order of Water Rats was less than a decade old.

On Monday, 21 March the Martinettis received this letter
from Crippen:

39 Hilldrop Crescent, N.
Sunday, Mar. 20/10

Dear Clara and Paul,
    Forgive me not running in during the week but I have
really been so upset by very bad news from Belle that I
did not feel equal to talking about anything, and now I
have had just a cable saying she is so dangerously ill
with double pleuro-pneumonia that I am considering if I
had better not go over at once.
    I do not want to worry you with my troubles but I

felt I must explain why I had not been to see you.

I will try and run in during the week and have a chat. Hope both of you are well with love and best wishes.

Yours sincerely
Peter

Paul called in on Crippen at work and said, 'Look here, Peter, if I were you I would take the first ship I could get hold of and go to America.' Crippen shrugged his shoulders and said nothing in response, a typical gesture of his, thought Martinetti. When Crippen returned the visit, the following day, Clara said she could not understand how Belle had caught double pneumonia and Crippen said she was always a girl who was self-willed and would go out, even after having a cold.

Next day, the day of the weekly Guild meeting, Clara told the committee about Belle's illness. She and another committee member saw Crippen as they were leaving and he told them he was expecting another cable any minute to say she was gone. They crossed the road together.

CRIPPEN: If anything happens I shall go to France for a week.
CLARA: Whatever for?
CRIPPEN: I could not stay in the house and should want a change.

Crippen had already told his assistant Long that he was going away for a few days. He had not mentioned that Ethel Le Neve was going too, though Long would note her absence at the same time.

The telegram arrived at the Martinettis' the following morning:

24 MARCH. VICTORIA STATION.
BELLE DIED YESTERDAY AT 6 O'CLOCK. PLEASE PHONE
ANNIE SHALL BE AWAY ABOUT A WEEK
PETER

Crippen had sent the telegram on his way to France with Ethel Le Neve. She would later say that she did not find out about Mrs Crippen's alleged death until they got back, five days later. Where was she standing when Crippen wrote out and sent the telegram?

Clara took it with her to Albion House and showed it to Crippen's dental partner.

RYLANCE: I know nothing about it.

CLARA: What? Does he not confide in you? Didn't you know Mrs Crippen was ill?

RYLANCE: Mrs Martinetti, I don't know anything. The doctor does not confide in me as to his private affairs.

CLARA: Dr Crippen told me he was going away to France for a week.

RYLANCE: I don't know where he has gone.

CLARA: And the typist?

RYLANCE: Oh, she's gone on her holidays.

Rylance was obviously being protective towards Crippen. He would later say, in court, that Crippen had told him a few days before that he was going to France and that Ethel Le Neve was going too, with her aunt (the detail of the aunt obviously intended to protect Ethel's honour and suggest the role of chaperone).

Clara showed the telegram to her Guild friend, Annie Stratton. They both thought it was very strange. She showed it to William Long too. Crippen never once mentioned his wife's death to Long.

It was Easter weekend and on the Saturday there was a notice in the stage paper, *The Era*, on page 17:

DEATHS

Elmore – 23 March, in California, USA, Miss Belle Elmore (Mrs H.H. Crippen).

Meanwhile, Crippen and Ethel were having a lovely time in

Dieppe, staying at the Vachers Hotel. Ethel sent a series of postcards and letters recording her pleasure. There was a quick postcard to her sister Nina sent on the very first day, just saying they had arrived safely after a pleasant journey. And another to her friend Lydia Rose, who was in service in Hampstead: 'Darling, arrived safely after a splendid journey across. Love E.' Then about Easter Monday there was a letter to Nina saying what a charming place Dieppe was, with beautiful valleys and weather, so different from cold, chilly England. The letter went on to report Belle Elmore's death. Hubby had heard that morning that she was dead, that she had caught cold going across (to America), result pneumonia. Was it not sad that one in the prime of life should be so cut off (or words to that effect, as Nina would later recall).

Hubby? Yes, hubby, because by now Ethel had told her family and friends she was already married to Crippen. They thought the trip to France was her honeymoon.

Ethel had sent a typewritten note to her friend Lydia Rose a couple of weeks earlier. 'You will be very surprised to hear I was married last Saturday, about 12 March 1910.' The note had gone on to say that she and her husband were so busy they could not get away until Easter but would then have a honeymoon at Dieppe. The note had been signed: Eth Crippen.

Though her true feelings are not recorded it is reasonable to assume that Lydia Rose probably *was* surprised – but she can't have been all that surprised because Ethel had told her as far back as January that she was engaged, though she did not say to whom and Lydia Rose had not asked. This must have been at Ethel's small birthday party, her twenty-seventh, which she held at her lodgings, 80 Constantine Road, in Hampstead. Lydia Rose's mum, who was also called Lydia Rose, had been there too and also remembered Ethel saying that she was engaged.

It was certainly prescient of Ethel to know as far back as January, even before Belle's murder, that she could safely be announcing her engagement. There was no marriage, of course. It was all a deception. But Ethel must have been desperate to achieve the status and respectability of becoming even a make-believe wife. Ethel, I think, wanted to be decent, perhaps even envied. Those were very Edwardian ambitions and, certainly for Ethel but also for thousands of other young women of the age, they were bound up in questions of class and social mobility.

FIVE

Though the exact date is unrecorded, Ethel's parents moved to north London from rural Norfolk towards the end of the nineteenth century. They may well have been following a general migratory trend from the country to the cities in the late Victorian age. The cities offered opportunity, the possibility of making good. The rural way of life was being eroded by mass production and metropolitan expansion.

Ethel's parents were to have six children and certainly needed some space of their own. They are on the 1882 census at 109 Sandy Lane in the small Norfolk market town of Diss, living with her mother's family in a home for ten people. The head of the household is Ethel's maternal grandfather, William Jones, aged fifty-six, a horse-breaker. His wife, Clara, is forty-seven and they have seven children still at home, including Charlotte, twenty-two and, in addition, Charlotte's husband Walter Neave, who is also twenty-two and listed as a railway clerk from Palgrave, Suffolk.

Walter and Charlotte were Ethel's parents and she was their first child, born on 22 January 1883, by which time Walter and Charlotte had moved to their own home, a tiny cottage in nearby Victoria Road. At the end of that same year they had a second child, the beautifully named Adine True Neave, who was born on 15 December and so was eleven months younger than Ethel Clara Neave. Adine would ever after be known to Ethel as Nina. Ethel would later say that the family moved from Diss to London when she was seven, which would be in 1890.

Ethel's father seems to have been a man with aspirations to a better station in life. He took the name Le Neave, he would later explain, because he used to sing in choirs at Norwich

Cathedral and also at the Norwich Festival and other concerts. He said Ethel used to sing at those concerts too, but she was Le Neve, without the 'a'. That must have been Ethel's extra affectation. Among the family only Ethel and her father took assumed names, but the youngest boy, Sidney, actually had the name Le Neave on his birth certificate. He was always plain Neave in later life and would complain that Ethel's notoriety had deprived him of his real name.

There must have been much more to it than merely using these names for concerts, or why would Ethel and her father continue using them long after their performing days were over? Being Le Neave or Le Neve sounded grander, obviously, and must have fitted their own ideas of where they really belonged in the world and where they hoped they were heading.

Late Victorian and Edwardian London was full of people searching for ways up the social ladder. You could see them all in the morning, flocking to the centre from the inner and outer suburbs. The rush hour was a relatively recent phenomenon, still fascinating, even thrilling to contemporary reporters with their florid turns of phrase:

London Bridge! It is the climax, the apotheosis, as it were, of all thus far seen. So crowded is the canvas, so full of movement, it dazes one. Life sweeps over the bridge like the rush of the sea by the sides of a ship – always Citywards. In thousands they advance, leaning forward, with long, quick strides, eager to be there! Swiftly they flash past, and still they come and come, like the silent shadowy legions of a dream. Somehow they suggest the dogged march of an army in retreat, with its rallying point far ahead, and the enemy's cavalry pressing on its rear. Looking down upon the swarming masses, with the dark sullen river for a background, they fuse into one monstrous organism, their progress merges in the rhythmic swaying of one mammoth breathing thing. Stand in the midst of the mighty current of men! A wearied, languorous feeling creeps over you, as face follows face, and eyes in thousands swim by. It is the hypnotic influence of the measureless, the unfathomable, the you-know-not-what of mystery and elusiveness in life, stealing your senses away.

Individually, this mysterious horde dissolved into junior managers and clerks, agents and brokers, sales representatives, shop assistants, typists and shorthand-takers and secretaries. All these roles were newly available on a wide scale and had served to help create a fresh social order, the lower middle class, whose pretensions and ignorance were much mocked and satirised by those who saw themselves as superior.

The Diary of a Nobody by George and Weedon Grossmith featured Charles Pooter, who lived with his family in a house not unlike 39 Hilldrop Crescent, and not far away from it either, beside a railway line in Holloway. Mr Pooter was an anxious clerk leading a decent boring life which he recorded in painfully fine detail. Among Pooter's worst traits were his vanity, his pomposity and his snobbishness – all of which it was possible to detect in Walter William Le Neave, although, sadly, Walter did not seem able to quite match Pooter's firm grip on the lower-middle rungs of the class ladder.

The theme of London's suburbia, and the many secret worlds within it, was addressed in kinder terms by the well-known Edwardian journalist George R. Sims in an article called 'Behind the Blinds':

A doctor has been compared to the driver of a hansom – he knows his way about the streets, but he cannot tell you what is going on inside the houses. But the great life of London is lived as much – nay, it is lived more – behind the blinds of the quiet houses than it is in the busy thoroughfares. In the streets, except on rare occasions and in isolated cases, we are all more or less 'supers' [he must mean 'extras'] in the great crowd. Our individuality is merged in that of the moving stream of humanity. Our joys and our sorrows are concealed behind a mask. It is only in the house that we take the stage and act out the story in which we are intimately concerned.

The Edwardian age is usually caricatured as a 'golden age' of gaiety, after the long, stern years of Victorian repression, embodied in the frivolous lifestyle of the new King and his aristocratic companions. But J.B. Priestley eloquently articulated a more realistic picture of class conflict and tensions arising from the social changes that were already under way. In his view a large proportion of the upper and lower middle classes might have still been Victorian in their outlook, values and judgements but, behind their 'imposing mask of moral indignation' was fear, and it was all the more fiercely expressed because they were unsure of themselves.

In Priestley's analysis, the upper middles felt that their property and their position were being threatened. The lower middles were concerned to guard their newly acquired respectability. They were often recent arrivals from the working class and feared 'sliding back into the jungles and bogs of the workers'. Priestley remembered his own father's cry of, 'What are the neighbours going to think?'

There was a general anxiety that the traditional beliefs – church, family, social and political stability – were being challenged by the middle classes with their clever men, their shameless women and their modern ideas (such as women's suffrage). This atmosphere of amorphous, undefined fear, argued Priestley, found its expression in the irrational belief, which mushroomed in the approach to 1914, that the Germans were about to invade. The aliens, as ever, were not really the foreigners but the people themselves, freshly seized by aspiration and losing their grip on the certainties of the past.

There is a press photograph, taken in 1910, of Ethel's parents and her young brother Sidney in what appears to be the parlour of their flat in Camden. They are posed in front of a pine dresser hung with crockery, Charlotte sitting in a chair, buttoned up to the neck in a blouse with frills, hands clasped

delicately in her lap. Sidney, all of eleven, sits to one side of
Charlotte, stroking a terrier sitting in his lap; he is wearing a
stiff collar and a bow tie and has hair slicked back. Walter
stands beside them with his hands in his pocket, his legs apart
and his chest puffed, and his moustache waxed to a fine point.
He too is wearing a stiff collar and a bow tie, with a white
waistcoat and chain and cufflinks on his shirt, as though he is
just about to put on his tuxedo and go out for the evening.
They are doing their best to look dignified. You would never
know their daughter was suspected of involvement in a foul
murder, which is the very reason why the photograph was
taken.

The accompanying text contains an interview with Charlotte in which she says there was a time when the family were
in better circumstances than they are now. In those better days
she and her husband had spared neither pains nor money to
give their daughters the best education. It had been harder for
the four boys, who had had to rough it, though they were all
doing well now, two in offices (one with a solicitor) and the
youngest, Sidney, still at home.

Charlotte said that when they had come up to London from
the country she had paid the girls' way through private school
and later sent them to a board school, Christ Church School in
Hampstead. They were trained in music too, under a special
master, though Ethel had never taken to the piano like Nina.

Ethel was obviously a disappointment and had clearly been
in her younger sister's shadow:

'Those two girls were inseparable. There is only eleven
months between them and they did everything together
from the very first. Nina got the upper hand, however,
always. She was stronger and perhaps cleverer and at school
they always thought she was much older than her sister
instead of the other way round.

'Ethel was more timid and nervous and gave in to her
sister. She was delicate in health and constantly catching
cold. She was very quiet in manner. Both girls were loving

and affectionate when they lived at home. They always put
their mother first in everything.'

When the time came for them to leave school Charlotte had
sent them both to Pitman's to learn shorthand and typing.
Both girls had picked it up quickly and Charlotte still had
Ethel's certificate for eighty words per minute of shorthand.
They used to spend the day over the shorthand and learn the
typing in the evening. Everybody said what quick, clever girls
they were and that they would be sure to make a good thing
out of it once they started in business. As you know, said
Charlotte, they both entered Dr Crippen's service together.

Well, this was almost right.

When the case blew up, that summer of 1910, Charlotte's
husband had not contributed anything so routine as a brief
interview but had lost no time at all in selling his own version
of Ethel's story to the popular magazine *Answers*, to be
serialised over no less than four weeks. He claimed he did it to
pay for her defence. It was clear that this had greatly upset
Ethel. On the other hand, there was a distinct chill, already,
between Ethel and her parents.

Walter agreed with his wife – in episode one of *Answers* –
that Nina had always been cleverer and in better health than
her older sister. Though it was Ethel, he said, who used to play
the piano and accompany him when he sang oratorios. Walter
took all the credit for getting his girls into Drouet's (that
esteemed medical practice). He had seen the advertisement for
the position of shorthand typist and he had applied, not for his
oldest daughter, but for Nina, no doubt because she was
cleverer and perhaps more personable too. Having got the job,
said Walter, Nina then introduced Ethel.

There was abundant evidence of Ethel's frequent indisposi-
tions. Dr Rylance the dentist said she was famous at Albion
House for her reply to any casual greeting: 'Not very well,
thank you.' He clearly did not think much of her and said it
passed his understanding how Crippen could have thrown
over Mrs Crippen in favour of his typist. Ethel's landlady, Mrs

Emily Jackson, who had been very fond of Ethel, also had plenty to say about Ethel's neuralgia and anaemia and her various considerable pains and weaknesses. She said her fingers twitched nervously when she was afflicted by the neuralgia.

It sounded, frankly, as if Ethel was a bit of a nervous wreck, though it is often the case that people who affect to suffer mental or physical pain, or both, can turn out to be the toughest characters of all. Walter Neave also wrote in *Answers* that Ethel was a living advertisement for Crippen's dental partnership, having had more than twenty teeth removed in one go and the same number of false teeth fitted, as a gift from Crippen. Neave implied that Crippen had conducted the extractions. Whoever took them out, for whatever reason (maybe they thought it might help her neuralgia), it certainly suggests that Ethel had hidden reserves of courage.

Ethel herself, in her own life story, painted a self-portrait of a hardy tomboy child. She had no longing for dolls or other girlish toys, she said, and with her chief companion, her uncle, who worked on the railway, she would often go to see the trains, so that even to this day there were few things which interested her more than an engine. How her uncle used to laugh when he saw her climbing trees, or playing marbles, or shooting with a catapult. Amazingly, there was no mention anywhere in Ethel's life story of her mother and father, except for one line in the newspaper serialisation. This was removed, the only line that was removed, when it was immediately re-published as a book: 'I had had a great deal of family worry, unconnected with Dr Crippen, for the past six years.'

Though Nina and her husband later had financial problems, which troubled Ethel, these had not been going on for six years. It may be that the 'family worry' is a reference to her father's problems with alcohol. There is anecdotal evidence from surviving descendants that he was an alcoholic and, if true, this must have been a pressure on all his family.

The 1901 census has them living at 61 Gayton Road in Hampstead, all of them down as Le Neaves. It is tempting to picture Walter standing over the census-taker with his clipboard as he writes the names down – 'we spell that capital L-e-space-capital N-e-a-ve . . .' – in longhand on the printed form which survives to this day.

Walter William Le Neave is now the head of his own household, a dairyman's manager aged forty-one. Charlotte Anne is forty-two, Clara Ethel (her names are back to front) is eighteen and a typewriter, Adine True is seventeen, typewriter and shorthand, Claude, fifteen is a clerk in a provision shop, Bernard is eleven and Sidney is four. There is a child missing: Wilfred Montague Le Neave, aged nine, born Hampstead, appears on the 1901 census in Wales, at the home of his aunt Gertrude in Blaenavon, Monmouth. Gertrude, who is probably his father's sister, has married a Valentine Narracott who lists his profession as Conservative agent. There is no explanation as to why Wilfred is there: perhaps he was recovering from an illness, or maybe he had been causing problems with his behaviour.

By 1910 Walter William Le Neave was describing himself as a commercial coal agent. This was not a grand title for the man who carried the sacks but a white collar job: he went around offices in London obtaining orders for fuel on behalf of a company called Wallace Spiers.

It was about the time of the 1901 census that Nina, and then Ethel, joined Drouet's in Regent's Park. Crippen arrived shortly afterwards. The first exposés of the company appeared early in 1903, and in the summer of that year Nina left to get married, at nineteen, to Horace Brock, a thirty-three-year-old fruit broker's clerk from Kentish Town. His father was a retired solicitor, so that was social progress. Ethel was a witness at the wedding. They were very close, those two sisters, and there must have been some awkwardness between them, at least a little, that Nina the younger was marrying first.

It was said by Walter in his *Answers* serial that Ethel replaced Nina as head of the ladies' department at Drouet's and this may have been true, but given that there were only three people working there by 1905, this perhaps makes it sound more important than it was.

Ethel later wrote that she was lonely when her sister left Drouet's to get married and that Crippen was lonely too, in his marriage, and that was what drew them together and 'deepened' their friendship.

Crippen would recall their beginnings in one of a series of eloquent and deeply moving letters which he wrote to Ethel from his condemned cell: 'I see ourselves in those early days of our courtship, having our dinner together after our day of work together was done, or sitting sometimes in our favourite corner at Frascati's by the stairwell, all the evening listening to the music. The dinner too with Nina with us, in anticipation of her marriage; and ah! How even in those early days we began to realise how near and dear we were to become to each other . . .'

Frascati's Restaurant was at 26–32 Oxford Street, near Tottenham Court Road and not far from Albion House. It had opened in the 1890s and was a popular, sprawling place with various areas: a winter garden, a café and a grill room. There was often live music and, later, in the twenties, dance bands performed there.

> 'One Sunday, how early I came for you – six years ago last summer it was [that would be the summer of 1904] – and we had a whole day together, which meant so much to us then. A rainy day indeed, but how happy we were together, with all sunshine in our hearts. It is good to think, darling wifie, that even in those early days before our wedding came that we were always in perfect harmony with each other. Even without being wedded.
>
> 'Then came those days when hub felt, and wifie too so earnestly felt, it was impossible to live on and not be all in all to each other, and from our wedding day all has been a perfect honeymoon of four years to Dec. 6 next.'

That date, 6 December next, was a day that Crippen already knew he would not live to see, the letter having been written in Pentonville on Sunday, 6 November 1910, seventeen days before he was hanged. I wish I could say with certainty that Crippen had not written those letters with an eye to their later publication. So much did get sold at the time that it is hard to be sure. And they did find their way into the public domain. Still, it does not negate the tenderness of the phrases and the true sentiments I'm sure they express.

Crippen and Le Neve never did marry. The date he refers to as their wedding, 6 December 1904, is undoubtedly the day they first had sex: on that day they became 'all in all' to each other and, ever after, were hub and wifie in the coded language of their own private world, the 'marriage' unknown to another soul, except, by implication, to Ethel's landlady.

Ethel at least told her sister Nina about Crippen, though probably not that they had begun a sexual relationship. She said the doctor had asked her to go out and about with him and wait for him until such time as he could get a divorce, as he and his wife did not live happily together. The doctor's wife was always nagging him and some man in America wanted her. With hindsight, Nina was sure she must have sympathised with her sister in her unfortunate love affair, as Ethel was not free to love the doctor.

Crippen would say in court that his wife had always treated Ethel with the greatest courtesy, so he did not think she knew of his relations with her – though there was the statement of Maud Burroughs that Belle had said she did not like (perhaps, did not trust?) her husband's typist. But Crippen said there was never any obstacle to him seeing Ethel, his time was his own, he went as he liked and often stayed away from business whole days at a time. He had told Ethel that if his wife ever went away and got a divorce he would marry her, certainly, and she had seemed very happy with that position.

Ethel did not seem to know at first that Crippen even had a wife. She had told her friend Lydia Rose about an actress coming to visit the doctor at the office, but she was sure that couldn't have been Mrs Crippen. She found out the truth soon enough, though, because, according to her life story, Crippen collapsed at the office one day after an angry visit from his wife, and Ethel had to revive him with some brandy. He had told her then that Belle was his wife in name only and that they went their separate ways. Ethel said that 'quite by chance' she saw some of Bruce Miller's letters to Belle and that they (very conveniently) relieved her of any misgivings she might have had about having a relationship with Belle's husband.

It seemed important to Ethel to emphasise in her life story that she had only ever had one landlady, as if staying in a succession of different lodgings would have been somehow disreputable. Ethel lived with her parents for a while at another address in Hampstead, Willow Cottages. Then she moved into Nina's marital home – Nina lived first in Willesden, where her first child, Ronald, was born in 1904, and then later moved to Clonmell Road in Tottenham. Ethel was with her for around eighteen months and left not long before September 1908, when she went to lodge with Emily Jackson, at 80 Constantine Road, in that area of Hampstead not far from the Heath which is nowadays known locally as South End Green.

Crippen later told the police he had frequently stayed with Ethel at hotels but was never away from home at nights. There seems to be a contradiction in this statement – did he stay with her or did he go home? – but, in any event, there is no other evidence of visits to hotels before Belle's murder.

There is, however, evidence of rooms he rented at 82 Wells Street, just north of Oxford Street, not far from Tottenham Court Road, under the assumed name of Mr Franckel. He initially only rented a letter-box there, in June 1906, telling the landlord he was an ear specialist. Then in October 1906 he rented an office there, for six shillings a week. That was just before he and Ethel became hub and wifie. A year later he took an office and a bedroom at twelve shillings and sixpence a week, telling the landlord he expected to have a typist there. This arrangement continued until mid-1908, when he gave up the office and just retained a small attic bedroom which he partly furnished. The landlord sometimes heard movement there at 1 am but otherwise said the room was rarely used at night, though he occasionally saw a girl coming down the stairs during the day. 'Mr Frankel' had asked him to forward any letters for Miss Le Neve to Albion House, and so he did. It is reasonable to assume this place was their 'love nest'.

Ethel gave Crippen's name as a referee when she applied to lodge at Mrs Jackson's in September 1908. They were to become very close, Ethel calling Mrs Jackson 'Ma' as if she did not already have her own 'Ma'. The intimacy must have been hastened by the miscarriage Ethel went through, within two weeks of arriving at 80 Constantine Road.

The miscarriage is absent from Ethel's life story and was never mentioned by anyone else. Maybe no one else knew, apart from Crippen. The only account is from Mrs Jackson, who described it in one of her police statements and also alluded to it, indirectly, in court. Mrs Jackson said she never saw the baby but called a doctor, a Miss Ethel Vernon of 11 Grosvenor Road in Wetsminster. Mrs Jackson was there when Dr Vernon asked Ethel where the baby was and she at first said she didn't know but eventually said she had gone to the lavatory and while she was there felt something come from her. Both Dr Vernon and Mrs Jackson had questioned her closely on who the father was, but Ethel would not say.

She had remained in bed about a fortnight, asking Mrs Jackson 'to send' to Albion House to tell Dr Crippen she was ill. He had called at the house two or three days after the miscarriage and asked to see Ethel, showing Mrs Jackson his business card at the door. She let him in and he only stayed a few minutes. He called again a week later and again stayed only a few minutes.

Not long after this, Ethel started 'walking out' with a young man, a chemists' and druggists' clerk, called John Stonehouse, who came to lodge at Mrs Jackson's in January 1909. He said he considered Ethel was a very nice girl and they had treated each other as friends, nothing more. After he had been at Constantine Road for two or three months they started going on walks together, regularly visiting the Coach & Horses in

Heath Street and also the Stag on Fleet Road. They used to stay half an hour, or longer sometimes, and Ethel would have a bottle of stout or a glass of port wine.

When they had been walking out together for some weeks, Stonehouse heard a rumour that Ethel had borne a child for someone, unknown. Then one night when he was at the Stag his landlord, Mrs Jackson's husband, made a complaint to him that Ethel was implicated with someone else, though Stonehouse could not find out who it was.

He must have been curious, though, because when they were in the West End one evening, near Oxford Street, Ethel pointed out Albion House and told him that that was where she worked and afterwards he looked it up in the directory and found a Dr Munyon was based there. He asked if that was her employer and Ethel said it was. Stonehouse had noted how 'the doctor' was always to the fore in her conversation, although he never really knew who he was or what they did in business. He never heard the name Crippen.

Ethel went away without telling him, and he did not hear from her for some time until she wrote from an address in or near Brighton saying that her uncle, who was living there, was indisposed and that she was staying to help her aunt.

He then had a letter from Albion House saying she was back in London – though she had not returned to Constantine Road – and asking Stonehouse to make an appointment. They met in Hampstead one Saturday evening and, when he took her home, Stonehouse discovered that she was living in Store Street off Tottenham Court Road. As they stood at the door talking he realised she was uncomfortable there and when he got back to Hampstead spoke to Mrs Jackson, who seemed not unwilling to have Ethel back. He mentioned this to Ethel when he next saw her and, even so, was surprised when he got home a few days later, to find Ethel already back there in her old room.

Things went on as usual, Stonehouse told the police in his statement. He and Ethel started walking out again and he treated her in the same friendly style as before until he moved to new lodgings in October 1909, when they stopped seeing each other. 'There was never any undue familiarity between us,' Stonehouse assured the police.

According to Mrs Jackson, Ethel left her in March 1909 and went to stay with her aunt, Mrs Benstead, in Brighton. She returned to Mrs Jackson's in September (or maybe it was August, as Jackson mentioned both months in different statements). Where was she, for up to seven months?

There is no corroborating evidence of her whereabouts, or what was going on, except that Crippen's assistant, William Long, said that in March 1909 he became suspicious that there was something not quite right between Crippen and Ethel by their general demeanour. This is not explained, so could mean it was at this time he realised they were having an affair, or it could mean there was some tension or frostiness between them. He had, after all, been with them at work for much of the decade, time enough, you would think, to detect their intimacy, even if they were doing their best to hide it.

One earlier account of the case dates this as the time of Ethel's miscarriage, but the writer did not have access to Mrs Jackson's statement, which clearly places it at the time Ethel began lodging with her.

It's possible that there was another miscarriage. Or perhaps Ethel was using her dates with Stonehouse to signal to Crippen that, following her pregnancy, she was not prepared to carry on being a dishonest woman. Although Crippen would later write that there had never been a cross word between them, perhaps Ethel left London for a while after a falling-out with him.

Ethel never mentioned this interlude in her life story, and although it's possible that the version she told Stonehouse was the truth and her uncle really was ill, there must be some doubt that she was ever in Brighton. The Bensteads gave brief statements to the police but never said she had stayed with them. She did visit them at weekends so could then have posted a letter to Stonehouse. She may have been holed-up in

London the whole time, perhaps trying out co-habiting with Crippen, or maybe hiding something else.

One possibility is that Ethel did become pregnant again, in the six months following the miscarriage. By coincidence, her sister Nina's second child was registered as being born on 20 September 1909, at just around the time Ethel returned to Mrs Jackson's. Nina made Ethel her daughter's godparent and named the child Ivy Ethel Brock. The place of birth was given as the Brocks' home, 43 Clonmell Road, Tottenham. Could this have been Ethel's child, taken on by Nina?

In support of the possibility are one or two inconsistencies. Nina's husband served in the army during the First World War and his military record also records family details, including a date of birth of 30 August 1909 for Ivy on one page and, on another page, the date on the birth certificate, 20 September. The contradiction has been flagged with question marks, presumably by a War Office clerk.

Ivy grew up and married and had one son and lived on until 1992, when she died – on 19 September – at the age of eighty-two. She had always told her son she was born in Diss, Norfolk and this was recorded on her death certificate, even though her birth certificate recorded her place of birth as Tottenham. Like others among Ethel's surviving family, Ivy never spoke about her relative's infamous association with Crippen. She did not even tell her son, Roger, until six months before her death, when she told him she had never disclosed it to her husband, Jack Palmer, who was still alive at the time but died without ever knowing Aunt Ethel's true identity. The family obviously inherited Ethel's facility for keeping secrets.

While Ivy was still a baby there was ample evidence from Nina of the times when she visited Ethel, or met Ethel in the park or was visited by Ethel and showed her the baby and how delighted Ethel was to see it. There was never any mention of Nina's other child, her son Ronald, or that Ethel was delighted to see him. Of course, none of this means that Ivy was really Ethel and Crippen's child. It's all just circumstantial. Such an arrangement would almost certainly have required the collusion of Ethel and Nina's parents and it is hard to imagine their father, Walter, keeping that to himself and not spilling the beans in *Answers*. It would surely have required the collusion of Crippen too – if Ethel was in Store Street he must have been involved in that rental – and he wrote in one of his prison letters, 'If only I could have left you well provided for I would have wished our little one had lived that you might have had what would have been part of both of us. But, like other things, it was not to be.' This must be a reference to the miscarriage and suggests that there was only one pregnancy.

Still, I think of Ethel on the door-step at Store Street with her young man, John Stonehouse, around September 1909, with only four months to go to the murder, and wonder what or who it was, inside the house, that made her uncomfortable. I think of those missing seven months and wonder where she was and what she was up to. And I can't forget what an accomplished liar she was.

'A real piece of work,' as the American academic, Julie English Early, who has studied the case, describes her.

On that same day in September 1909, the 20th, Crippen also began trading from Craven House on Kingsway as the Aural Remedies Company, in partnership with Eddie Marr.

Crippen was obviously undeterred by the failure of Drouet's and the legal fall-out that followed. He had written to Marr a year earlier to ask if he had a few minutes to talk about a new Deaf Institute along the same lines. They had met, but nothing had been settled. Crippen had written to Marr a couple of weeks later and they had met again, but this time Marr told Crippen he was too busy to take on any fresh business. Crippen, apparently anxious for more work, had written to Marr again in January 1909 and Marr must have finally relented because they then started meeting regularly to discuss the new enterprise.

To start with, Marr agreed to pay Crippen a one-off fee of £10 for writing a booklet – 'The Otological Gazette edited by H.H. Crippen, MD, USA'. He would then be paid £2 a week to manage 'the technical part' of the correspondence with a modest commission of $2\frac{1}{2}\%$ on excess profits. He had gone to Marr's offices at Vine Street every Friday to collect his wages, until his escape in July 1910. He never received any commission.

Marr would later tell Chief Inspector Dew that he believed Crippen was earning around £10 a week, from all his businesses, which was a good salary without being astronomical. It was hard to see how this would have paid for Belle's furs, clothes and jewellery, or indeed their increasingly sociable lifestyle. Marr said he thought it was impossible on Crippen's wages.

Crippen used to go to Craven House on Kingsway each

morning at 9 am to collect the correspondence, draft replies based on his expert advice and see patients who had made appointments or simply turned up. The headed paper used by Aural Remedies did not specify a room number at Craven House and its advertising sometimes used different room numbers, so that at least one newspaper reported complaints from other companies in the building that they received both his mail and his visitors. It was the visitors who were the most problematic – as they were usually stone deaf they were hard to direct to Crippen's office. His name appeared on a plaque on the door of his room; this was quickly taken down when he became a wanted man. People seeing a suspicious-looking character unscrewing the plaque thought it might have been Crippen himself, covering his tracks, but it was actually Eddie Marr.

A number of Crippen's typewritten Aural Remedies' letters signed by him have survived. He employed a different typewriter there, Ena Balham, so the handiwork was not Ethel's. The letters are essentially attempts to hustle the recipients with testimonials, discounts, cast-iron assurances of a cure and any other bamboozling that will strip them of their money. Each is a mini-masterpiece of aggressive marketing. And funny too, from a distance of ninety-five years. Here's one sent in January 1910, which begins, as do most of the examples I've seen (perhaps only men were deaf in the Edwardian age – most likely it was only their deafness that mattered):

Dear Sir

As I have received no answer to my letter of a few days ago I can only conclude that your hesitation in deciding to adopt my treatment is due to previous unfortunate experiments which have very naturally caused you to harbour suspicion against all so-called cures, and a strong disinclination to spend any more money without some stronger assurance of receiving adequate return.

Since writing you, however, I have received the

following extraordinary testimonial from Mr J. Hanrahan, of Castlegrale, Clogheen, Co. Tipperary, who, after being deaf for no less than fifty-eight years, writes me as follows: 'I want to let you know that your remedies have entirely cured my Deafness. Yours is the very best treatment that was ever known. I had been deaf ever since I was seven years old, and my Deafness had thus lasted for fifty-eight years.'

I feel so confident that you will share the happy experience of Mr Hanrahan, that I am going to make you the following special offer. This places within your reach the possibility of being speedily and permanently cured, and I hardly need point out that I could scarcely make such an offer, were I not convinced of the efficacy of my Treatment.

If you will send me half the amount mentioned in my last letter, namely 7s 6d, I will at once forward the full and complete Outfit 'On Trial'. If, at the expiration of a sufficient time, say three weeks, you feel you have derived no benefit you can return what is left of the Outfit and need not pay me another penny. On the other hand, if you I feel you have been benefited by the treatment, you can then remit the balance of the purchase price, namely 7s 6d.

I believe you will agree that this offer is just as fair to both of us as I can possibly make it. By assuming the risk of no further payment, I want to make you feel that I believe my treatment will do what I claim for it. I need hardly point out to you the desirability of taking advantage of this concession without delay.

Yours faithfully
H.H. Crippen [signed with a flourish]

It did not take the anti-quack campaigners long to pick up on the new company. The periodical *Albion Magazine*, which was produced for a deaf readership, reported on Aural

Remedies in its October 1909 issue. Their investigator had evidently met Dr Crippen before, at Drouet's in 1904:

> I remember the man very well indeed mainly on account of his get-up and incidentally because of the story to be read in his face. I think Crippen is the only 'physician' I ever met who wore a frock coat together with a remarkably 'loud' fancy shirt, and his 'diamond' studs would have been worth a fortune – if real. His face and eyes told the story of a life miserably misspent. Like some other medical men (happily few in number), he has come down badly, until he touches the lowest depth to which it is possible for a medical man to come. Today he is a quack, and as a quack he is ready to do anything within the limits the law permits to quacks.

This was certainly an invitation to Crippen to sue for libel. No doubt, *Albion* would have argued that it was true – he was a quack – and that after working for Drouet's he had no reputation left to lose. Anyway, Crippen did not sue and there is no record that he ever reacted to any adverse publicity.

The other magazine, *Truth*, which had fought the libel trial against Crippen's fellow doctor at Drouet's, published an annual 'cautionary list' and in 1910 this included the following entry: '117. Aural Remedies Co., Craven House, Kingsway, London WC – A firm which runs a treatment for deafness on the lines of the late Drouet Institute. It has for "consulting specialist" one H.H. Crippen MD, a graduate of an American Homoeopathic Hospital College, who was at one time connected with the Drouet Institute, and has also been interested in other quack remedies.'

It is intriguing that Crippen was beginning to enjoy some notoriety, as it were, long before he became notorious. Even after he had become a fugitive, in July 1910, his advertisements were still appearing in the very publications that were just getting started on the acres of coverage they would devote to his case. Here is *Answers* of 16 July 1910 with its third column on page 255 shared equally by two advertisements, the top half promoting 'The New Cream Custard – One Quart Packet Free To All Ladies. Send a postcard today . . .' and beneath it:

WONDERFUL NEWS for the DEAF
New Publication containing Complete Description of Marvellous Discovery for the Cure of Deafness Given Away Free . . . [a lot of text here on the progress of science, etc.] . . . the onward march of scientific progress [blah blah] . . . this latest triumph of scientific investigation [blah blah blah] . . . every reader of this paper who suffers from Deafness, Head Noises, or Ear Disease in any form is cordially invited to send their name and address to the Aural Remedies Co., 825, Craven House, Kingsway, London, WC. By return they will received a copy of the Booklet
ABSOLUTELY FREE

And that was how he reined them in, those sufferers in search of hearing.

Not that Crippen was by any means the lone shark in this murky pool. The newspapers were full of similar advertisements and there is only a little – very little – evidence of newspapers showing any discrimination or self-censorship. It must have been earning them a fortune. No wonder one of Crippen's other enterprises was the Imperial Press Agency (owned by his alter-ego Mr Frankel) which acted as a broker for placing this kind of advertising: Consumption Can be Cured; I Have Found the Cure for Fatness, Hunyadi Janos Nature's Own Inimitable Remedy For Constipation, Free to the Ruptured; How I Got Rid of my Superfluous Hair; Wincarnis, the World's Greatest Wine Tonic; Junon Hair Tonic Restores Gloss and Brilliancy, Stops Hair Falling, Grew New Hair in 30 Days, Actually Grows Hair and Corrects all Scalp and Hair Troubles (to quote a selection of the advertisements from a few random pages of *John Bull*, September 1910).

As Crippen would say in court, he never completed

prescriptions because he didn't have to. His activities, like those of Marr and everyone else in patent medicines, were still completely unregulated. The British Medical Association published damning studies of patent medicines in 1909 (*Secret Remedies*) and in 1912 (*More Secret Remedies*), when Parliament set up the Select Committee on Patent Medicines and uncovered many more bogus claims for impossible cures of diseases such as cancer and inducements to abortion, which had often resulted in blackmail of the correspondents. The Committee's 782-page report of this 'grave and growing evil' had the misfortune (good fortune if you were Eddie Marr) to be published in August 1914, right at the start of the Great War when Parliament became preoccupied with other matters. Controls were introduced by the Pure Food & Drug Acts in the United States in 1909, and further tightened with an amendment in 1912, but in Britain those regulations were a long time coming, and were not properly in place until after the Second World War.

In late 1909, Crippen must have been trying to find ways to survive without Munyon's. At the beginning of December he gave Munyon two months' notice that he would be leaving altogether, following his earlier switch from salaried employee to agent on commission. At the same time he began the partnership with the dentist Gilbert Rylance. This too had been vigorously pursued by Crippen. Rylance said he pestered him for months after their initial discussion, which had taken place when Crippen invited Rylance to watch the royal procession from his office window when the Kaiser came to London on a state visit. Rylance had agreed very favourable terms, having no liability, no financial stake, and half of all the profits. He would later say that, although Crippen put all the money in, he never took anything out of the partnership. He had to pay the assistants too, who would have been Ethel Le Neve and William Long.

Earlier that year Belle had banked the last of a series of payments which she and Crippen had been making to deposit accounts at the Charing Cross Bank. The payments had begun three years earlier, in March 1906, and now amounted to £600. (That would have bought a house in Hilldrop Crescent, with money to spare.) On 15 December 1909 Belle gave notice to the bank that she wanted to withdraw the whole lot. The money was on twelve months' notice so would not be available until the end of next year, 1910.

In court, as in all accounts of the case since, this was portrayed as Belle acting alone, without her husband's knowledge, apparently intending to take the money for herself. On this basis, it was presented as evidence of her getting ready to leave him and defraud him, since it was his money too, or, if not, as money she had received from gentleman friends. It was further evidence of her gluttony and, in court, it was suggested that this was part of the financial motive for her murder.

According to Adelene Harrison, however, Belle was worried about money that Christmas because the doctor had revealed to her that business was bad and he was in want of funds to carry on his various enterprises. He had suggested realising a portion of the stock which she held at the bank and disposing of some of her jewels. Adelene would write that Belle was 'evidently not prepared to accede to this request'. But it seems she was wrong: Belle *was* prepared to help and had given the bank notice of withdrawal. In this version, Belle and Crippen are working together, not against each other, and it is no longer an indication that she was planning to leave him and take his money with her.

Perhaps Adelene was right, though, when she suggested, albeit in somewhat melodramatic language, that Belle was 'seized with a horrible fear' for her little world and was haunted by the thought of having to give up some of her outward glitter. She was surely over-egging the pudding when she described how Belle's 'little material soul shuddered. She forgot he was the man who had given her everything in the past. Perhaps if she had stood by and helped him she would have lulled some of the fiendish passions within him.'

In Adelene's account of the Crippens' life she creates a plausible distinction between their public face of cheerful unity and their private struggles. She describes them keeping up a brave show and trying to appear more wealthy than they really were. 'The world must not know,' as Adelene puts it.

But what is the truth of their finances? The messages are very mixed. Yes, Crippen appears to have been struggling. On the other hand, he also seems to have been extremely proficient at creating new enterprises. And, there was always that £600 on deposit at the bank, an enormous safety net, plus Belle's hoard of clothes and jewellery. In the absence of any evidence that Belle ever received money from other men, or that she ever earned very much as a performer, everything they had must have come from his earnings, which were evidently far greater than Eddie Marr realised. Perhaps Crippen was adept at siphoning off the profits and that was how they had accumulated such a susbstantial deposit at the bank, while at the same time paying for all Belle's luxuries. There is no other persuasive explanation, and while money issues might have heightened the tension between them at the time of the killing it does not seem like much of a motive. He could have just divorced her if it was money he wanted. Murder seems a drastic solution to a not very serious problem.

Adelene also picked out the shadow cast by the couple's inability to have children and the way they doted instead on their cats and treated them as any protective parent might, never allowing them further than the garden and, even then, placing them in a cage which Crippen had built at Belle's urging, so that they could not escape or come to harm while they took the air. But for the most part Adelene homes in on Belle's domestic sluttishness. Not that she would have deployed that word herself. She merely implied it, forcefully, and here her words seem to have been written with a poisoned pen. Adelene seems personally affronted by Belle's refusal to employ servants. For Adelene life without servants must have been unimaginable. It is as if Belle was letting the side down and betraying her class – whatever that class was, American boho having not yet entered the lexicon. 'In contrast to the lavish expenditure on her person, she exercised the most rigid economy in her home. The cost of one day's purchase of finery would have been more than sufficient for the upkeep of a well-regulated household for a week. In fact, to such an extent did she carry economy that it became parsimony.'

When they moved in to Hilldrop Crescent, Adelene said, Belle had taken two of the largest bedrooms in the house for dressing-rooms in which to place a portion of her gigantic wardrobes. Her gowns, mantles, hats, furs, laces, rolls of silks and satins, unmade robes in dozens, overflowed every room. During one visit to the house Adelene had been shown the new ermine and guipure coat (guipure is a kind of lace) which had just cost the doctor £85. The doctor had 'smiled blandly' at Belle's childish delight in her new treasure. She had also showed off several new gowns and a costly silver tea-tray which he had bought for her.

What really got to Adelene, however, was this: 'There was no system in the household. She [Belle] disliked fresh air and open windows. There was no regular household cleaning. Only when she "received" were lights seen in the hall or living rooms. They lived practically in the kitchen, which was always in a state of dirt and disorder.' (Actually, the windows must have been open sometimes as a neighbour would later recall missing hearing Belle singing – maybe rehearsing – at upstairs windows.)

Belle might be having a cup of coffee and a slice of bread and butter in the kitchen for lunch and then that same evening would be in a Parisian gown at the Savoy or the Trocadero, hosting a lavish dinner party. It was clear that the Crippens maintained the habits of their homeland, with the American cocktails they mixed for guests, and the coffee they always drank, which they made with condensed milk. Crippen said they always had coffee in the mornings, never tea. He usually had breakfast on his own, before going to work at about half past eight. Belle would still be in bed and once in a great while, but seldom, he took her a cup of coffee in bed.

Adelene also could not help noticing how Belle would go to market to buy her own greengroceries with a little cloth bag slung on one of her fingers containing hundreds of pounds' worth of diamonds and other jewels. She went to the cheapest shops for meat and to the Caledonian Market to buy cheap fowls, always trying to save the pence, while scattering the pounds. Some of Belle's other friends had seen that bag too, or perhaps a different one, Melinda May describing a leather wash bag which Belle used to transport her jewellery to and from the safe deposit where she kept it on Chancery Lane. In May's recollection it was not swinging from Belle's fingers but hidden under her bodice. But then, Melinda May thought the Hilldrop house was magnificently furnished. It was obviously all in the eye of the beholder.

For Adelene there was nothing magnificent about the house at all: 'The basement, owing to want of ventilation, smelt earthy and unpleasant. A strange, creepy feeling always came over me when I descended; it was so dark and dreary, although it was on a level with the back garden.' (The benefit of hindsight here, you may think). She had followed Belle into the kitchen one morning when she was busy, and even though it was a warm, humid day the windows had all been tightly closed. On the dresser Adelene had spied a 'heterogeneous mass' comprising dirty crockery, edibles, collars of the doctor's, false curls of her own, hair-pins, brushes, letters, a gold-jewelled purse and other articles. The kitchener (the fuel-burning heater) and the gas stove had been brown with rust and cooking stains. The table had been littered with packages, saucepans, dirty knives, plates, flat irons, a washing basin and a coffee pot.

In one article, Adelene described seeing a lovely white chiffon gown, embroidered with silk flowers and mounted over white glacé, thrown carelessly across a chair. In another article she had seen a twenty-two-guinea dress thrown carelessly across the dresser side by side with edibles and crockery. There were dresses everywhere. 'But when she [Belle] received her friends the whole scene changed. The table in one of the reception rooms was elegantly laid with a lace-bordered table cloth, dainty serviettes, gleaming silver and expensive flowers.' It seemed to be the contrasts and the contradictions that caused Adelene the most anguish. That and the disorder created by Belle's atrocious kitchen hygiene.

Still, she could not forget seeing the Crippens together at the house on one of the last occasions, side by side on the sofa, his arm around her waist, in the 'sweetest domestic intimacy'. There was no indication that it was for 'appearance sake', for he showed his love for her in every action of his life. In Adelene's experience no one had ever known them to be otherwise than loving and affectionate towards each other.

The layout of 39 Hilldrop Crescent was typical of the grander semi-detached villas that had been built in the area during the middle of the nineteenth century. It was on four floors altogether, beginning with the basement at garden level comprising two rooms, a breakfast-room and a kitchen, and a corridor leading down to the small cellar beneath the outside steps which led up to the front door of the house. The cellar had a hatched opening as a coal-hole at the side of the steps. The first floor had two sitting-rooms, the second floor had a front bedroom and behind that a bed and sitting-room. At the top were three small bedrooms, one at the front and two at the back together with a bathroom and lavatory.

According to one of the Crippens' lodgers, the house had a beautiful garden and was in a quiet street, one of the better streets in the neighbourhood. This was back in 1905, soon after they moved into the house. Belle was not performing much around this time, their social life yet to be transformed by the connections she would make through the Music Hall Ladies Guild. It sounds as if their lives were on hold and they must have advertised for lodgers almost straight away, apparently in the *Daily Telegraph*.

A young German student, Karl Reinisch, seems to have been the first. He was certainly established in the house by Christmas 1905 and was there to witness Crippen's gift of an expensive gramophone for his wife. She was, said Reinisch, already a good piano-player and and was 'pleased as a child' at the attentiveness implied by the gift of the gramophone. Reinisch regarded Belle as childlike in other ways too. She was, for instance, very competitive at cards and would get extremely angry if she lost a halfpenny at whist. Crippen would sometimes ask Reinisch to let her win. But, in general, the lodging had been just what Reinisch wanted, providing him with the society of two cultured people, the conversations by the fire being varied, stimulating, interesting.

Crippen had seemed quiet, gentlemanly, sensing his wife's every wish which, so far as Reinisch could see, he hastened to fulfil. She, by contrast, was high-spirited, with an opulent figure and a pretty face. She spoke a lot about her former artistic career and Reinisch could see she was still very ambitious. She had cooked well – unlike many English women, in Reinisch's experience.

The marriage had been harmonious during his time there but they had lived quietly, so that it had been a curious condition of his lodging that he should remain at home during the evenings and make company for the Crippens. He had not objected to the arrangement and was pleased that they had made him feel at home, so perhaps he was disappointed to be given his marching orders early the next summer. He kept the letter Belle had written, which was dated and timed at 23 June 1906, 9.30:

Mr Karl Reinish [sic]. Dear Mr Reinish, as my sister is about to visit me I regret exceedingly I shall want the house to ourselves as I wish to do a great deal of entertaining and having paying guests would interfere with my plans. I therefore hope you will find comfortable quarters elsewhere. Kindly do so at your own convenience as I do not want to rush you and want you to remain thoroughly at home while you remain with us. I hope you will honour me with your presence at my weekly receptions while my sister visits me. Believe me, yours sincerely, Cora Crippen.

Crippen would give evidence at his trial of a visit by Belle's half-sister, Louise Mills, though the date was not given. Belle had always seemed closer to her than to her full sister Theresa, he would say, but when Mrs Mills was visiting they had not agreed at all.

Later lodgers claimed to have witnessed a different kind of domesticity which, at first sight, was more in keeping with the unfolding drama. There was a Richard Ehrlich, another German student, who was at the house for five months from December 1906 and said Belle seemed bored to death at home and missed the stage, which her husband had made her promise to give up on their marriage. The house had been quiet, with few visitors, and though the doctor had been calm he had disapproved of her theatre friends and she had lost her temper, with open quarrels, frequent bickering and stinging sarcasm from her. The doctor remained even-toned, but Ehrlich would see him clenching and unclenching his hands. There had been two other lodgers, said Ehrlich, during his time there and after he left Belle had written to him in a series of postcards, again making reference to the imminent arrival of her sister, and jokily warning him not to 'get awfully fond of the nice girls'.

No lodger gave evidence at Crippen's trial and, while Reinisch did not disclose his association for many years, Ehrlich's account appeared promptly in a French journal, *Le Petit Parisien*, from which it was lifted by several English newspapers. It was a singular story, unsupported by other accounts of their life. Of course, Belle had been performing long after their marriage; there was no suggestion anywhere that Crippen resented Belle's music-hall friends – except perhaps Bruce Miller, who was long gone by now – and no one else could say they had ever argued in front of them, though Crippen himself would describe similar scenes.

In one book about the case, Crippen is said to have come home unexpectedly and caught Belle in bed with one of the lodgers. The book does not source the anecdote and I have been unable to find any information that even hints at such an incident. It must have been an invention. There is no evidence that Belle was ever unfaithful with anyone, other than Bruce Miller, and even then, the case is far from proved.

Although the couple seem to have stressed companionship as the true reason for taking on lodgers, there may well have been a financial motive too, which they were too proud to acknowledge. It is left, once again, to Adelene Harrison, to sketch a sorry picture of Belle and Crippen looking after the lodgers, Belle doing much of the domestic work with occasional help from a cleaner, and Crippen getting up early to fetch the coal, lay the table for breakfast and even clean the lodgers' boots, all in time to get to the office for eight.

Harrison was a near neighbour during some of this time and recalled the Crippens calling at her home one Sunday morning after Mass and inviting the Harrisons to supper that evening. It was then that the doctor told them his wife had converted him to Catholicism, and they were now regularly attending the Catholic church in Kentish Town. For Adelene this was yet another example of his subservience to his demanding wife, falling in with her plans. She made him sound pleasant, if somewhat downtrodden, perhaps even a little emasculated and unmanly:

> He was delighted with the air up at Camden Road and he chuckled with delight when he told us his clothes were becoming too small for him, and that he was getting quite fat. Within a few months he put on flesh and appeared quite jolly and lively. They were about a great deal together and their garden and the embellishment of their house seemed a source of great interest.
>
> He was a man with no apparent vices, or even the usual weaknesses or foibles of the ordinary man. Restraint was the one and only evidence of firmness in his character. He was unable to smoke; it made him ill. He refrained from the consumption of alcohol liquor in the form of wines and spirits as it affected his heart and digestion. He drank light ale and stout, and that only sparingly.

He was not a man's man. No man had ever known him to join in a convivial bout; he was always back to time, and never came home with a meaningless grin on his face at two o'clock in the morning attended by pals from a neighbouring club. He never paid compliments to women, or flirted even in a jocular spirit.

His eccentric taste in the matter of neckties and dress generally may be attributed to the fact that it represented feminine taste. His wife purchased his ties, and decided on the pattern of his clothing. She would discuss the colours with the tailor, while he stood aside looking on, without venturing to give an opinion.

Filson Young clearly relied heavily on Adelene Harrison in his own influential account of the case, seeing the characters in simplistic, black and white terms. For Young, Crippen had come to London as the 'insignificant-looking little man he always remained, small and short and slight in stature with a sandy moustache, prominent eyes that looked at you through gold-rimmed spectacles, and a large domed forehead. His role in the social life was that of a spectator. He was the silent member of the gay little companies that were entertained by him and the bird of paradise. He was always courteous, always hospitable; apparently contented to look on at and enjoy his wife's little social triumphs among her friends.'

Young was certainly right about Crippen's plain appearance: a little jowly, with a thick shaving brush of a moustache and thinning hair on top. It was his eyes that captivated observers, who described them in varying degrees of bulginess.

The actor-manager Sir Seymour Hicks claimed to have spent half an hour in Crippen's company once, although he remembered him in his memoirs as 'Charles Hawley Crippen'. He said the bulge of Crippen's eyes was further magnified by his thick glasses to such an extent that Hicks was by no means sure that he was not talking to a bream or a mullet. Crippen had generously given a Munyon's cure to Hicks's companion, who was suffering from toothache. Even after Crippen's crime

– his terrible dissection of his wife's body – had been disclosed, Hicks was one of many who could not help feeling some sympathy for him.

All the witnesses testified to Crippen's kind heart, his courteousness and his even temper. Adelene Harrison said he was the last man whom anyone would ever associate with any criminal act, thought or intention. His dental partner said he had never met a more humble, unassuming little man and it seemed unthinkable to Rylance that he could commit such a dastardly crime.

That was Crippen of the popular imagination, the little man, long-suffering at his wife's demands and complaints – that appalling woman, as Filson Young would have us believe, with her 'inordinate vanity' and her vitality of the loud and aggressive kind that seemed to exhaust the air around it; living the 'somewhat squalid existence' described by Adelene Harrison; the avenue to her affections being neither very narrow nor difficult of access. She was fat, too – plump or stout by popular description.

And she had poor taste. Belle had once seen green wallpaper in a friend's drawing-room (this was another Adelene Harrison anecdote, so maybe it was Harrison's drawing-room) and had exclaimed, 'Gee! You have got a hoo-doo here. Green paper! You'll have bad luck as sure as fate. When I have a house I won't have green in the house. It shall be pink right away through for luck.' (This was the kind of thing writers liked to quote, for its dramatic irony. She said that and she was the one who ended up under the cellar floor!)

Hilldrop Crescent had been nearly all pink, according to Filson Young (though it's not clear how he knew), and alongside the wardrobes and baskets stuffed with her clothes had been the various mounted paintings and photographs which Belle had adorned with velvet bows. One commentator said that could have been produced in court as mitigating evidence. Anyone seeing those ribbons might have killed her.

How the house must have been transformed, no longer sombre and quiet but bustling with the Crippens' new life, when they began to socialise regularly after Belle joined the Ladies Guild. Not any mundane kind of socialising either, but something thrilling and elite, in among the aristocracy of the music-hall profession, whom they had come to know.

In January 1909 there was even a servant at number 39, a Rhoda Ray who did not live in but came every morning at 8.30 and stayed until 6.30 or 7 pm unless there was a party, in which case she would remain until 11 pm. Mrs Crippen used to go out every day from 1 pm to 3 pm – shopping, no doubt, shopping and socialising – and though Rhoda did not have much to do with the doctor she gathered that the couple were not altogether friendly towards each and spoke very little. Rhoda never heard any quarrels and never saw any marks of violence, nor heard Belle complain.

Rhoda must have been there for the party Belle hosted at 39 Hilldrop Crescent to celebrate the ninetieth and last birthday of George Washington 'Pony' Moore in February 1909. Moore had been one of the most popular vaudevillians of the Victorian age, but by the time of his ninetieth birthday he had only months to live – his obituary would shortly be appearing in *The Era* of October 1909. Pony was the father of the Crippens' friend Annie Stratton. Having been born of one blackface singer, also known as a nigger minstrel, Annie had married another, namely Eugene Stratton, who had been more successful even than old Pony, as he was affectionately known, in the field of coon songs.

Stratton's popular hits had included 'Lily of Laguna', 'Little Dolly Daydream', 'The Idler' and, most famous of them all, 'The Dandy-Coloured Coon'. He had been King Rat twice, in 1896 and 1900, but was now more or less retired and living quietly with his wife Annie in Boundary Road, St John's Wood, in the house which they had named Coon's Rest.

They were at Belle's party for Pony Moore, of course, along with Mr and Mrs Fred Ginnett and many others. It is not recorded whether Pony or anyone else had performed at the party, perhaps rendering some of the old coon songs. Belle too, had sung them on stage in her time, but Pony had been the pioneer, a New Yorker like Belle, who had run away to join the circus, getting his nickname from his skill with the circus horses before the craze of nigger minstrelsy had got him in its grip and he had first blacked-up (using the traditional burnt cork) at the age of around twenty.

He had been in London since 1859 and performed regularly in a long-running show at St James's Hall in Piccadilly (now the site of the Piccadilly Hotel) with his unique Ethiopian Minstrelsy. *The Era* would write that the advance of the halls had brought minstrelsy into disrepute (not, I think, on the grounds that it was racist but simply that it had become hackneyed) and Pony had retired from St James's Hall in 1894.

There had been one final performance by Pony, at the age of eighty, at the London Pavilion: 'I don't know whether I laughed or cried when I smelled the burnt cork and made up for the stage. I sang "Ada with the Golden Hair" and "Hear Dem Bells" and gave a few steps of a dance and then finished up with an old trick of mine, running across the stage and jumping into my seat just as the orchestra gave a big crash. The people gave me a fine welcome. I was glad they had not forgotten old Pony.'

The Crippens' new neighbours had also helped out at the party, William and Jane Harrison having moved in to 38 Hilldrop Crescent with their friend Jane Cowderoy, to act as caretakers. They used to see the Crippens in the garden together and thought they always seemed happy and comfortable, never rowing or exchanging a cross word.

There was an apocryphal tale, from around this time, of Belle being back on stage, during a performers' strike, crossing a picket line and being heckled by none other than Marie Lloyd, who called, 'Let her through, she'll soon clear the hall.'

This is not a convincing story. Belle, having joined the Ladies Guild to help poor women performers, would hardly be likely to cross a picket line, much less with the admired and feared Marie Lloyd standing there. The story seems to emerge from the popular version of Belle's unpopularity, which gained ground during the case and afterwards, somewhat cruelly, you might think, in view of what happened to her. There is another story that seems more likely, of Belle being on stage at the Euston Music Hall during the strike and 'retiring amid a storm of hisses', to be comforted by a fellow performer who was just about to go on with a sketch and was indignant on Belle's behalf. This was Weldon Atherstone, real name Thomas Weldon Anderson, who would be murdered in Battersea the same weekend in July 1910 that Crippen and Le Neve took flight, and fight them for column inches in the newspapers.

It was at Pony Moore's home, at another party, that Belle had first met Clara Martinetti. They were both at Coon's Rest in March 1909 celebrating Annie Stratton's birthday. Belle told Annie about her old operation. That summer Belle was invited to stay the weekend at the Martinettis' bungalow, Clariscio, near Staines. The doctor only came down on the Sunday and did not stay over but left that night, supposedly because he had to go to work early on the Monday. Belle had stayed the extra night.

The weekend would become memorable, in retrospect, when Clara was asked if she had ever seen a scar on Belle's body. Well, of course, she had, during that weekend, catching sight of it while Belle was wearing a dressing-gown. It had seemed like something substantial, and Clara had said, 'Oh Belle, does that sometimes hurt?' And Belle had put her two hands to it and said, no.

It was perhaps among these new theatrical friends that Belle could give full rein to her flamboyant style and feel appreciated for the generosity and kindness that they would later remember her for. All those women seemed in thrall, not just to Belle's large-hearted, high-spirited personality, but to her appearance as well. As Melinda May would say, Belle was an attractive woman in her prime. Lil Hawthorne said Belle had a 'fascinating' look, accentuated by her extravagant clothes and jewellery. She had a habit, said Lil, of jerking her head backwards. This must have emphasised her dramatic head of hair, which also seemed to fascinate her friends.

She was naturally dark but took to dyeing her hair blonde. Adelene Harrison (of course) even knew where she bought the bleach – at Gillingwaters on Upper Street in Islington. She used curling pins at home, Hindes curling pins, shorter ones for the front and longer pins for the back, to create rings of luscious golden curls. Belle had told Adelene that Crippen himself had initially dyed her hair for her some years earlier. It grew out quickly, and Adelene had sometimes seen it down first thing in the morning, with the natural dark colour emerging from the roots.

Clara Martinetti said Belle wore her hair thrown over, not like a fringe but like when a lady brushed her hair down and then threw it back, leaving it in a puff. That was how she would have worn it at the Ladies Guild dinner that autumn, when she was fêted and rewarded for all her efforts. She must have felt loved and valued that night, among her celebrated friends and colleagues. Then it was out with the old and in with the new year, 1910, with American cocktails at the top of the steps of number 39, and Lil Hawthorne's chauffeured car parked at the kerb and those 'strangely moving noises' of Melinda May's description.

And after the guests had gone at half one in the morning, Belle must have sat at a dressing-table in front of a mirror and put her hair up for the night with the Hindes curling pins.

SEVEN

Crippen actually ordered the poison that probably killed Belle on either 15 January or 17 January 1910, from the chemists, Lewis & Burrows at 108 New Oxford Street, just across the road from Albion House.

The chemist who served him, Charles Hetherington, knew Crippen well as a regular customer. In the three years that Hetherington had worked there, Crippen had often ordered cocaine, morphia, mercury and other drugs which were all perfectly normal for a chemist to dispense. Crippen always signed the Poisons' Register. So far as Hetherington could remember, Crippen had said, 'I want five grains of Hyoscine Hydrobromide' and the chemist had asked him, as he was obliged to do for the Register, why he wanted it, and Crippen had said he would be using it for 'homoeopathic purposes'.

It was not an extraordinary thing to order, but it was unusual, especially in that quantity. Lewis & Burrows did not keep more than about a fifth of a grain of that particular form of hyoscine in stock. They had about two grains of what the chemist called 'trituration' (a fine powder, by definition) which was a mixture of hyoscine with milk and sugar but that was not enough either, and it was not what Crippen had asked for. The quantity might seem small – half an ounce comprised about 219 grains – but it was a significant measure for a poison.

Hetherington knew hyoscine was sometimes used as a sedative in nervous cases. He telephoned the order through to the wholesaler, British Drug Houses over near City Road. They were then the biggest druggists in London and traditionally kept around half an ounce of hyoscine in stock, which they supplied at 9d a time, commonly in orders of a single grain to chemists but sometimes five or even fifteen grains to a hospital. The wholesaler got its supplies of hyoscine from the German drug company Merck.

Hetherington at Lewis & Burrows thought it was 17 January when Crippen placed the order, but the British Drug Wholesaler recorded receiving Hetherington's telephone call on 15 January. There was no dispute that Crippen returned to collect the five grains on 19 January. He signed the register and the crystals were handed to him in a small tube or box. He did not record the purchase in Munyon's own register.

This being a Wednesday, the Guild met at Albion House, and later Belle and Crippen joined the Martinettis and the rest of the committee at a farewell dinner for Lil Hawthorne and John Nash, who would soon be off to the States. Belle complained of a headache before dinner but refused a medicinal brandy because, she said, Crippen had already given her something for her head. She said she had felt dizzy and fallen the day before, but otherwise seemed all right.

Was this illness a trial run by Crippen or an early attempt to kill her, or just coincidence? There was no way of knowing, though the Guild women would certainly look back later at this event and wonder, as they would at another incident Belle had mentioned a few days earlier.

On 7 January she had gone to Albion House, where she and Crippen had met Guild committee member Louie Davis (one half of the double-act Ward & Davis), who was celebrating her birthday. Belle had given her a coral necklet as a gift and then said, 'I didn't think I should be able to come to give it to you as I woke up in the night stifling and I wanted Peter to send for the priest. I was stifling and it was so dark . . .' She turned to Crippen, 'Didn't I, dear?' Davis knew she always called him dear. Crippen had said, 'Yes, but you're all right now.'

They had gone to Lyons for tea and Belle had repeated the story and put her hand to her throat saying she would never forget what happened, it was so terrible. Crippen had said, 'It's the worry of the Guild. You must resign.' Belle had said she didn't think that was the problem.

It must have been about three days after Crippen collected the hyoscine that Ethel was telling her friends, Lydia Rose and Lydia Rose senior, that she was engaged, during her small birthday party at her lodgings in Constantine Road. 22 January was Ethel's twenty-seventh birthday. She must have been 'feeling her position' as the phrase goes. She had even shown the younger Lydia Rose her engagement ring. Who knows what was in her mind or what she knew of Crippen's plans or what pressure he was feeling from her?

At the least, it's a remarkable juxtaposition of events, that a woman in a long-term affair with a married man should tell her friends she is engaged and show them a ring, and then nine days later the married man murders his wife.

According to the full account she wrote down on 20 July 1910, sitting in her weekend bungalow near Staines, Clara Martinetti first received the invitation to supper from Crippen on Monday, 31 January 1910 between four and five in the afternoon, when he had called at her apartment on Shaftesbury Avenue. Peter had said Belle wanted them to come down to their home that evening and take pot-luck dinner with them. Clara had said, Oh, she'd like to very much but, you know, it is Paul's doctor day today (meaning he went to his doctor by appointment) and when he came home he always felt very queer and weak (he had been to the doctor several times and Clara knew its effect) so she didn't think he would care to go to supper.

PETER: Oh, make him, we'll cheer him up and after dinner we'll have a game of whist.
CLARA: Well, I'll see what Paul says and if he cares to go, we go. I don't expect him back before six o'clock.
PETER: Well, I have a little more work to do at the office and I'll call again.
CLARA: All right, Peter.

When Paul Martinetti came home at about six o'clock, Clara told him about Peter's visit and the invitation and said he was coming back, but that Paul did not have to go if he didn't want to. Almost as she was saying this, Peter knocked at the door again and so they talked it over and Clara reminded Paul that they didn't have to go out if he didn't feel well enough and he said, 'I feel rather queer, but we'll go.' Crippen turned to leave and Clara asked why they didn't all go together, but Crippen said he thought he ought to go ahead and tell Belle they were coming. Clara said they'd be there about seven.

When Peter had gone, the Martinettis went into Paul's study and Paul asked Clara to give him a little whisky and water, which she did and then, while he was putting some letters in the desk, she said she thought she'd go and get ready, and they left soon after. Not seeing a taxi on Tottenham Court Road, they took the motor bus to Hampstead Road, opposite Maples, then crossed over the road to take the electric tram that took them to the corner of Hilldrop Crescent. As they walked to the house they saw Peter at the door, and as they got nearer Belle appeared too, shaking her hand at them in mock annoyance and saying, 'You call this seven o'clock?'

Belle asked Clara to go upstairs and take her hat and coat off in the front bedroom. Peter helped Paul out of his coat in the hall, then Belle excused herself saying she was still a little busy in the kitchen and Clara said she hoped she hadn't made any fuss with the cooking, as Peter had told them it was to be a pot-luck dinner and Belle said it was only a little soup. By the time Clara came down Paul and Peter were chatting in the parlour (this must have been the front room on the first floor) and Belle called up from the kitchen, telling Peter to look after them and she would be up in a minute. Clara said they were in no hurry.

Belle appeared with some glasses, asking what they would like as an appetiser, and Paul took a little whisky while Clara, feeling rather thirsty, had a gin soda. Belle went back down to the kitchen, Clara calling after her to ask if she could help. Belle said, 'Oh no.' They talked a while about nothing memorable and Paul took another whisky, then Belle called them down to the kitchen where she tried to show them how funny her bull terrier was, complaining that he was not clean, being only a puppy, but she liked him and Clara saw that she made a fuss of him.

They walked through to the dining-room which, as Clara said, was really the breakfast room, but Belle and Peter took all their meals there. Belle asked Clara to make sure nothing was missing from the table and Clara and Peter checked it was properly laid before they sat down and Belle came in with the soup. When they had finished they put the plates together and Belle carried them out, telling Clara not to trouble when she followed her with some more things. There was a joint of beef which was placed in front of Crippen for carving, while Belle and Clara served the salads and other side dishes. Belle offered drinks and Clara took a glass of ale while Peter had a stout and Paul said he would wait and have a whisky afterwards.

The main course was eaten, the plates cleared and Belle produced two or three different sweets. Clara said she'd gone to a lot of trouble and they hadn't needed all that, but Belle only laughed and asked which she'd like and they all took some dessert. Belle went off again and came back with coffee on a tray and offered liqueurs. Peter said they didn't agree with him. Clara just had coffee and resisted Belle's coaxing to take a liqueur.

There was a box of cigarettes and Belle wanted one of a particular brand (the name of which Clara had forgotten) and said, 'Peter, where are the so and so cigarettes?' And he said they must be with the others. Paul took a cigarette and passed the box on to Peter, who declined. They chatted for a while before the men went upstairs and Clara tried to insist on helping Belle clear up but she said just to remove the necessary soiled things and she would leave the rest for the morning. She told Clara to go ahead upstairs and tell Peter to get the cards ready, and when Belle came up soon after they began a game of whist, Belle and Paul partners against Clara and Peter.

They played several games and had some drinks and Clara thought the room began to feel hot so Crippen reduced the stove, but Clara noticed Paul was growing quiet and worried that his pain was coming on again. He got up, excused himself and left the room, Belle calling after him that there was a light upstairs. When he'd gone Clara said she didn't think he felt so well and that it would have been better if they'd stayed at home.

Clara (without disclosing what the illness was) said that both Peter and Belle knew what was wrong with her husband, as he had told them one evening at the Martinettis' flat. When Paul came back he complained of feeling cold and looked white. Clara felt his hands, which were cold, and he began to tremble and asked how they'd get a taxi and Peter said, 'Well, Paul, you always get away from here all right.'

Belle said, 'I'll give him some pure brandy,' and with that she poured him a measure and said, 'Here, drink that, Paul' and Clara said, 'Oh Belle, that's too much, I don't think he ought to have brandy after the whisky he's had.' Belle said, 'Let him have it,' but Clara said, 'No Belle, I'd rather not, I have to take him home.' Belle said, 'You let him drink it, I take the responsibility.' Clara said, 'Then give him some pure whisky, I don't really care for him to mix his drinks.' Paul was given a whisky and Belle turned to Peter and said, 'Well, will you get him a taxi, dear,' and Peter went out into the street to find one.

He was gone so long it seemed he would never return and several times Belle went out of the door to listen for him or looked out of the window to see if she could see him. He came back alone saying he had walked very far trying to get a taxi but had not seen one. Paul was feeling worse, if anything, and Belle invited them to stay the night but Clara said, 'No, Belle, thank you, if Paul got very ill I'd rather he was at home.'

Belle turned to Peter and said, 'Can't you see anything else? A cab or a four-wheeler?' She turned to her guest and said,

'Would that do, Paul?' Paul said, 'Anything, anything' and so Belle turned back to Peter and said, 'Perhaps there will be something now, go and see,' and so he went out again, returning soon afterwards with a four-wheeler which they could see through the window.

There was a cab stand near Hilldrop Crescent on York Road (nowadays it is York Way), where Crippen would say, at his trial, he had gone looking for a cab without success. In 1904 there had only been two 'motor cabs' in London and 11,055 horse-drawn cabs. In 1906 there were still only 96 motors. By 1910 there were 4,941 'motor cabs' (the taxis the Martinettis would have preferred to use) and fewer than 4,000 horse-drawn cabs, comprising 1,200 two-wheeler Hansom cabs, only suitable for two passengers and 2,500 four-wheelers, with greater passenger capacity. Four-wheelers were also known as growlers. When Belle suggested a cab or a four-wheeler she obviously meant a Hansom or a four-wheeler, anything, in fact with a horse at the front of it.

When Clara saw the cab through the window she quickly ran upstairs for her hat and coat, while Belle and Peter helped Paul into his. Then Peter helped Paul down the front steps and into the cab, Clara following behind and turning to Belle as she started to follow her down the steps, saying, 'Don't come down Belle, it is too cold, you only have a thin blouse on.' Clara kissed Belle and walked down the steps, down the path and out the gate and into the cab, Belle calling after her to take care of Paul. Peter stood at the door of the cab to help Clara inside. She said goodbye to him – she did not say, in her account, whether she had kissed him – and he asked if she'd like a rug for Paul and Clara said, no, he could have her sable fur. And with that, they went. It was now about half one in the morning.

Belle was as good as dead, already.

When asked about the supper, nearly six months later, Clara would recall it as quite a nice evening, the Crippens happy and natural, Peter's manner as usual. Paul would say that from the time they entered the house until the time they left the

Crippens had been as the Martinettis always knew them: kind, pleasant and seemingly on the best of terms. There had been no quarrel between them.

Crippen would later tell Chief Inspector Dew, and repeat it at his trial, that Belle had immediately gone into a rage and started abusing him, after the Martinettis had left, ostensibly for not showing Paul to the lavatory, when he'd gone during the evening. According to him, this was such a familiar pattern that he did not take much notice. She was always finding fault with trivial things, threatening to leave him and saying she would go to a man who would support her better. If he could not be a gentleman, she had apparently said, she would no longer stand it. This was the finish of it, she had said this time, according to Crippen, she would leave him tomorrow and he would never hear of her again. There was only one new thing she had said, Crippen would conveniently claim, and that was to tell him he would have to cover up the scandal as best he could when she was gone.

You can almost imagine the outbreak of bickering as soon as they were alone. That's happened a million times to a million couples. He might have cracked, finally, lost control, released his tight grip on himself in one cataclysmic moment and killed her and then tried to disguise it. But that theory, of course, did not fit the facts – certainly did not explain the purchase of the hyoscine two weeks earlier, or the traces of it found in her remains.

When she thought it through afterwards, Melinda May from the Guild was sure that Crippen must have deliberately kept away from the house while he was supposedly searching for a cab, having already administered the poison and expecting Belle to be dead by the time he got back. That may be so, but Crippen could not have anticipated Paul Martinetti's sudden turn for the worse and his wish to leave in a cab.

In normal circumstances the Martinettis would probably have walked away to find a cab themselves. In Clara's account Crippen was apparently with them the whole time. It was Belle doing the fetching and carrying and serving the drinks. So there was no opportunity for Crippen to have slipped the poison into Belle's drink. And there were other reasons, which became apparent during discussion of the effects of taking hyoscine at the trial, why it might have been risky to poison Belle with the guests still in the house.

Although none were ever called in evidence, perhaps because they were inconclusive and might have distracted from the few hard facts that were available, there were statements given to the police by several neighbours that might have shed some light on what happened. They did not recall the events until more than five months later, so some allowance must be made for the unreliability of recall, and any normal witness's natural desire to help. The statements are here entering the public domain for the first time.

In particular, there were the people at 46 Brecknock Road, whose upper windows overlooked the gardens of 39 Hilldrop Crescent (though 48 Brecknock Road was the house whose garden directly backed on to the garden of 39). Mrs Lena Lyons, who lived at number 46, had distinctly heard two shots one morning at the end of January or the beginning of February, between 7 am and 8 am. There had been an interval of several seconds between the shots. It had been dark at the time and they had startled her. They had definitely come from the direction of 39 Hilldrop Crescent.

Almost immediately after the first shot, Lena Lyons's lodger Mrs May Pole had come running into her room. 'Did you hear that shot, Mrs Lyons?' Mrs Lyons had barely had time to say yes, before they heard the second shot. The two women had been alone in the house and Mrs Pole, being pregnant, had been particularly nervous, sitting on the end of Mrs Lyons's bed, where it was so dark they couldn't see each other. They had waited there together until daylight.

They could be quite sure of the time because Mrs Lyons's husband always went to work at 6.30 am and Mr Pole followed him out of the house at 7 am. The shots had been heard soon after Mr Pole had left. Mr Lyons had been dismissive when his wife told him what they had heard, saying that it must have been a motor. She had more or less kept the story to herself after that, especially when the case broke in the papers and Mrs Glackner in the oil shop at 30 Brecknock Road came forward and said she'd heard screams and people started calling her an old gossip.

Even the police hadn't bothered with Louisa Glackner or, if they had, her statement had not survived. She had been left to tell her story to the *Islington Gazette*, who added insult to injury by getting her name wrong and calling her Mrs Blackner. She said, when interviewed in July, that she had heard the screams four or five months earlier. She had been woken up in the night by a piercing shriek and had got out of bed and opened her window, when she heard a repeated cry of 'Oh don't, oh don't'. She was certain the sounds had come from the direction of the Crippens' house and her son had heard them too, because he had mentioned them to her the next morning.

Another neighbour, at 54 Brecknock Road, had also heard screams but, after five months, thought the date must have been either 28 January or 4 February, a Friday night when he had returned home in the early hours after a night out with friends at the Orange Tree pub on Euston Road. This was Frederick Evans, who also used to enjoy hearing Belle sing while she was standing by the upstairs window of her home.

He always checked the time by the clock in the window of the jewellers at the corner of Brecknock Road as he passed, so remembered it had been 1.15 am when he was adjusting his watch and he had arrived home about three minutes later. He had heard a screech 'which terminated with a long dragging whine'. The sound had come from Hilldrop Crescent but he was sure it had come from out of doors. He was startled and immediately thought of the Ripper murders (albeit the last one had been in 1888, twenty-two years earlier). He knew that 'Parmetes Row' (this is how it was written in his statement, though I have been unable to find any record of it), a turning out of Hilldrop Crescent, was frequented by prostitutes and thought it might be one of those 'poor creatures' in trouble. Checking that his wife was still asleep, he put his hat, coat and boots back on and went round there. The private gate to Parmetes Row was closed but he looked down and saw nothing. He walked around the nearby streets for a while but saw no one apart from a couple in Camden Road.

The screech so impressed him that he bought the local paper the following Friday to see if any charges had been reported. There was nothing that explained the terrible sound he had heard.

EIGHT

Ethel usually arrived home from work at about six and had tea with Mrs Jackson and her husband. They would then sit together until about nine, when they had supper. Mrs Jackson noted that Ethel was always lovable and affectionate towards her. Sometimes they would sit and talk, just the two of them, in Ethel's bed-sitting room. The Jacksons treated her like one of the family.

Around the time of the murder, Ethel had appeared very depressed and seemed ill and unhappy, eating hardly any supper and going straight to her room afterwards. When she came in one evening looking very upset and went directly to bed, Mrs Jackson waited a while and then went in to try and talk to her.

EMILY: I am sure you have got something on your mind, do tell me what it is.
ETHEL: It's nothing between you and me.
EMILY: Whatever it is it must be something awful or you would not be in this state. You will go mad if you don't relieve your mind.

Ethel did not reply. She sat up in bed, did up her hair then undid it, pulling and clawing at it, looking straight into the corner of the room as she did so. She shuddered violently. Mrs Jackson again pleaded with her to say what it was. 'Go to bed,' Ethel told her, 'I shall be all right in the morning.' Ethel lay down in the bed and Mrs Jackson got beside her and lay with her a while until she thought Ethel was asleep. It was two in the morning when she finally left her.

The next day, Mrs Jackson took a cup of tea in to Ethel, first thing, as she usually did. After Mr Jackson had left for work, Ethel came out of her room dressed for business and sat in the kitchen for breakfast but did not eat much, only a sandwich, and could barely hold a cup of tea for trembling. Mrs Jackson decided to take decisive action and told her to sit down while she telephoned to Dr Crippen and told him that Ethel was too ill to go in. She had to leave the house to make the call and when she spoke to the doctor he said, 'I am sorry, tell her not to worry.' Mrs Jackson returned to the house.

'For the love of God,' she said to Ethel, 'tell me what is the matter. Are you in the family way again?' Ethel assured her she was not and said she would tell her the whole story after dinner. After a couple of hours Ethel said, 'Would you be surprised if I told you it was doctor?' Mrs Jackson assumed this was a reference to the miscarriage. 'No,' she said, 'why worry about that now, it's all past and gone.' Ethel burst out crying and said, 'It's Miss Elmore.'

Mrs Jackson had never heard that name before and didn't know who it was. Ethel had not told her Crippen was married. Ethel said, 'She is his wife, you know, and I feel it very much when I see the doctor go off with her after the other affair.' Mrs Jackson took 'the other affair' to mean the miscarriage. Mrs Jackson said, 'If he is a married man why do you keep on with him?' Ethel said, 'He is taking steps for a divorce.' Mrs Jackson advised Ethel to give him up and tell him she had told her all about it. She said she would.

When she came back from business the following evening, Ethel said she had told the doctor what Mrs Jackson had suggested. Crippen had told Ethel that as soon as he could free himself she would be his little wife. A few nights later Ethel had come home more pleasant than Mrs Jackson had ever seen her. 'Somebody has gone to America', she said. Mrs Jackson knew whom she meant. Ethel brought home a short brown fur coat and gave it to Mrs Jackson. 'Doctor thought you would like to have this,' she said. Soon after, the doctor himself appeared in person and spoke to Mrs Jackson. 'I have come to thank you for all you have done for my little girl,' he said. 'I am sorry I have been unable to thank you before.'

Belle Elmore was never mentioned again in Mrs Jackson's hearing.

Mrs Jackson was to tell this story several times, in two or three police statements, at the inquest into Belle's death and finally at Ethel's trial. The details differed each time, just a little (in one version Ethel first said there was something wrong with the accounts at the office) and so, critically, did the timing of when the night of hysteria occurred. It was such an important moment. She might have been hysterical because she knew Belle had been killed, or was about to be killed, or simply because she was unhappy with her place in Crippen's life. Her declaration to him, at Mrs Jackson's urging, could have been the trigger for the murder.

In her first statement to the police, on 15 July 1910, Mrs Jackson said the incident had taken place in late January or early February. She added a further statement three days later, adding this time that she thought it was the beginning of February – this could, of course, have been at the prompting of the police. At the inquest she again placed it at the beginning of February, but then agreed this was merely guesswork.

At Ethel's trial, that October, giving her evidence in chief, Mrs Jackson would say it had been in 'the latter part of January'. During cross-examination by Ethel's barrister, F.E. Smith, she would push the date back even earlier, agreeing with Smith that it could have been 'somewhere about' 25 January. She also said Ethel had been miserable and unhappy from earlier still, 'something like' 5, 6 or 7 January, at Smith's rather blatant leading of his witness.

Smith would claim this as a decisive victory in Ethel's acquittal, his skilful probing producing the key admission that it must have been well before the murder, and therefore not *because* of the murder, that Ethel became hysterical. Perhaps Smith did not know, or did not care to dwell on the fact that the Crown, by that stage, had no interest in convicting Ethel Le Neve, and was simply going through the motions.

Mrs Jackson was equally unable to say when it was that Ethel had started staying out regularly overnight. She had sometimes told her she was staying at her sister's. Then, in early February, when she was staying out four or five nights in the week, Ethel said she had been up at Hilldrop Crescent, helping doctor to search for a bank book, for an account which contained £200, which they eventually found. She said they had been up until midnight, searching. (If there was such a bank book, and such an account, its existence was unrecorded.) Ethel also said the doctor had found a diamond tiara and some rings, on which the doctor had raised £175 in the West End, putting the money into his business to place it on a firmer footing.

One evening in the middle of February Ethel turned up at Constantine Road wearing a diamond solitaire ring which she showed Mrs Jackson, saying it was her engagement ring. So that put the relationship on a firmer footing too. She subsequently appeared wearing another similar ring and again showed it to her landlady, but this time said (or boasted), 'Do you know what this cost?' Mrs Jackson said she had no idea. Ethel said, '£20.' There was another ring, which she said Dr Crippen had had made for her. She said all these rings had belonged to Dr Crippen's mother.

Mrs Jackson also saw the three bracelets Ethel began wearing, one chased and one set with amethyst stones, which she noted was much too large for Ethel, who said they had been bought for her by the doctor. Then there were the two gold watches, one of which, said Ethel, was a present from the doctor. And here again was that famous star-shaped brooch which Ethel had worn to the Ladies Guild ball. In her life story, you may recall, Ethel had said that the doctor selected it for her from a handful of jewellery in his pocket while they were together in the office on the day after Belle's disappearance. When she showed it off at her lodgings she told Mrs Jackson she had previously seen it at the house in Hilldrop

Crescent and had thought she could get it out of the doctor with a little persuasion, and she had.

While she was collecting the jewellery, Ethel made free with Belle's wardrobe, dispensing items from it in all directions, giving them away to friends and family and of course Mrs Jackson, who later tallied her haul as a short brown fur coat, a black feather boa, a long cream coat, a long brown coat, a long black coat, a black voile blouse and skirt, a grey and black striped coat and skirt, a mole coat and skirt, a yellow under-skirt, a black under-skirt, a black skirt length accordion-pleated, a heliotrope costume length, a white lace blouse, a blue and white silk and lace blouse, two black combs, a heart-shaped locket with blue stones, a lizard brooch with green and white stones, three new nightgowns, two brown hats, two old black blouses, ten pairs of stockings of different colours and a pair of pink shoes.

Ethel told Mrs Jackson the doctor wanted her to have these things. Most of the clothes had been previously worn and Mrs Jackson had gone on to wear some of them. She had only pawned a few small items – some grey silk, a lace collarette and a small piece of pink trimming – for three shillings. Mrs Jackson believed she had been given Belle Elmore's cast-offs following her sudden trip to America.

Ethel gave another of Mrs Jackson's lodgers, Caroline Rumbold, some fake jewellery and lace for her two children, as well as some shoes, stockings, a pink waistband, a couple of collarettes and two bottles of scent spray. She gave Lydia Rose a white feather boa, a comb with an imitation pearl handle, a string of imitation pearls, a chain bag, an old blouse, a white fur muff, a hat, a lace summer coat, a pink feather ruffle, a linen dress, a belt and a piece of chiffon. Lydia Rose senior received a parcel of four worn blouses with a note inside from Ethel saying she could use them to make up things for her children.

Naturally, Ethel gave her sister Nina some of Belle's clothes, sending her a large cardboard box containing a black dress, a black silk petticoat, a maroon velvet costume, a gold silk dress and a heavily braided black coat. She also received a cream-coloured cape with long stole ends, a white ostrich neck wrapper, a gold silk hat, a blue hat with two pink roses, two black ostrich tips, a brown fuzzy-looking feather, a pair of ladies buttoned boots and some pieces of embroidery. When she next saw her, Nina said to Ethel, 'Fancy going away and leaving such lovely clothes behind.' Ethel said, 'Yes, Belle must have been wonderfully extravagant.'

Even Ethel's mother was a beneficiary, receiving some linen material, which she pawned (using her maiden name, Jones) after having a pair of trousers made up from it for her husband. That was in July, when he must have wanted to look smart to receive the representatives of the press.

Ethel and Crippen arrived at her lodgings one day in a cab, with a large dress basket full of beautiful, unused lengths of material which they pulled out in front of Mrs Jackson. Ethel took some of the material round to Caroline Elsmore, a dressmaker who lived and worked nearby on Fleet Road. She told Elsmore that the material was from Dr Crippen's aunt who had lived at 39 Hilldrop Crescent until February when she left for America.

Elsmore gave rich descriptions of the clothes she had made for Ethel in her statement to the police: a blue serge costume of a coat to the hips trimmed with heavy braid about half an inch wide around the edge over the shoulders to the pockets, which were also trimmed with the braid, three large braid buttons down the front about the size of a florin and three small ones on each pocket and two on each cuff, with a skirt in a corselet pattern with several rows of stitching around the bottom; a light grey shadow stripe costume in serge trimmed with grey moiré silk instead of braid; a white princess robe trimmed with gold sequins; a mole-coloured striped costume with black moiré silk collar; a dark vieux-rose cloth costume trimmed with black velvet collar. She had also cut a light heliotrope dress down to size for her. Ethel settled her account with a postal order.

The new clothes and the jewellery certainly caused something of a transformation in Ethel's appearance. She told Mrs Jackson they were gifts from Crippen in advance of their wedding.

An actress, Kathleen York, who was having her teeth fixed at Albion House by Dr Rylance, over a series of appointments, gave an otherwise inconsequential statement to the police in which she described seeing Miss Le Neve in the surgery and noting how well dressed she was and wearing plenty of jewellery, especially several diamond rings and one in particular, a gent's large single stone diamond ring.

You could say that Ethel's behaviour was, in some respects, a little creepy, but that word does not perhaps quite do justice to Ethel's inhabiting of the cloths and clothes and jewellery of her lover's ex-wife, whom he had recently murdered, with or without her knowledge and/or assistance. She appeared to be emulating Belle's personal style, as well as moving into Belle's house with Belle's husband. She told Mrs Jackson she would be leaving soon and getting married.

Ethel moved out of 80 Constantine Road on 12 March 1910, a landmark day for Ethel, surpassing her modest origins and finally outstripping her sister in the stakes of wealth and status. It was a day to celebrate, and they did. Dr Crippen and Ethel arrived in a cab and collected her box, which they sent on, then inviting the Jacksons to join them at the Mansfield Hotel where doctor bought a quart bottle of champagne which they all drank together. They parted on the pavement outside, Ethel and the doctor heading back to Holloway in a tramcar.

When Mrs Jackson visited Ethel at her new home a few days later Ethel told her the doctor had been teaching her how to shoot his little nickel-plated revolver. Over in Brecknock Road, Louisa Glackner would say she often heard shots from the direction of 39 Hilldrop and this may have been Crippen giving Ethel target practice.

Mrs Jackson couldn't help noticing that there was a very strange smell all over the house, particularly downstairs. It was a damp, 'frowsy', stuffy sort of a smell and Mrs Jackson thought it might have resulted from the damp and dirt. She mentioned it to Ethel, who agreed the place was very damp and in a filthy condition, and that was how Belle had left it before she went away to America. Crippen had reported a broken pipe causing damp to the landlord. It was quite possible, however, that the smell was caused by the body beneath the cellar floor.

Several neighbours noted all the burning that had been going on in Hilldrop Crescent. One man grew suspicious because it continued over several mornings, and he looked over the neighbouring gardens to see where it was coming from and saw that the culprit was number 39. He thought at first that it must be leaves and then wondered if it was old wallpaper. He mentioned it to another neighbour, who said his mother had seen the old gentleman at 39 carrying a burning substance in a white pail, putting it into the dustbin and stirring it all up. He had returned several times to the dustbin from the house with the pail and there had been a lot of smoke.

Yet another neighbour told one of the binmen in the second week of February that she thought they must be moving, at 39, because they'd been burning so much in the garden. The binmen went to 39 that Wednesday as usual and collected the usual binful plus four or five baskets of burnt items. There were traces of partly burnt clothes, such as petticoats, but a lot of pure white ash that did not seem like the normal ash you'd get from a grate or from burning clothes. This had gone on over three weeks. On one occasion Ethel had called from a window of the house and said, 'Here you are, dustman, get yourself a drink,' and handed over 3d.

Right at the end of February Ethel and Crippen had called in to see Ethel's sister Nina and her husband. They did not stay long, not more than half an hour. Ethel and Nina went upstairs, apparently to have some "girl" talk alone. Nina had already received a letter from Ethel telling her of Belle's trip to America. Now Ethel said Belle had already divorced Harvey (which was Ethel's familiar name for Crippen, his middle name) and they would be getting married in about three weeks. Nina said how glad she was that the way was clear to marry. Ethel said, 'Yes dear, I think I shall be very happy and I shall try and make the doctor happy.'

When they'd gone Nina told her husband that Ethel was getting married in three weeks and Horace said, 'Oh, doctor tells me about five or six weeks.' Nina said that perhaps they had not settled the point yet.

A week later, about 5 March, eighteen days before Ethel and Crippen's holiday to Dieppe and the public announcement of Belle's death, Nina received a letter from her sister: 'Dear sis, we have been and gone and done it, as the advertisement says.' The letter had been sent from 39 Hilldrop Crescent, though Ethel hadn't even moved in yet. She also told her mother she was married about this time, and her father, Walter, must have been sceptical when his wife passed on the information because he told her to ask Ethel for the details and to see the marriage certificate. His wife tried several times, without success, to get the certificate and could only establish that the wedding had taken place at St Pancras register office in the presence of two of the doctor's intimate friends.

Walter was openly annoyed that Ethel had gone ahead with her wedding without consulting her parents. He thought they'd gone to Dieppe for their honeymoon and, when the chance arose, he asked Ethel about the doctor's wife and Ethel told him she had died and one of the doctor's friends had come from America just to tell him the sad news. Still, though he was disgusted by the marriage and refused to discuss it further, Walter never doubted that any of this was genuine.

NINE

Ethel told the police that it was either the night they returned home to Hilldrop Crescent from Dieppe, 29 March, or the night after that the doctor finally told her his wife had died. He said, according to Ethel, that he could not get to the funeral as it was too far and she would have been buried before he could get there. 'I was very much astonished,' Ethel's police statement recorded her as saying, 'but I don't think I said anything to him about it. I have not had any conversation with him about it since.'

Perhaps the doctor had not wanted to spoil Ethel's holiday with such tragic news, except that he would have known Belle's death would not be so tragic to Ethel. There seems to be no other reason why he would have kept it from her. It seems more likely that she already knew, which might explain why, despite her professed astonishment, she could tell the police she had not said anything to the doctor about it at the time and not mentioned it since.

Crippen told his partner Dr Rylance that he had not sent him a telegram about Belle's death because he had not wanted to spoil Rylance's holiday. In fact, he had not mentioned Belle's death at all to Rylance, after his return to work, until Rylance disclosed that he had seen the telegram Crippen sent to the Martinettis. Crippen said he had kept the news back in order not to upset him. He explained that he had received a cable from America saying his wife had died suddenly of pneumonia. That was the last time Crippen spoke to Rylance about Belle.

Rylance realised that Crippen and Le Neve were very much together now, going out to dinner openly. They must have been very discreet before, perhaps always leaving the office separately or arriving separately so as not to draw attention to their affair. One morning, not long after the Dieppe holiday, a man rushed into the dental rooms and asked to see Mrs Crippen. Rylance said she was dead and the man said, 'Oh no, there is another Mrs Crippen,' so Rylance asked Crippen and he pointed at Ethel and said, 'Yes, this is my wife.' That was also how William Long would discover the marriage. He was never told, until a client called, asking for Mrs Crippen. The new Munyon's manager, Marion Curnow, asked Crippen how he had enjoyed his holiday and he said, 'As well as I could under the circumstances.' She asked if it was true that Belle had died and he bowed his head and didn't answer.

It certainly seems that the Ladies Guild became very suspicious now about what had happened to Belle, even if they stopped short of imagining the unimaginable. At the first Guild meeting after Easter on 30 March Clara Martinetti and Mrs Smythson went to see Crippen in his office, ostensibly to offer their condolences. When Clara said how sorry she was he shrugged his shoulders.

Crippen told them that Belle's illness had begun on the boat over to America, and that she would not look after herself sufficiently and would go out. Pneumonia had ensued and she had died. They asked where she had died and he said in Los Angeles, in the presence of his son. Clara asked for the address so that the Guild could write and send a letter of sympathy and a wreath. Crippen said that was not necessary, the Guild was unknown to his relatives in America. Mrs Smythson said the ladies wished to send an everlasting wreath to the grave. Crippen said there was no grave, Belle had been cremated and the ashes were on their way to London so they could have a little ceremony here. Clara again asked for the address and Crippen relented and wrote it out in pencil: H.O. Crippen, 1427 N. Hoover Street, Rural Delivery, Los Angeles, California. Louise Smythson wrote a postcard to the address straight away and it was later followed up with a letter from Melinda May on behalf of the Guild.

The next day, Mrs Smythson went to Scotland Yard. The

visit must later have represented quite an embarrassment to the police and that must be why it does not feature in any of the official accounts – it is not recorded in any statement given by an officer and was not brought up at the trial. There would be enough complaint, anyway, of police incompetence without the further revelation that they had completely ignored this early alert to the murder. There is no coherent version of precisely why she went and whom she saw. In her own statement to the police she said she simply went to find out how a death in America would be registered and was redirected to the US embassy, where she was given the address of a court official in California to write to.

Mrs Smythson wrote to a trade paper, *The Performer*, in July, apparently stung by a public accusation from Lil Hawthorne's husband, John Nash, that the Guild ladies had sat back and done nothing while their treasurer was lying dead under the cellar floor. In *The Performer* she said she had seen an unnamed police inspector and told him the story of what had happened to Belle and he had said the police could not get involved unless she made a definite charge. She obviously wasn't ready for that step, so he gave her some names and addresses of shipping companies (who might confirm Belle's crossing) and the address of the American embassy. She went straight there while another committee member began exploring the passenger lists. In one of the studies of the case it is said that when she went to Scotland Yard, Mrs Smythson saw Chief Inspector Dew, but this information is unsourced and seems to be supposition.

Mrs Smythson and Louie Davis also went to Hilldrop Crescent and knocked at number 39, no doubt out of curiosity and to see what would happen. But nothing did happen and there was no reply. They knocked at some of the neighbours' houses but that didn't get them very far either.

When Crippen called at the Martinettis' (for the last time) Clara said she could not understand why Belle was being cremated and Crippen said her mother had been cremated and they had made a pact that, whoever was the first to go, the other would oversee their cremation. He told Paul he was going to sell the house (the house he only rented), that he had always hated it and would sell it with all the furniture except the good things which he was going to pack up. Paul said that would be a very lonely task and, having nothing to do he would be glad to help. Crippen seemed thrown by this. Oh no, he said, don't trouble.

The Guild could not let the matter rest. Clara and Annie Stratton, together with a nephew of Annie's who went with them for some reason – safety, perhaps – took a cab to Hilldrop Crescent and found Crippen at home. He came to the door and stood at the top of the step talking to them, noticeably not inviting them inside. They wanted the name of the ship that had taken Belle across the Atlantic. Crippen was hesitant. Wait, he said, let me think. Then he said a name which Clara promptly forgot, something like *La Tourne* or *La Touvée*. There was in fact a French transatlantic ship called *La Touraine*.

The ship's name was passed on to a man asked by Guild treasurer Lottie Albert to look into Belle's vanishing. Michael Bernstein said he was a translator and interpreter but was hired as a private investigator. He had met Belle himself and was told she had disappeared in mysterious circumstances and that the ladies had been to Scotland Yard, who refused to take the matter up. He began searching the passenger lists of a French shipping agent and looked at every French ship that had crossed from the beginning of February onwards. Of course, he found no trace of Belle on any list.

When the Crippens' former neighbours from Store Street, John and Maud Burroughs, heard about Belle, they immediately wrote a note of condolence to him from their new address at 169 City Road, EC. The letter was dated 2 April 1910. The sceptical tone is barely concealed:

Dear Peter,
    Both Maud and myself were most inexpressively shocked and astounded to learn of poor Belle's death.

We hasten to send our heartfelt condolences on your great loss. As two of her oldest friends, why ever didn't you send us a line?

Do please give us some details of how and where she died. Maud is very much upset and so anxious to hear. Only quite casually we heard that she had suddenly left for America and were daily expecting a letter or card from her.

Maud couldn't understand it as Belle always wrote her on such important occasions so could only think Belle wanted to cut all her old friends. And now to learn she is no more. It is all so sudden that one hardly realises the fact.

We should so like to send a letter of condolence to her sister of whom she was so fond, if you would kindly supply her address.

Yours very sincerely,
J.H.B.

Crippen cannot have been oblivious to the mounting number of inquiries coming at him from various directions. He had already been forced to write to Hawley Otto Crippen to cover his claim that Belle had died beside him, a rare communication between father and son – he told Hawley Otto he had given this out in error. Now here was Burroughs threatening to contact Belle's sister.

He replied to Burroughs on 5 April; the letter was addressed from Albion House and was framed in black for mourning. Crippen himself was framed discreetly in black at this time, daily sporting a black hat-band and a black armlet.

My dear Doctor,
I feel sure you will forgive my apparent neglect but really I have been nearly out of my mind with my poor Belle's death so far away from [sic]. She was not with her sister but out in California on business for me and,

quite like her disposition, would keep up when she should have been in bed with the consequence that pleuro-pneumonia terminated fatally. Almost to the last she refused to let me know there was any danger so that the cable she had gone came as a most awful shock for me. I fear I have sadly neglected my friends but pray forgive me and believe me most truly appreciative of your sympathy. Even now I am not fit to talk to my friends but as soon as I feel I can control myself I will run in on you and Maude [sic] one evening. I am of course giving up the house and every night packing things away.

   With love to both and again thanking you for your kindness.

   I am as ever

   Yours
   Peter

Presumably uncertain that he had prevented an inquiry to Belle's favoured sister, Louise Mills in New York, Crippen wrote to her almost at once. The letter was posted at 10.30 in the morning on Thursday, 7 April addressed this time from 39 Hilldrop Crescent, N. London, England. It's a frighteningly convincing portrayal of its writer's supposed grief, as well as a further exercise in quelling or pre-empting suspicion.

My dear Louise and Robert,
   I hardly know how to write you my dreadful loss, the shock to me has been so dreadful that I am hardly able to control myself. My poor Cora is gone and to make the shock to me more dreadful I did not even see her at the last. A few weeks ago we had news that an old relative of mine in California was dying and to secure important property for ourselves it was necessary for one of us to go and put the matter in a lawyer's hands at once. As I was very busy Cora proposed she should go

and as it was necessary for someone to be there at once she would go straight through, from here to California, without stopping at all and then return by the way of Brooklyn and she would be able to pay all of you a long visit.

Unfortunately, on the way out my poor Cora caught a severe cold and not having, while travelling, the chance to take proper care of herself, it settled on her lungs – later to develop into pleuro-pneumonia. She wished not to frighten me, so kept writing not to worry about her that it was only a slight matter and next I heard by cable she was dangerously ill, and two days later, after I cabled to know should I go to her, I had the dreadful news that she had passed away. Imagine if you can the dreadful shock to me, never more to see my Cora alive, nor hear her voice again. She is being sent back to me and I shall soon have what is left of her here. Of course I am giving up the house, in fact it drives me mad to be in it alone, and will sell out *everything* in a few days. I do not know what I shall do, probably find some business to take me travelling for a few months until I can recover from the shock a little, but as soon as I have a settled address again I will write to you. As it is so terrible to me to have to write this dreadful news, will you please tell all the others of our loss. With love to all, will write soon again and give you my address, probably next in France.

From,
'Doctor'

That week's edition of *Music Hall and Theatre Review* carried a modest but apparently genuine tribute to Belle from the column of her future chronicler, Adelene Harrison, under her pen-name, Marjorie. The column was called 'Frocks & Fancies – a woman's view of variety'. It was with deep regret that Marjorie recorded the death of Miss Belle Elmore, the wife of Dr Crippen, the late Hon. Treasurer of the Music Hall

Ladies Guild. She had passed away in California, USA, on 23 March. She had been an old and valued friend of Marjorie and the good work she did for the Guild and her kindness to all would leave a tender remembrance in the hearts of those who knew her, mingled with sincere regret for the doctor, who was devoted to his bright little wife.

By accident or design, the devoted doctor had chosen to announce Belle's death on the very day, 23 March, that Lil Hawthorne and her husband John Nash had left for New York. Lil set off from Waterloo bearing a bouquet of flowers presented by a Guild posse led by Melinda May. The sad news was waiting for the couple when they arrived, delivered by the recent Guild president, Isabel Ginnett, who was already there with her husband Fred.

Clara wrote to the Nashes while they were away and must have expressed some of her doubts, which the Nashes seem to have shared with Mrs Ginnett. John Nash would later say that Mrs Ginnett 'did not like the look of affairs' and so wrote to the authorities in Los Angeles to try and confirm the death. The reply was dismissive and so she contacted her local police in New Jersey and they wrote an official letter of inquiry about Belle to California. The reply was that no one called Belle Elmore or Crippen had died there. Nash said they all thought it a mysterious affair.

One Wednesday afternoon, Crippen walked in on the Guild committee with a handful of photographs of Belle and asked if they would like to keep any. Melinda May went through them and saw one with the name Motzki, the old stage version of Belle's family name, which Melinda May said she would like, but Crippen took it back and returned it to the pile. Perhaps he was trying to prevent further contact with New York.

Meanwhile Ethel was busy playing house at 39 Hilldrop Crescent. She invited her sister Nina to spend the day with her and Nina arrived in the early afternoon with baby Ivy – no mention of her son Ronald – and did not leave until five or six o'clock. The doctor was there to begin with but left to go back to business. Belle's death was not mentioned and Nina did not like to bring it up, assuming it was a delicate subject. She did not ask where the wedding had taken place and Ethel did not tell her. There was no certificate, of course, but Nina was shown and admired Ethel's wedding ring though she really thought it was of a rather peculiar sort as it looked more like a band. She preferred the diamond rings Ethel was wearing and the round brooch that sparkled a great deal.

Ethel took Nina on a guided tour of the house and Nina made some comment about how hard it must have been to keep clean without a servant. Ethel said she didn't think Belle could keep a servant as she kept them short. She sent Nina home with a few clothes.

Even Walter, Ethel's father, secured himself an invitation. No doubt he had noticed how Ethel had risen in the world. He showed her the two rather good pictures he had in his possession, one an oil-painting of a fox-terrier killing a rat and the other a steel engraving of an Irish castle. Ethel thought she might like them for her new home and suggested Walter bring them in a taxi to show the doctor, and stay for lunch, bringing young Sidney too.

Walter had arrived ready to insist on seeing the marriage certificate, but once there his resolve melted. Crippen was the soul of politeness, and allowed Walter to do most of the talking. Knowing Walter was musical, Crippen produced his gramophone and played some of the finest records Walter had ever heard. Walter saw how Crippen was waited on by Ethel. She called him dear and he called her darling and Walter could see that his daughter was happy as a lark. Sidney played hide and seek round the house and in the cellar until it was time to leave, when Crippen sent Walter away with a box of cigars. Walter must have left the pictures without securing any money for them, as intended. He would remember them soon enough, however.

Over the Whitsun holiday in mid-May, Ethel and Crippen went to Boulogne for a long weekend, apparently with the intention of hiring a French maid. They stayed in room 16 of the Margate Hotel, as Dr and Mrs Crippen. The Edwardian age had ended nine days earlier, with the death on 6 May of King Edward VII from bronchitis. He was sixty-eight years old and had not come to the throne until 1901, when he was already sixty, the period of his reign finding an echo in the time-span of events in the case of Crippen. Looking back from later years, the case would be seen as one of the key Edwardian events, even though it did not come to public attention and notoriety until just after the age had ended.

Crippen and Ethel had just about six weeks of unfettered domestic life ahead of them, as they returned from France, having asked the owner of the hotel to find a servant for them. She produced Valentine LeCoq, the seventeen-year-old daughter of Eudoxie LeCoq, a Boulogne cook. Valentine would be met by 'Mr and Mrs Crippen' when she arrived at Charing Cross Station the following month, to begin her residency at 39 Hilldrop Crescent at £1 a month. It was destined to be a short-lived term of service.

Having earlier given his landlord notice that he would vacate the house in late June, Crippen now asked to stay on until the end of September. There was no explanation for this change of plan. Perhaps, much as he must have wanted to escape his wife's corpse, he also knew the risk of abandoning it and feared it would be discovered. In that way, Crippen and Belle remained tied together, the bond almost greater now in death than it had been in life.

The lies and deceits poured forth as the pair went about their lives. There were casual encounters with members of the Guild committee, such as Mrs Smythson who bumped into them in a shop in Tottenham Court Road. She was sure Ethel saw her and left the shop first. Mrs Smythson asked Crippen if he'd had further news of his wife's remains and he said that, yes, he had her ashes at home now.

Clara Martinetti and Annie Stratton met Crippen in New Oxford Street. Clara could see he was in a hurry to get away, which must have been an unpleasant change from their former friendship. They watched him after he left them and saw him

39 Hilldrop Crescent,
Lower Holloway,
July 1910.

The basement of the
house showing the
excavations in the
cellar.

The remains of Belle Elmore uncovered beneath the cellar floor.

The police team who dug out the basement, led by Chief Inspector Walter Dew (far left).

WANTED poster issued 16 July 1910.

The victim, Belle Elmore – Crippen's wife – depicted in studio photographs.

Dr Hawley Harvey Crippen.

Ethel Le Neve recreated for a
newspaper photograph the
disguise she adopted to
escape with Crippen.

The SS *Montrose* and its captain, Commander Harry Kendall.

Detective Arthur Mitchell sets off to Canada on 4 August 1910 with Holloway Prison wardresses Foster and Martin who will accompany Ethel Le Neve back to England.

Crippen arrives
back in Liverpool
after his arrest, 27
August 1910. He is
helped down the
gangplank by Chief
Inspector Dew.

Crippen and
Le Neve in the
dock at Bow Street
Police Court,
29 August 1910.

Crowds outside the Old Bailey on the first day of Crippen's trial, 18 October 1910.

Crippen in the dock during his trial, which lasted from 18–22 October 1910.

Ethel Le Neve poses for a photograph to accompany publication of her life story in *Lloyd's Weekly News*, November 1910.

joined by Ethel, the two of them getting on a bus and disappearing from sight. Ethel appeared to be wearing one of Belle's furs.

Ethel called in on Lydia Rose senior and her husband, showed off her wedding ring and invited them to tea at her new home in Hilldrop Crescent. The Roses went to number 39 the following week, where they had a couple of hours of general chat with no word spoken about the wedding. The Roses had no idea that Crippen had been married before and had two dead wives.

'My dear Ma,' Ethel wrote to Mrs Jackson, just before the new servant arrived:

> You will be wondering when I am going to reply to yours, dear, which I was indeed pleased to get, but sorry to hear of your illness. From your letter I guess you must have hurt yourself internally during the morning & you poor dear must have had a bad turn of it. Well, dear, I do so hope you are much better. Let me have a line as soon as you can spare the time. Have been ever so busy with the wretched house and think you would hardly recognise same. Shall be indeed glad when we are able to move, which will be in June. It's real hard work to keep it anywhere near clean and to spend the afternoon at Biss [business]. It gives me very little time to myself. Still, notwithstanding the hard work am indeed happy.
>
> Shall love to see you, dear, & shall try and fix a date next week for paying that long promised visit. Poor Fred, give the little bairns a kiss, and tell Fred indeed I do want a scratch badly. Pardon this scrawl, dear, but I feel so tired & felt I must not put you off another day. Perhaps if you are better you could meet me at Westminster. This is where I get the car, don't I. Write me, dear, when you feel able. How's Bot [sic] also Mr J. Give my kindest regards to both. Now must close with much love to your dear self and the boys.

Affectionately Yrs,
Ethel

PS Dr sends his kindest wishes to both & hopes you
have recovered.

Mrs Jackson did not hear any more from Ethel, until the
next letter, which was dated Sunday, 12 June, the day after the
servant's arrival, and this time began, 'My dearest Mum.'

Here comes another epestle [sic] hoping, dear, it will
find you well and quite fit also the boys and & Mr J.
Now for the next item. If fine will you come up &
spend the best part of the day with me Wednesday. I
will meet you from the office, say 11.30, as I must go up
for an hour, then we can come straight along and have
dinner in the Summer house if the boys like.
Now for No. 2. Will you bring me a few pieces of
my music. I have nothing to play & should love to have
some of it if you cannot find all. This I will relieve you
of when we meet, dear. If wet I shall not expect you.
Bye [sic] the way I have at last got a girl which I am
thankful for. She is only eighteen yrs. But seems anxious
to learn & willing enough.
The poor girl, however, hasn't hardly a rag to her
back, not a black blouse or anything & as Dr is asking
some friends to dinner next Sunday, I feel I must rig her
out nice and tidy. I know, dear, you will give me a few
ideas. Well, dear, no more until Wednesday and please
pardon scrawl.

Love, dear,
Ethel

PS Write per return, dear.

It seems possible that Ethel chose Wednesday because it
was the day of the Guild meeting and she was happy to absent

herself from the members' curiosity and disapproval. There was still one more letter to come, to 'My dear Ma', sent and delivered the day before the visit:

Yours to hand with many thanks shall look forward to a real good chat tomorrow Wednesday. Dear, will you please come straight here as am having rather a bad turn again so do not think it wise to go to the office at all. I dare say you will come by the Motor Bus to Camden Town then Finsbury Pk Car. Excuse pencil writing in bed. Leave all news until we meet. Heaps of love to your own dear self & the boys.

  Always yrs
  Ethel

PS Dr sends his usual kind wishes.

When Mrs Jackson finally made her return visit to 39 Hilldrop Crescent that day she immediately noticed that the smell had disappeared. Ethel said it was because she had cleaned it from top to bottom. Did you clean it all yourself? Oh yes.

The Sunday guests were Crippen's dental partner Gilbert Rylance, together with one of his dental assistants, who would say they went to lunch, not dinner, having been invited to attend at two o'clock. 'Dinner' was the working-class version of the midday meal, and what the middle classes ate in the evenings, so Ethel was betraying her origins. Crippen and Ethel were just like a man and wife, thought Rylance while he was there.

Mrs Jackson must have brought the music Ethel wanted – sheet music, presumably – because the next among this last little flurry of social events was a musical evening attended by Lydia Rose junior the following Sunday. She arrived at four o'clock and took tea downstairs in the 'morning room' with Ethel and the doctor. They then returned to the sitting-room for the 'enjoyable musical evening'. Lydia was invited to go back a fortnight later, on 10 July. Instead, she would get a note the night before, from Ethel, putting her off.

Mrs Jackson spent the evening there on 1 July and met the new maid. Ethel told her, in front of the doctor, that they would soon be leaving the house to go to a top-floor flat in Shaftesbury Avenue (that was where the Martinettis lived). They had already taken the flat but it would not be ready until the end of July. There is no evidence that a flat was ever rented, though Crippen too had spoken of such a plan. Perhaps Ethel was keen to get away and hoped to hasten the move by speaking about it to someone else in front of Crippen. Or maybe she was just being grand with Mrs Jackson.

Ethel's aunt and uncle from Brighton, the Bensteads, also came on a visit that weekend and Ethel saw them off at Victoria Station afterwards. During the next week she called in to see her mother and invited her little brother Sidney, who was thirteen, to come and spend the day with her the following Saturday, 8 July.

But Ethel's days as a north London hostess were already over. The next caller would be Chief Inspector Dew.

There had been no reply for many weeks to the Guild's attempts to reach Crippen's son. When the letter finally arrived on 24 May it was clear that he had other things to worry about.

Los Angeles
9 May 1910

Music Hall Ladies Guild
Miss Melinda May

Dear Madam
    Received your letter forwarded to me from the County Clerk, 23 April 1910, but owing to many

misfortunes, sickness and death of our son, I overlooked your letter until this date. The death of my step-mother was as great a surprise to me as to anyone. She died at San Francisco and the first I heard of it was through my father, who wrote to me immediately afterwards.

He asked me to forward all letters to him and he would make the necessary explanations. He said he had, through a mistake, given out my name and address as my step-mother's death-place. I would be very glad if you find out any particulars of her death if you would let me know of them as I know as a fact that she died at San Francisco.

Yours very sincerely
H. Otto Crippen
1612 Holenby Avenue
Los Angeles
Calif. USA

Otto's son had died soon after birth. He did not have any more children.

This was the first time San Francisco had been mentioned and was clearly a completely different account from the one Crippen had been giving out in London, saying his son had been with Belle when she died. That was hardly something you could make a mistake over. Crippen had obviously not stopped to think that these two distant facets of his life – his son and the Guild – might ever come together. Or he may have been too desperate to worry about it, prepared to say or do whatever was necessary at the time to keep a step ahead of discovery.

The Nashes had sailed for London from New York on 5 June, seen off at the quayside by Mrs Ginnett. They had promised her that they would talk to Crippen as soon as they were home. Back in London they talked to their friends, who had also been the Crippens' friends, and realised that none of them believed his account of how Belle had died. They went to see Crippen in his office at Albion House on Tuesday, 28 June, to offer their condolences.

John Nash would later describe how Crippen had seemed cut up and had sobbed with grief. Crippen would deny in court having sobbed. Nash also said Crippen was very nervous and twitched a bit of paper in his hands all the time they talked. When Nash asked where Belle had died Crippen said that it was some little town near San Francisco with a Spanish name, he thought. Unluckily for him, Nash had lived in northern California for two years. Nash suggested some names. Alameda? Alamaio? Something like that, said Crippen, he wasn't sure.

NASH: Peter, do you mean to say you don't know where your wife has died?

CRIPPEN: I can't remember, I think it was Alamaio.

NASH: I hear you have received her ashes?

CRIPPEN: Yes, they're at home in my safe, as we had decided to be cremated.

NASH: Where was she cremated?

CRIPPEN: There are about four cemeteries about San Francisco and it was one of these but I cannot tell you which one.

NASH: Surely, you received a certificate?

Nash could see Crippen's nervousness increasing and felt sure now that something was wrong. How could a man not know where his wife had died or where her ashes had come from?

NASH: When did she sail and by what ship?

CRIPPEN: I don't know as she went to France on business for me, but I think it was a French ship with a name like *Lorraine*.

NASH: *La Touraine*?

CRIPPEN: I think so.

NASH: Why didn't she call and see Mrs Ginnett on her way through?

CRIPPEN: She was in too much of a hurry to get through.

Lil asked about Belle's relations in New York. Crippen said there was a Mrs Mills, the wife of a soap manufacturer, living in Brooklyn.

When the Nashes left Albion House they went directly to Scotland Yard. They apparently hoped to see their friend, Superintendent Frank Froest, but he was unavailable and, rather than see anyone else, they left without making any report after making an appointment to see Froest two days later.

TEN

Walter Dew was forty-seven that year, just about the same age as Crippen, whose forty-eighth birthday fell in July. Dew had been born and raised in a Northamptonshire village with the eloquent name of Far Cotton and had served nearly thirty years as an officer of the Metropolitan Police since giving up his job as a railway porter at the age of nineteen. As a young detective in Whitechapel in 1888, Dew had worked on the investigation into the 'Jack the Ripper' murders. He had been a Chief Inspector since 1906. He had three daughters, one named Ethel, and a son who would be killed at Givenchy in 1914. When he published his memoirs in 1938 they were called *I Caught Crippen*. That's a clue to the importance these events would assume in Dew's life.

The police approach to investigating crime was evidently very different in those days. When the Assistant Commissioner Sir Melville MacNaghten published his autobiography in 1914, *Days of my Years*, he could proclaim on the first page, without shame or professional embarrassment, 'I never kept a diary, nor even possessed a notebook so that, in what I write, I must trust to memory.' A police officer without a notebook? Relying on his memory? That must be why MacNaghten makes so many mistakes in his account of the Crippen case. And why he forgets to mention Walter Dew, whose name is oddly absent from MacNaghten's story. MacNaghten may, of course, have been jealous of the attention his Chief Inspector enjoyed afterwards. Or he may have felt that Dew's conduct had brought Scotland Yard into disrepute.

According to Dew, he was called to Frank Froest's office on 30 June so that John Nash and Lil Hawthorne could repeat for him the sequence of events they had just relayed to Froest.

The Nashes once again went through the details of Belle's disappearance and her husband's suspicious conduct and apparent lies. Nash was quite open now in saying he believed there had been 'foul play'. Froest said, 'Well, Mr Dew, that's the story, what do you think?'

Dew said he would make inquiries personally, though he seems to have set off at a fairly leisurely pace, taking just a few statements before he and a sergeant, Arthur Mitchell, called at Hilldrop Crescent eight days later, at about ten o'clock on Friday morning, 8 July.

Valentine LeCoq opened the door and Dew asked if Dr Crippen was there. Valentine, no doubt struggling with the language, said he was, when in fact he wasn't, he was on his way to Albion House having already made his regular weekly call to collect his wages from Eddie Marr. According to Ethel in her life story, she overheard Valentine on the doorstep and was annoyed at her for saying the doctor was in. 'What a stupid creature that is!' Ethel said she thought to herself.

Valentine left the officers on the door-step and went to fetch Ethel, who came to the door. Dew again asked if Crippen was there and this time was told he wasn't, which seemed a little suspicious to Dew. She invited him to look over the house but he eventually accepted her word. He had immediately noticed that Ethel was wearing the brooch he had heard so much about from John Nash and the Guild women he had interviewed. She seemed agitated when he said they were police officers and told them she was the housekeeper. Dew said, 'Aren't you Miss Le Neve, Dr Crippen's typist?' Dew saw Ethel hesitate before admitting she was. Dew said he must see Crippen, and where was he? Ethel said she didn't know but would try to find him if they could call back later. Dew said, no, he had to see him about his wife and wanted them all to go together to Albion House.

The officers waited while Ethel got ready and then the three of them went and caught a bus to Tottenham Court Road. They walked round to Albion House and, as they began to walk up the stairs, Ethel asked them if they'd mind waiting and ran ahead to fetch Crippen from his office. He came out into the stairwell and Dew introduced Mitchell and himself and said, 'Some of your wife's friends have been to us concerning the stories you have told them about her death, with which they are not satisfied. I have made exhaustive inquiries and I am not satisfied so I have come here to see you to ask if you care to offer any explanation.'

Crippen said he supposed he had better tell the truth and Dew said, yes, he thought that would be best. He must have wondered what was coming then, what truth Crippen was about to tell. They went through to Crippen's office and Ethel went to her desk. Dew could see her flitting back and forth outside the room while the men talked.

Crippen now said the stories he had told people about his wife's death were untrue. So far as he knew she was still alive. Dew stopped him and said any explanation he wanted to make would be written down in his own words. Perhaps it would be more convenient if he told the officers all about himself?

They began taking the statement at about midday and, said Dew in his memoirs, it was a big job. By lunchtime they had barely got past the introduction and, not wanting to lose sight of Crippen, Dew invited him along for lunch at a small Italian restaurant only a few yards from Albion House. Crippen 'made a hearty meal', according to Dew. He ordered beefsteak and ate it 'with the relish of a man who hadn't a care in the world'. Dew would be wounded later by the allegations that they had gone to eat at the grand Holborn Restaurant and that he and Crippen had lunched together more than once. Just silly rumours, he said. Even so, there could not have been many occasions, before or after, in the history of the Metropolitan Police, when a detective went for lunch with a murderer. That was not a good start to the case. It certainly looked as though Dew was taken in by Crippen.

When they returned to his office to continue the statement Crippen said he believed his wife had left him and gone to Chicago to be with Bruce Miller, who was in another business now, but his stage show had been 'a musical instrument turn'.

Crippen said Belle must have taken some clothes in a theatrical travelling basket that was now missing and also some jewellery. He said he had never pawned or sold anything belonging to her before or after she left. This of course was a foolish and demonstrable lie – unless he was playing a semantic game, on the grounds that he had paid for the clothes and the jewellery and they were therefore his. He did tell Dew that he had bought all Belle's jewellery. He said he had treated her sometimes with homoeopathic remedies for bilious attacks.

They did not finish with Crippen until well after four o'clock and then the officers took a statement from Ethel. Her statement was short, just two pages when typed, as opposed to Crippen's which ran to ten pages. Dew would note in his memoirs that her statement showed Ethel had nothing to hide. He must have admired Ethel's candour when she told him: 'My parents do not know what I am doing, and think I am housekeeper at Hilldrop Crescent.' A telling lie – Ethel's statement, like Crippen's, leaving out any mention of a marriage between them.

According to Ethel, it was from Dew that she now found out Belle was still alive and the story of her death had been Crippen's invention. She was stricken, she would say in her life story, with grief, anger, and bewilderment at his deception.

It must have been while Dew was busy with Ethel that Crippen was already thinking of escape, or even arrest. At about half past four he asked Marion Curnow if anyone else knew about the two envelopes he had placed in her safe. 'No,' she said, and he said, 'If anyone asks, say nothing and if anything happens to me please give what you have there to Miss Le Neve.' 'All right,' said Marion Curnow, who did not like Ethel.

Gilbert Rylance asked Crippen who the two men were, and Crippen said they were Scotland Yard officers come to see if Belle had any estate in England to pay taxes on.

When he had finished with Ethel, Dew wanted to see the house so the four of them went together in a growler to

Hilldrop Crescent, Crippen and Ethel sitting side by side and, as Dew put it, doing nothing to 'disguise the affectionate relationship between them'. At this stage, Dew said, he was not suspicious of murder but knew that Crippen had lied to him. His statement had been ingenious, half false, half true. Crippen's very frankness, said Dew, was misleading. Dew was clearly misled.

When they arrived at the house Ethel sent Valentine out to buy some vegetables for supper. Dew and Mitchell were shown all round the house and made some search of cupboards and drawers. Dew said he saw enough ostrich feathers to stock a milliner's shop. There were many pictures of Mrs Crippen on the walls and he saw that in some rooms everything was packed up ready for removal. When they went downstairs, Crippen and Ethel stood in the doorway of the cellar, while Dew struck matches to poke around inside and sound the floor.

In his memoirs Dew would say he was not sure that he would have lived to tell the tale if he had discovered the body at that moment. He believed Crippen had a loaded revolver in his pocket and was ready to shoot him. They later found Crippen's gun in a bedroom drawer, but it had not been there that day, when they searched.

They finished in the breakfast room next to the kitchen, where Dew said he would like to see Mrs Crippen's jewellery and Crippen said, 'with pleasure' and went off and came back with four rings and the rising-sun brooch. As Dew noted, Crippen had readily agreed to everything and seemed to have nothing to hide. Even so, Dew told him, he should have to find Belle to clear the matter up. Crippen said, yes, he would do everything he could. Could Dew suggest anything? Would an advertisement help? Dew said he thought that was an excellent idea. So the two men sat down at the dining-table and composed a form of words which Crippen said he would place as an advert in various newspapers, apparently in America, since dollars were offered: 'Mackamotzki. Will Belle Elmore communicate with H.H.C. or authorities at once.

Serious trouble through your absence. Twenty-five dollars reward to any one communicating her whereabouts to [the draft ended here]'.

Dew and Mitchell left Ethel and Crippen at about eight o'clock. According to their servant, madame cried when the police had gone. They had supper and went to their bedroom on the first floor where they talked for a long time. Ethel would say she was profoundly hurt and angry at the doctor's betrayal. She described herself saying 'For mercy's sake, tell me whether you know where Belle Elmore is. I have a right to know.' 'I tell you truthfully,' Crippen replied, in Ethel's account, 'that I don't know where she is.'

Of course, if Ethel had really believed Belle was dead from natural causes, from pneumonia, she would not have bothered inventing a sham marriage. She could have had a real marriage instead. Her version of these events is implausible. It seems astonishing that the two journalists who 'ghosted her story' – both would go on to be eminent in their fields as author and barrister – could have been taken in by it.

In reality Crippen and Ethel must have been discussing what they would do. It must have been an agonising conversation, in the looming shadow of the gallows. Perhaps the doctor was planning to escape alone – hence his request to Curnow to pass on the envelopes to Ethel. He may have thought that going alone would distract the police from Ethel and suggest her innocence. Then perhaps, Ethel would not be left behind but insisted on going with him, being afraid to stay behind and carry on lying alone. Or maybe the reverse, that she wanted to stay and he didn't trust her to maintain the deceit alone. It's possible that they considered staying in the hope that Dew could be satisfied and the storm would pass.

Ever after, people who followed or studied the case would say that if Crippen had stayed put he would have got away with it, that Dew would not have bothered making further inquiries. But Dew himself said in his memoirs that there was no question of his letting the matter drop. He had to find out where Belle was to complete the inquiry, as Crippen must have realised.

In Ethel's life story, when they woke up on Saturday morning, 9 July, Crippen said that now everybody would know he had made up stories about Belle's disappearance and did not know where she was. The Guild members would be talking and gossiping and neither he nor Ethel would be able to face the office again. He was only thinking of Ethel, she said he told her. The scandal would be far worse for her than for him and he would do anything to save her from it.

Crippen then said there was only one possible thing to do and that was to get away. They had to leave all those prying people who would talk about Ethel and go somewhere until the whole affair had blown over. The worst of it was, the police would try to hold Crippen there until she was found. This was an echo of what Crippen would say at his trial. His best explanation for why he had run away – running away being generally taken as a clear expression of guilt, of having something to hide – was that he ran because he knew he would be accused and put in jail because Belle could not be found. He could not say what crime he would be accused of. Accused of losing his wife, maybe.

Ethel described how Crippen suggested that a disguise would be necessary. 'What sort of a disguise?' she had asked. 'Well,' he said, 'you do very well as a boy. You have often told me how you played the tomboy in your early years.' Ethel had not liked the idea at all. She had thought her tomboy days were over and was not sure she dared go about in boys' clothes. The doctor had said to leave it to him, he would take care of everything. They should slip away with as few things as possible.

Valentine saw the doctor for the last time at about half past eight that Saturday morning as he left for work by the side door, apparently as usual, carrying an umbrella. She said Ethel was very nervous in the house and went white with fright when there was a knock at the door. 'Oh, oh,' she said. It was the milkman. Ethel told Valentine to get on with her work, urging her to hurry, hurry, hurry.

Ethel left about an hour after the doctor, carrying a small, flat bag. She left a note for Valentine to give to Sidney, her teenage brother, when he called later that morning. He arrived about eleven and Valentine gave him a card which said, 'Dear Sid, am sorry to disappoint you today; have been called away. Will write you later. My love, dear, to you and all and kisses. From your loving sis Ethel.' Sidney stayed at the house all day – apparently waiting for Ethel to return – and played in the garden with Valentine, practising his French.

When William Long arrived for work at Albion House he was surprised to find the doctor already there, ahead of him. Crippen was overhauling his desk. He seemed worried. Long asked if there was any trouble. 'Just a little scandal,' said Crippen. 'If anything happens to me, or any letters come for me or Frankel, please deal with them.'

Long at first told the police the morning then went on as usual, until about one o'clock, when he realised the doctor had disappeared. He was interviewed by the police on Monday, Tuesday and Wednesday. On Monday he said things went on as usual. On Tuesday he said Crippen had asked him to go out and buy a grey felt hat, which he had bought at Horne's for 3s 9d. On Wednesday, finally, he told the police what had really happened. He cannot have liked the police very much to have held out for so long. Or he must have been loyally trying to protect Crippen – perhaps give him a head start.

The true story was that Crippen had called Long into his office at about ten o'clock on Saturday morning. He asked if Long would do something for him. Yes. He had given Long £2 and a list of boy's clothes and asked him to go to a menswear shop, Charles Baker's, and buy them. Long had gone to Baker's on Tottenham Court Road and bought a brown tweed suit at 24s 9d, a shirt at 2s 6d, a tie at 6½d, two collars at 6d, and a brown bowler hat at 3s 11d. On his way back to the office he had bought a pair of size 5 black boots from a shoe shop in Tottenham Court Road. He had left the things in room 91, as asked by Crippen. He must have gone out again later to get the felt hat from Horne's.

Long saw Ethel arrive some time after his return from shopping. She was wearing a hat which he later found with the suit Crippen had worn to work, hidden in the back of the forceps cupboard.

Crippen was clearly tidying his business. He wrote some letters and asked Marion Curnow what he owed her for the dentistry ads she had placed. She said about £3 and he gave her the money in postal orders. He asked if she was going out and she said, yes, about midday, was there something he wanted? Yes, he wanted to settle up with her and also talk to her before she went out. When she went into his office at 11.15 he showed her his banking passbook with a credit of £37 19s 4d and asked if she would cash him a cheque for £37. He asked her not to pay the cheque in until Monday. She agreed and he gave her the cheque which was also signed by Belle. The signature was apparently genuine, it being common practice to ask spouses who were joint signatories on accounts to sign several cheques in advance. (That would be especially handy if you planned to murder them.)

The dentist, Dr Rylance, saw Crippen when he arrived for work at about 11 am. He saw him about midday and never again after that, having waited until two o'clock for him to return from lunch. 'He never told me he was going or wished me the time of day,' as Rylance would later put it.

Ethel had taken a taxi to Tottenham to say goodbye to her sister, Nina. She kept the cab waiting while she went inside. She asked Nina if she was alone and Nina was telling her how pleased she was to see her when she noticed Ethel was staring at her intently and assumed it was because her hair was untidy.

'Don't look at my hair,' she laughed. 'I have been busy and have not been able to do it up properly.'

'Oh, I am not looking at your hair. Look at mine. I scraped mine up in a hurry.'

Nina now realised something was wrong and said, 'Oh,

dear, what is the matter?' Ethel's lips quivered as if she was about to cry and Nina put her arms around her. Ethel told her two detectives had called yesterday not long after Harvey had gone to work. Belle Elmore's friends didn't seem to think she was dead and did not believe Ethel was his legal wife.

'Who am I?' Ethel said. 'Everybody will think I am a bad woman of the streets.' She again began to cry but pulled herself together and stopped. She said she couldn't stay long with Nina but couldn't go without coming and saying goodbye. Nina asked where she was going but Ethel couldn't, or wouldn't, tell her. She said that as soon as she knew and was settled she would be in touch.

Nina asked why she had to go. Ethel said, 'What good is it for me to stop without means and my character gone? I told detectives I was only Harvey's housekeeper.' Ethel told Nina that Harvey was going away, either to find the person who sent the cable saying Belle was dead, or Belle herself. 'For all I know she may not have gone to America at all and may still be in London and have got somebody across the water to send a bogus telegram informing of her death and keep in hiding till we got married and confront us with bigamy.'

Ethel must have forgotten she had told Nina she was married *before* she told her Belle was dead. Had Nina forgotten, as well? What she made of all this, sadly, is not recorded. Ethel only stayed about fifteen minutes but found time before leaving to go upstairs and kiss baby Ivy goodbye. Ethel would describe this visit in her life story, omitting any mention of marriage or bigamy. She would, however, say that she left in a very distressed state and felt awful on the way back to Albion House.

Back at the office, her life story continued, Crippen showed her the boy's brown suit and said she would look a perfect boy in it, especially with her hair cut off. Ethel cried, 'Have I got to cut my hair?' 'Why of course,' said Crippen 'gaily', 'that is absolutely necessary.' Ethel said she slipped out of her clothes and left them in a heap on the floor just as they fell from her, and changed into the suit. It was a poor fit and she immediately split the trousers down the back. She could not help laughing as she changed into the whole costume: shirt, braces, waistcoat, trousers, jacket, collar and tie, boots and bowler hat. Crippen was just as gay, as he took the large office scissors, saying, 'Now for the hair.' Her 'mop' fell to the floor with one or two snips. She had not minded, she said. It was all part of the adventure.

She put on the hat and walked back and forth in the office saying she would never be able to face the world in those things. Crippen said she would do famously: 'No one will recognise you. You are a perfect boy.' Ethel said that she fairly soon felt at ease, though missed the habit of holding her skirt for quite a while to come. She lit a cigarette and dangled it on her lips to complete the disguise. She said the cigarette was a novelty. Relatives in later life would remember her as a heavy smoker.

They arranged to meet at Chancery Lane tube station and Ethel set off downstairs alone and out into the street. She felt very self-conscious but no one paid her any attention, even as she stood waiting nervously at the tube station. Crippen eventually arrived after shaving off his trade-mark moustache.

You can sense the thrill, a sexual frisson almost, something fetishistic, in Ethel's description of her cross-dressing, her hair cut, the cigarette hanging from her lips. She says Crippen told her what a pretty boy she made. Perhaps it really was like that, and not frantic or sordid, as you might imagine it would be, with Crippen and Ethel running for their lives. There is, of course, no other testimony to these events. Crippen never spoke of them.

They took the tube to Bank and then went to Liverpool Street Station, where they found they had just missed the boat train to Harwich, which the doctor had planned to take. They obviously intended to head for mainland Europe. The next train did not leave for several hours so the doctor suggested taking a bus ride, 'hiding' in plain sight, to pass the time. Ethel thought they went out to Hackney, taking the top deck on the way and travelling inside on the way back. She said little for fear of being betrayed by her voice. 'Strange as it may seem, I was now quite cheerful and, indeed, rather exhilarated in spirits. It seemed to me that I had given the slip in fine style to all those people who had been prying upon my movements. I had gone in disguise past their very door in Albion House, and no longer would they be able to scan me up and down with their inquisitive eyes.'

Here was some indication that Ethel must have felt the judgement and disapproval of others in recent weeks. No doubt she was referring to office colleagues, such as Marion Curnow, and surely the women of the Ladies Guild too.

They caught the train to Harwich and crossed over to the Hook of Holland on the night boat, taking a train to Rotterdam after breakfast. They spent the day, Sunday 9 July, sightseeing, watching the Dutchmen in their baggy trousers and big wooden shoes, visiting the parrots in the zoological gardens. At Crippen's insistence, Ethel went to a barbershop so that she could have his rough cuts tidied. He sat and watched while the barber used his clippers. Good gracious! How startled Ethel was when she first felt the little instrument running up and down her head and her hair scattering on the floor. She left the chair with 'a poll as closely cropped as Jack Sheppard' (Sheppard was a Georgian criminal, a popular hero for his repeated escapes from prison). When they went to sit in a café two Dutch girls admired the 'pretty little English boy'.

That evening, they went to Brussels and checked into the Hotel des Ardennes, where they remained for the next eight nights. Crippen signed them in as John Robinson, a merchant, aged fifty-five, born Canada, resident Quebec, arriving from Vienna, and his son, Master Robinson, aged sixteen, born Canada, resident Quebec. The son did not say much, on check-in or afterwards. John Robinson said the boy was deaf and mute because of a throat infection.

The same-day post was a marvel of the age. It delivered

Long's letter to his home in Camden Square at about seven o'clock that Saturday evening.

> Dear Mr Long,
>   Will you do me the very great favour of winding up as best you can my household affairs. There is £12 10s due to my landlord for the past quarter's rent, and there will be also this quarter's rent, a total due to him of £25, in lieu of which he can seize the contents of the house. I cannot manage about the girl. She will have to get back to France, but should have sufficient saved from her wages to do this. After the girl leaves, kindly send the keys with a note explaining to the landlord; address Messrs Lown & Sons, 12 Ashbrook Road, St John's Villas, Holloway. Thanking you in anticipation of fulfilling my wishes, I am, with best wishes for your future success and happiness,
>
>   Yours faithfully,
>   H.H. Crippen

Long's letter enclosed a key to the door of number 39. He and his wife Flora went round there and found Sidney, Ethel's little brother, still there with Valentine, who had just received her own letter, which had been posted at 4.15 pm:

> Valentine,
>   Do not be alarmed if we do not return until late as we shall go to the theatre this evening.
>
>   H.H. Crippen

Mrs Long asked Valentine if she had received a letter and Valentine said she had. Mrs Long told her she must return to France. 'Why?' asked Valentine. 'Is madame vexed?' 'No,' said Mrs Long, 'madame has gone away. I will sell some of her dresses to pay your fare.'

Long took Sidney home and that was where Walter Neave, Ethel's father, found him when he returned home later that evening. Long told Neave he had been given written authority to sell the doctor's effects and settle his accounts, but had wanted to see Walter before he went ahead. Walter was suspicious – what was going on? – and said he would not express an opinion on the subject. Later he remembered his paintings, still at number 39, and went round there the next day and left a note in the keyhole for Long, asking him to collect him when he next went to the house.

Neave and Long went to the house that evening, where Walter saw all the clothes that had been left and was again puzzled. He asked Long if he knew where they were but Long couldn't help him. He wondered if they'd gone to the Bensteads in Brighton. He was suspicious, but couldn't work it out. He wondered if Crippen had run off with the company funds.

Flora Long went to the house on Monday to take Valentine some food and to pick some clothes to sell for Valentine's return fare to France: seven pairs of cotton and wool ladies undervests (white and cream), eight pairs of light cotton and wool ladies combinations, two pairs of short Merino white combinations, four champagne-coloured cotton and wool undervests, a light blue cotton and wool undervest, a cream cotton and wool camisole, a Holland skirt, a white linen embroidered skirt, a white lace petticoat, a coloured voile dress and kimono, a silk petticoat, a coloured muslin frock, a brown linen skirt, a cream silk petticoat, a cotton petticoat, a feather boa, a heliotrope dress, a grey costume, a silk blouse and two pairs of stockings.

She packed the things in two parcels and took them to Mrs Seymour's second-hand shop on Camden Street. Mrs Seymour gave her 24s. Mrs Long returned to the house, where she noticed the note Dew and Crippen had written as a missing person's ad for Belle. She was still there when Dew arrived with Sergeant Mitchell.

*

On Saturday, while Ethel and Crippen were fleeing the country, Dew was circulating a description of Belle to every police office in London. He said he made various other inquiries. On Sunday, he read through and considered the statements he had taken from Crippen and Ethel on Friday.

On Monday, 11 July, in the late morning, he and Sergeant Mitchell returned to Albion House. He never would say why he went back there. He saw Gilbert Rylance, who showed him the letter that had been waiting for him when he arrived at work that morning. The letter was dated Saturday, 9 July.

Dear Dr Rylance,

I now find that in order to escape trouble I shall be obliged to absent myself for a time. I believe with the business as it is now going you will run on all right so far as money matters go – Plucknett's last account you will find in my desk, as to rent, you only have to send Goddard & Smith, £10 12s 6d as I have already paid them off £40 12s 6d (this is in advance up to Septr 25th). If you want to give notice you should give 6 months notice in my name on Septr 25th 1910. Long knows pretty much all of the business, and can take over the book-keeping, there will be several paid bills to enter on my file on my desk, the key of which you will find in the upper drawer of the little cabinet in Coulthard's office. I shall write you later on more fully.

With kind wishes for your success.

Yours sincerely,
H.H. Crippen

PS I am enclosing Plucknett's account which you can attend to yourself personally.

Marion Curnow opened and showed Dew the two letters that Crippen had asked her to keep in the safe. One envelope contained all the deposit notes for the £600 the Crippens had invested at the Charing Cross Bank. The second contained a watch and a brooch.

Dew also saw Long, who showed him his letter from Crippen and gave him the key to the house. Long did not, of course, mention the boy's clothes he had bought on Saturday.

Dew and his sergeant went to Hilldrop Crescent and found Valentine there with Mrs Long. Sergeant Mitchell went to Camden Street with Mrs Long to collect the clothes she had sold there earlier. The two officers began to search the house. Dew dug up the garden a little and examined the floor of the cellar by candlelight, kicking at the bricks with his heel to see if any were loose, which they weren't, even though they were not cemented into place, merely lodged in the clay beneath.

In a wardrobe drawer in the bedroom Crippen and Ethel had used, at the front on the first floor, Dew found Crippen's revolver which was loaded. Downstairs in a cupboard in the breakfast room, Mitchell found a box of .45 cartridges and several cardboard targets. There was also a sheet of paper with Belle's signature written on it several times, as if in practice.

Dew now circulated two more descriptions. In a couple of days they would be dressed up and elaborated upon for a handbill with photographs under the lurid heading: 'Murder and mutilation'. But for now, they were just a few descriptive words, going not just to London police stations but to ports all over the United Kingdom and Europe.

Dew returned to Hilldrop Crescent on Tuesday the 12th, tapping the cellar floor with his feet but still missing what lay beneath it. He arranged a search of the drains and sewers in the street and had the left-luggage lockers at the main railway stations checked for putrid smells, but none were detected. He looked for signs of luggage having been sent from the house since January, and discovered the transport that William Long had arranged. He checked the cases that could be found, without success.

Dew must have guessed that Long was holding something back because he pressed him repeatedly, and finally, on Wednesday, Dew told Long he didn't feel he was telling him everything he knew, and got out of him the story of the clothes Long had bought. The two officers again returned to number 39 and went back to the cellar.

There was just a little coal on the cellar floor and some rubbish such as cuttings from trees and an old chandelier. It was late in the afternoon of Wednesday, 13 July 1910. According to Dew in his memoirs: 'I was armed with a poker. Presently a little thrill of excitement went through me. The sharp point of the poker had found its way between two of the bricks and one of them showed signs of lifting.'

Giving evidence at Crippen's trial he would say, 'I again searched the coal cellar ... I went down with Sergeant Mitchell on to my knees and probed about with a small poker which I had got out of the kitchen. I found that the poker went in somewhat easily between the crevices of the bricks, and I managed to get one or two up, and then several others came up pretty easily. I then produced a spade from the garden and dug the clay that was immediately beneath the bricks. After digging down to a depth of about four spadefuls I came across what appeared to be human remains.'

No one could be in any doubt that Dew himself had wielded the poker and found Belle's remains. He would talk in his memoirs about how he was fascinated by the cellar at the end of the dark passage, as if there was some mystical element which had drawn him to the discovery. That and the eventual arrest were his future claim to fame. He had found the body and caught Crippen.

Sergeant Mitchell did not give evidence at the trial and never wrote his memoirs. He did however give a formal statement that September, in which he gave his own version of events. The statement is in a box of case papers in the National Archives: 'We dug parts of the garden and then with a small poker probed parts of the floor and basement. We then went into the coal cellar, and on probing the brick floor, which was covered with coal dust, I dug the poker between two of the bricks in the centre of the floor. I loosened and removed them, and Chief Inspector Dew then dug the floor up, and uncovered some pieces of human remains as described. This was about 5 pm.'

'I dug the poker . . .' It seems inconceivable that Mitchell would have made this up. He was just the Sergeant. So, even though the initial discovery had been his, he must have sat and watched from the sidelines later while his boss took all the credit. That must have been very galling, though Dew would be the target of plenty of criticism, too, for his sins.

As soon as they uncovered the remains a foul, overpowering smell was unleashed and they had to stop digging. Dew contacted Scotland Yard to notify his superiors and call for assistance. Some uniformed constables turned out. MacNaghten the Assistant Commissioner came in a car from Scotland Yard with his Superintendent, Frank Froest. MacNaghten said that before he left he grabbed a handful of cigars from the box on his desk, rightly thinking they might be appreciated to ward off the fumes. The divisional police surgeon for Kentish Town, Dr Thomas Marshall, was called and shown the remains, which were barely exposed at this stage. He went away and returned about nine o'clock when the digging had progressed.

It was a warm summer's evening in London, not far from the longest day in the year. Dew said they were driven out a second time from the cellar by the smell and, before going in a third time, they had some of the brandy which he'd called for, to fortify them. The digging was taken up by two constables, Frederick Martin and Daniel Gooch. They tried to remove only the clay, but it was an inexpert process and they could not help scraping off some of the remains, bits of flesh and clothing, including a tuft of hair, some portions of an undervest, some string and lumps of lime, which Dew appears to have placed in an aluminium bucket.

Dew sent another constable, Charles Pitts, to buy some disinfectant to try and further reduce the smell. Pitts went to Merrell's the chemist on Queen's Terrace in Camden Road and bought a bottle of Neville's sanitary fluid, which he took back and diluted, then sluiced around the walls of the cellar, at Dew's direction.

Nowadays that single action might have destroyed the case, allowing the defence to argue that the evidence had been contaminated. The disinfectant must have sloshed or at least splashed over the remains too. There was little or no system in the procedures and little or no attempt to preserve the integrity of the scene, which might have yielded further clues. These things were still many years from becoming common practice.

The digging continued until midnight, when boards were laid over the hole and the cellar door locked. Dew and the others went home, leaving two constables on night duty outside the house.

ELEVEN

A police photographer took a series of pictures of 39 Hilldrop Crescent, covering the front of the house from different angles, moving to the back garden, going inside to the corridor downstairs which led to the cellar and then to the cellar itself, photographed both from the hallway and from inside.

The front of the house is verdant with shrubbery, two plants are growing from pots mounted on the pillars at the bottom of the ten steps leading up to the front door. A small iron boot-scraper is embedded in the path at the side of the steps. Downstairs, there is a gas-light mounting in the small narrow corridor, a servant's bell above a door, a decorative plate, some drapes hung from the ceiling, and a substantial pile of earth just outside the cellar door.

The photographs of the cellar itself show how dark, cramped and claustrophobic it must have been in there, with bare brickwork and the low sloping ceiling formed by the under-side of the front steps. There is a candle in a holder, other candles stabbed into the earth, a couple of pails, a spade resting in the clay and, by now, a considerable cavity around the remains, which are not really discernible as human fragments so much as a mound of jumbled detritus.

There is a final picture, taken in the garden, of the six police officers involved arranged around a wheelbarrow: a well-dressed chap in a three-piece suit and a bowler, a uniformed officer in a helmet standing to attention and four men with their sleeves rolled up – two with their collars removed (one has a pipe in his hand) holding shovels, one wearing a dark waistcoat resting lightly on a pick-axe and the fourth, a taller, smarter figure standing just behind them. Sadly, I am not sure who is who, not even Dew, though the two without collars must be the constables Martin and Gooch. All except one of the men have bristling moustaches.

The cellar was a ten-inch step down from the corridor. It was three yards long and two yards and three inches wide. The remains were in the centre, slightly to the right of the door, beginning thirty-four inches from the wall by the door. They began eight to twelve inches below the surface, which comprised a three-inch depth of brick and between five and eight inches of clay. The remains were four feet and one inch in length and, at most, twenty inches wide.

Searching in the garden, down at the far end, Dew found a raised heap which had been covered with flower pots and other garden litter. Beneath that was a layer of ordinary soil which disguised a mound of clay similar to the clay from the cellar.

The police surgeon, Marshall, came back at about eleven o'clock the following morning with Dr Augustus Pepper, a consultant surgeon from St Mary's Hospital in Paddington, who would conduct the post-mortem with Marshall. The undertaker, Albert Leverton on York Road, was called and when he arrived was sent back again by the Coroner's officer to his shop and told to return with two shells. He came back with a shell and a large coffin, a shell apparently being a roughly made coffin-shaped box. He took them to the side entrance of the house and the two constables, Gooch and Martin, took the coffin inside, down to the cellar. Leverton watched them as they removed the remains from the ground and placed them, covered with some clay earth, in the coffin with their bare hands. Even the undertaker noticed the smell which he described as 'very bad'. The coffin was carried out into the back into the garden, where the remains were examined by Pepper and Marshall. There seemed to be no bones in the remains.

By now the hue and cry was up, the discovery public knowledge. A cover had been erected to shield the back of the house from the street but the crowd of reporters and other curious people out front, seeing the two caskets carried in, initially assumed that two corpses had been found. Instead, there was barely one corpse.

Leverton screwed the lid of the coffin down, as instructed by Dew, and then took it to the Islington Mortuary Chapel of Ease on Holloway Road in his van. He had some other remains on a tray. He handed them all over to the mortuary keeper, Arthur Robinson, who placed the coffin on two trestles, having been told by Leverton, on Dew's instructions, not to unscrew the lid without the proper authority.

Robinson would later be obliged to admit that, after the post-mortem and a subsequent inspection visit, he had left the remains open on the slab for five days. He had sprinkled them with carbolic powder, presumably to reduce the smell, and covered them with wallpaper lining paper.

The post-mortem, on Friday afternoon, took three hours and produced the beginnings of a definitive account of what had been found. Dew and Mitchell were both there while Pepper and Marshall carried out the examination. The first list of remains said they included, 'the left breast of a stout woman (apparently)'. This must have been Pepper's first thought, later withdrawn, as Marshall gave a statement shortly after saying, 'one object there was on which there had been a good deal of debate, but I am not prepared to say whether it is a female breast or not'. He obviously did not believe it was a woman's breast because he made it clear in his statement that he could not say whether the remains were male or female: 'Whoever committed the crime endeavoured to obliterate all evidence of identity and sex. He removed not only the pelvis, but also the external organs, and if he left one breast he certainly made a blunder.'

Marshall came to the conclusion that it was a homicide. He had no doubt a murder had been committed but there was nothing to tell him how the victim had met her death. He noted too that many of the organs were wonderfully preserved so that, although the quick lime had destroyed a good deal of the body, it seemed to have preserved some too. The heart, for instance, was in excellent condition, as were some other organs. He noted how much of the flesh had turned to a fatty mass, known as adipocere, which was the result of decomposition in moist places where there was no air, suggesting to Marshall that the remains had been under the cellar for many months.

Although there had been no noticeable bloodstains in the cellar (or elsewhere) he thought the work of dissection had been done in the cellar. He was never asked to explain why he thought this. No one else in the case was ever asked about this either. Exactly how, when, where and why Belle had died and how the bulk of her had been destroyed or discarded would never be known.

Although the gender of the human remains themselves could not be determined, there were heavy clues in the other items that were found. Dr Pepper had seen some of them while they were still in the ground, and had them removed on to the tray. There was a tuft of hair in a Hindes curler, the hair naturally dark brown but showing traces of bleaching. There was a small piece of fair hair in a man's handkerchief which had two corners tied together in a reef knot but was also torn through. There were two small pieces of cloth of reddish-brown colour and a portion of a woman's cotton undervest with lace collar, armlets and six buttons, one of which was fastened. And a piece of coarse, string-like material. These items had been thickly encrusted in a cement-like material. There was also one large single piece of flesh, composed of skin, fat and muscle. That came from the thigh and lower part of the buttock.

Everything was laid out on the slab for the post-mortem. It was quite clear now that there were no bones, not even any fragments of bones; there was no head, no genitals and no trace of any limbs apart from the piece of thigh, and another possible piece of a thigh. There were other pieces of skin, one about eleven inches by nine inches with fat attached which came from the upper part of the abdomen and had a small piece of brown paper attached and a smaller piece from the lower abdomen, about seven inches by six inches, with some hairs which Pepper thought were pubic hairs. That piece had a four-inch-long mark which Pepper would spend hours examining before concluding it was the scar of an old operation. Belle, of course, had been operated on years ago and had her ovaries and her uterus removed. These organs were also missing from the remains, while the scar matched the position of an ovariotomy incision.

There was a piece of a flannelette pyjama jacket with a collar and the label visible inside: Shirtmakers, Jones Brothers, Holloway Road, Limited, Holloway, N. The label matched the labels on two pairs of pyjamas that Chief Inspector Dew had found in a box under the bed in the front bedroom on the first floor, along with an odd pair of pyjama trousers for which no jacket could be found. Among the remains were two more pieces of the same jacket as the collar: a sleeve and a part of the front with some of the buttons intact.

The organs were also intact and all together, having obviously been eviscerated with some care – the heart, the lungs, the lower two and a half inches of the windpipe, the gullet, the liver, kidneys, spleen, stomach (which was empty) and the pancreas.

When the doctors had finished they placed some of the remains in five glass jars which they sealed. When the contents were examined later a second and then a third Hindes curler would be found. Nowhere was there any trace of disease or injury. In life, despite being 'stout', Belle had been surprisingly healthy.

All the medical experts would eventually agree that the dissection and dismemberment had been carried out with considerable dexterity by someone with skill and training. There were no unnecessary cuts or tears that betrayed a careless hand.

ISLINGTON GAZETTE, FRIDAY, 15 JULY 1910
THE GREEN CRESCENT OF THE CRIME
AN IMPRESSION: BY OUR OWN CONTRIBUTOR

Late last night a *Daily Gazette* man revisited the scene of the tragedy so gruesomely revealed by the spades of the police; and found the usual morbid crowd assembled in the street eager for a glimpse of the house which saw enacted within its walls so revolting a drama.

Hilldrop Crescent is a quiet suburban place, although in the inner ring of the Metropolis; and, reasoning superficially, it would be the last spot one would have dreamt of for the stage of a sordid murder. The exterior aspect of the quiet residential streets speaks of respectability; and in the placid atmosphere of well-to-do Suburbia the tokens of the grim deed seized the heart with a greater shock than they would have done in the denser and darker neighbourhood that lies not far away.

For this secluded crescent is situated just off the bustle and roar of several busy thoroughfares, and a stone thrown in any direction would fall in the thick of clustering human hives. It is no more than five minutes from Holloway Road with its ceaseless traffic; it is close to Caledonian Road with its constant goings-to-and-fro; on the other side the huge glass palaces rattle on their way to Tottenham Court Road. In a word, it nestles serenely in a back-wash of the whirling waters of modern Babylon . . .

It stands up, does that ill-fated house, behind large, spreading trees that almost conceal its frontage. In the sunshine of a summer day the green foliage gave almost a gay appearance to the scene.

Behind the umbrageous screen the house uprose – a large, commodious villa. The blinds were not drawn. There was none of that sinister air that enwraps a house whose face is blank with blinds. The curtains, looped well back, gave every appearance of habitation.

There was only one exception to this general view. Down

in the basement a large expanse of yellow blind betokened the sad mystery behind it.

A few minutes walk and I again emerged from this suburban retreat into the unheeding and hurrying life of the broad highways.

But one could not forget that away there in the silence and respectability of the green crescent a fair woman had lain buried and bloody beneath the stones that paved the cellar.

The *Islington Gazette* had extensive coverage of the case that day, responding at short notice on the first real news day of the freshly uncovered crime, the body having been found inconveniently late on Wednesday afternoon for the Thursday papers. This had given a brief edge to the papers in a different time zone in north America. 'Where is Dr H.H. Crippen?' the *Toronto Star* had asked on its front page. At the *Los Angeles Examiner* they had a local angle to exploit: 'Los Angeles Centre of Murder Mystery'. Myron, Crippen's father, was found, aged eighty-three, living in a boarding-house on Third and Flower.

Any lost advantage had been regained by the domestic newspapers in time for Friday's editions. They all covered the case at great length, even *The* Times running over more than a column. The *Daily Mail* with its several columns set the pace for its future coverage. In all the papers it was the North London Murder or the North London Cellar Murder, the case not yet associated with the name of its chief protagonist.

Everyone helpfully reported the descriptions that Dew had issued of the two suspects now wanted for murder and mutilation:

Hawley Harvey Crippen, alias Peter Crippen, alias Franckel, an American Doctor, age fifty, height five feet three inches, complexion fresh, hair light brown inclined to be sandy, scanty and bald on top, long sandy moustache, rather straggly, may be clean shaven, or wearing beard, eyes grey, flat bridge of nose, false teeth, wears gold-rimmed spectacles, may be dressed in dark-brown jacket suit, marked 'Baker and Sons' and grey round felt hat, 'Horne Bros.' inside, rather slovenly appearance, throws his feet out when walking, speaks with American accent, wears hat back of head, very plausible and quiet-spoken, speaks French, carries firearms, shows his teeth much when talking, and:

Ethel Clara Le Neve, will go as Crippen's wife, age twenty-seven, height five feet five inches, complexion pale, hair light brown, large grey eyes, good teeth, good looking, medium build, pleasant appearance, quiet, subdued manner, looks intently when in conversation, walks slowly, reticent, probably dressed blue serge skirt and blue serge three-quarter jacket, large hat, or may be dressed as a boy in dark brown suit, grey hard felt hat, native of London, shorthand writer and typist, absconded 9th, will endeavour to leave the country.

The police corrected their description some days later, pointing out that Ethel did not have good teeth but had a number of false teeth, probably around twenty.

In the ensuing days the suspects would be reported in all corners of Europe – except Brussels, where they were actually staying. Crippen was 'spotted' in Edinburgh, Glasgow and Aberdeen. He was seen by a barber in Liverpool and a deckchair attendant in Ramsgate, and in twenty other towns, plus the London suburbs of Streatham, Peckham, Walworth and Chingford.

There were reports of a suspicious-looking man in a straw hat in the south of France. Provisional warrants were sworn for the arrest and extradition of the suspects in France, Spain and Portugal, showing that the police took sightings in these countries seriously. It was suggested that a young woman who had killed herself in Paris on 13 July was Ethel Le Neve. Or alternatively, her inexplicable silence in the face of the media onslaught was taken as an indication that Crippen could have murdered her too.

A man and a woman were arrested in the Welsh seaside town of Llangranog and only released after the deputy chief constable of the region confirmed that they were not Crippen and Le Neve. In Willesden a man wearing spectacles was knocking on doors, accompanied by a young woman, looking for lodgings. A crowd said to comprise several hundred people in hostile mood surrounded them before they were rescued by the police and taken to the station, where their real identities were established.

Every police station in London took at least one report of a sighting. There was also an arrest in Chicago.

The case competed briefly for newspaper attention with the murder late on Saturday evening, 16 July, of an elderly actor, Thomas Weldon Anderson – stage name Weldon Atherstone – in the grounds of an apartment block near Battersea Park. He had been shot while apparently hiding in the shrubbery, staking out the flat of his ex-girlfriend. One of his two sons had been in the flat with the woman at the time. There would never be a conviction in the case, but the sons would be suspected of the crime and one of them would shortly be emigrating to New Zealand, where he would carve out a new life as a corrupt trade unionist. It would take the papers a while to catch on to the slender link between the two cases – Atherstone having once been on the same music hall bill as Belle and reputedly having comforted her when she was distressed after being jeered from the stage.

Over in New York the former Ladies Guild President, Mrs Ginnett, had made contact with Belle's sister Louise Mills. The two of them joined detectives at the pier to meet several transatlantic ships from Europe, scouring the arriving passengers for signs of Crippen and Le Neve. They paid special attention to the women, as there had been reports that Crippen had been seen in Normandy, northern France, dressed as a woman and could be disguised as Le Neve's mother.

As the search continued without success some of the newspapers reported criticisms of the police for having allowed Crippen and Le Neve to escape in the first place. There was even a question in Parliament. William Thorne MP wanted to know why the police had not kept close watch on Crippen during their investigation, since their pressing inquiries had caused him to vanish. The Home Secretary, Winston Churchill, left it to a junior minister to reply – a Mr Masterman at the Home Department telling the House that it was undesirable to discuss the case at present. The accusations caused discomfort at Scotland Yard, especially with Dew and no doubt with his superiors, Froest and MacNaghten – though at least they hadn't taken the murderer to lunch.

Dew would still be explaining himself in his memoirs, saying it was ridiculous to suggest that he should have arrested Crippen after interviewing him, when there was no evidence of a crime. While there may not have been hard evidence, there was an unexplained, suspicious disappearance and, as Dew himself acknowledged at the time, Crippen had lied to him – which could be evidence of guilt. As, of course, had Ethel. You could argue that there was a justification for arrest, if only Dew had not been blinded by Crippen's plausibility. It would soon be apparent that he was desperate to make amends and be seen to conduct the case properly. If only he could be given the chance. The truth was that, in those days before passports were needed, Crippen and Le Neve could have been anywhere. Even so, it seems remarkable that, in the eye of such a media storm, they evaded notice for so long.

False reports of their whereabouts continued to pour in from all quarters, so there must have been something about the telegram passed on from Liverpool police that seemed to Dew to be a genuine sighting. It was in his hands on Friday afternoon, 22 July, eleven days after his discovery that Crippen and Ethel had run off. The telegram had initially been received as a wireless message at the Liverpool office or agent of the Canadian Pacific Railway, from Commander Henry George Kendall at sea on the SS *Montrose*. The office had relayed it on to the Liverpool police and they had forwarded it to London.

Telegrams were still sometimes called Marconigrams, after Guglielmo Marconi, the thirty-six-year-old Italian founder of the system which he had developed in the mid-1890s. He had patented 'tuned or syntonic telegraphy' in 1900 as patent number 7777. In that year he had also formed Marconi's Wireless Telegraph Company Limited. He sent the first ship-to-shore messages in 1902, but they had only been in commercial use since 1907.

Piers, Liverpool
3 pm Greenwich meantime
Montrose, 130 miles West of Lizard
   Have strong suspicion that Crippen London Cellar murderer and accomplice are amongst saloon passengers. Moustache shaved off, growing beard. Accomplice dressed as boy, voice, manner and build undoubtedly a girl.

   Kendall

Dew had nothing else to go on and could not contact the ship in return. But he must have sensed and hoped that the information was good. He found out where the *Montrose* was going and discovered that a faster ship, the *Laurentic*, was also leaving Liverpool the next day for Quebec, Canada, and would reach the destination first. By now it was early evening and he contacted MacNaghten, who was at home dressing for dinner and told Dew to come and see him. MacNaghten was nervous about sending Dew off on the *Laurentic*, and taking such a serious step. It might have been a wild-goose chase. In the end he gave his permission, but, he would say in his memoirs, when he arrived at Scotland Yard the following morning he would find that Froest and other officers thought he had made the wrong decision. The papers would soon be reporting Scotland Yard's fears that Dew was on a fool's mission.

   The MP William Thorne also returned to his theme, charging Dew, by name, with grave neglect in not having the house watched after his interview with the suspects. Churchill responded in person this time, saying it was not fair to make a charge of dereliction of duty against a police officer who by reason of his being engaged on special duty abroad could not make an answer.

When the *Laurentic* sailed from Liverpool on 23 July, Dew was on board, travelling alone, having booked passage in the name of Dewhurst to disguise his presence from the press, which worked, briefly. By 25 July *The Times* had identified him and his ship, while reporting that Crippen and Le Neve were on the *Sardinian*, Crippen disguised as a priest.

Dew would have a frustrating time over the next week, spending hours in the *Laurentic*'s wireless room trying and failing to make contact with the *Montrose*, not really knowing what was happening.

TWELVE

There seems to have been just one genuine sighting of Crippen and Ethel during their week in Brussels, though the report did not reach London until some days after they had left. It was said that two suspicious people had ordered stout at a café in the Belgian capital and had asked for directions to the forest. The young one seemed to be a woman dressed as a man.

Ethel would say in her life story that they spent happy days in Brussels without a thought of peril or the horrors that were to follow (never mind, presumably, the horrors they had left behind in London). She got used to her boy's clothes and found them comfortable, so that she no longer worried about her disguise and was free to delight in their exploration of a new foreign city. They went north and south, east and west and in the country parts beyond. The doctor, she said, never showed any signs of nervousness or any desire to keep her locked up in their room at the Hotel des Ardennes. He showed no anxiety for her or himself at being in public.

They saw everything Brussels had to offer, going to the Exhibition several times, wandering about its palaces and side-shows and having good fun in the old Flemish fair watching the crowd of foreign people around them. They went to picture galleries, museums, public gardens. They window-shopped and stopped to listen to the bands and the songbirds on the Bois de la Cambre. It was all so very beautiful and peaceful.

Then Ethel said she got tired of Brussels – bored, presumably – and wanted to move on. 'Tired of Brussels already,' Crippen said, according to Ethel. 'Very well, we will push on. How about Paris?'

'No, not Paris,' said Ethel, according to Ethel. 'Somewhere else.'

She would claim that she never had any news of what was happening in England and was thus oblivious to the pandemonic fuss resulting from their flight and the discovery of what was left of Belle. The doctor used to read *L'Etoile Belge* and other Belgian papers, she said, but they were all Greek to Ethel with only her limited conversational French. She said she asked him several times to get an English paper but he never did. This is contradicted by the owner of the Hotel des Ardennes, who would later be quoted as saying he had found a copy of the continental edition of the *Daily Mail* in their room after they left, though he did say that to a reporter from the *Daily Mail*.

It was by chance, said Ethel, that they ended up on the *Montrose*. The doctor had the idea of crossing back to England, at Hull and then going to Liverpool and getting a ship to America. Then one day, during their wanderings, they saw an advertisement for the *Montrose* sailing from Antwerp to Quebec. 'That is what we will do,' said Crippen. 'Let us book berths on the *Montrose* and go over to Canada.'

In Ethel's version they inquired at the shipping office on 17 July and discovered that the *Montrose* would leave on the 20th. They checked out of the Hotel des Ardennes and left Brussels on the 19th, and boarded the *Montrose* the following morning, after spending the night in Antwerp.

Dew would later send a long handwritten letter to Scotland Yard from Canada, describing the arrest. He said he found that Crippen and Ethel had actually booked a passage on 15 July, though no vessel was mentioned. Across the ticket was written, as if in a change of plan, 'transferred to SS *Montrose*, 20 July, entire room (5), amount paid £31'. The passage was booked in the names of John Philo Robinson, aged fifty-five, merchant of Detroit, Michigan and John George Robinson, aged sixteen, single. It would be intriguing to know what the original booking had been for. Would it have made any difference if they had taken that journey instead? Was there ever a moment or opportunity when they could have got clean away?

There is a final discrepancy between Ethel and the known facts, in that the records of their Brussels hotel show they checked out two days before the departure of the *Montrose*, not one day, as Ethel said in her life story. Perhaps they spent the night in the forest.

She would say that she looked forward to the change of scene offered by the ship and she was quite easy and free from care as they boarded. The doctor too appeared calm and untroubled. He never once led her to believe that he feared arrest: 'Yet at that very time, I am told, all the great ports were being watched by detectives. If I had known of the frantic search that was being made for us, I should have understood that we were very badly prepared for a secret voyage. Our lack of luggage was in itself calculated to betray us. We only had with us the one handbag which we had brought from Hilldrop Crescent. As for myself, I had nothing beyond my boy's suit – not even an overcoat. The doctor was wearing his grey frock coat and his soft white hat. I think it was at this time that he left off his glasses.'

In the end it was not the lack of baggage that gave them away. The *Montrose* Commander, Henry Kendall, noticed them almost immediately, barely three hours and thirty miles into the eleven-day crossing, when he saw the boy squeezing the older man's hand, by one of the lifeboats. It seemed to him a strange and unnatural gesture and he at once thought they might be Crippen and Le Neve.

Once they had boarded the boat, Crippen and Ethel were trapped. Done for.

On 13 July, the day that Belle's body had been found, the *Montrose* was in London, at Millwall Docks, preparing for her next Atlantic journey. She had just made the regular reverse trip carrying several thousand cattle to England. She was not one of the more luxurious steamships, but just the sort of ship that two Thames Division police officers thought might suit the murder suspects they were searching for among the ships at quay on the river Thames.

Sergeants Francis Barclay and Thomas Arle of Thames CID had gone aboard the *Montrose* that same day with newly written descriptions suggesting that Ethel was probably dressed as a man. Sergeant Barclay must have been making his pitch for a share of the £250 reward later, when he made a statement describing the trouble he and his colleague had taken with their inquiries on board the *Montrose*. They had interviewed the ship's chief officer, Alfred Henry Sergeant, for nearly an hour after discovering that the *Montrose* would take on passengers at Antwerp, explaining the different ruses the suspects might adopt, such as Crippen dressing as a clergyman or Le Neve becoming a boy.

'Why I should have furnished the Officer with such a close and what appears to be an exact illustration of the method and plans undertaken by Crippen and his companion I cannot exactly tell but I seemed to be possessed with a presentiment that the two persons wanted would join the ship at Antwerp and I communicated my opinion to the Officer in question. . . . I do not wish to infer that myself or PS Arle have done anything extraordinary in this matter but I may respectfully submit that had it not been for our interview . . . it might have been possible for the fugitives to have landed without their identity being established.'

The detective's statement was even endorsed by his Divisional Inspector and his Superintendent, who said they wanted to draw attention to the statement 'as in all probability some claim will be put forward in respect of the £250 reward'.

Alas for Sergeant Barclay, he was in competition with a formidable adversary in Commander Kendall, who also had the reward in mind. Kendall was a Royal Navy reservist and had been with the Canadian Pacific Railway (a shipping company, in spite of its name) for eight years, rising up through the ranks and serving as a Commander for two and a half years. He lived on Moss Lane, Aintree, Liverpool. His

chief officer, Mr Sergeant, lived at Blundellsands near Liverpool in a house he had named Bermuda.

Sergeant had shown his captain the descriptions that
Wednesday. They left Millwall Docks at six o'clock on
Thursday evening, 14 July and arrived in the river at Antwerp
the following afternoon. The passengers came aboard five days
later, between 8.30 am and 10 am. There were no first-class
berths and just twenty second-class passengers, including Mr
and Master Robinson. With 246 passengers in third class and
a crew of 107 that made a total of 373 people on board.
Kendall had been ashore and bought a continental edition of
the *Daily Mail* – perhaps the same paper that Crippen and
Ethel had left in their hotel room in Brussels. Kendall had
seen the photographs and descriptions of the suspects in the
newspaper.

Once he had seen that strange and unnatural gesture, Ethel
squeezing Crippen's hand, Kendall paid close attention to the
pair. Crippen was wearing, not a grey frock coat but a brown
jacket suit and a dark grey soft felt hat, with dark canvas shoes.
He had several days' growth on his chin. She, of course, not
having anything else, was wearing the boy's brown jacket suit,
dark grey soft felt hat, white canvas shoes, collar and tie.

Kendall wished them the time of day and, after observing
them a little longer, felt quite confident that they were
Crippen and Le Neve. He decided not to do anything about it
straight away, however, for fear of making a terrible mistake.
He didn't even tell anyone else, until Thursday, when he sent
for his chief officer, Mr Sergeant, told him what he thought
and bound him to secrecy. He told Sergeant to keep it quiet
because it was too good a thing to lose. 'So we made a lot of
them. Kept them smiling.'

On Friday, 22 July, Kendall had his first conversation with
Crippen, discussing seasickness among the passengers and the
different remedies they carried as cures. Crippen used some
medical jargon in reply, which further gave him away. Up
close, Kendall could see the flat on the bridge of his nose, just
as the description had said and the deep ridge caused by his

spectacles. Kendall also overheard him speaking quietly in French to some French passengers; the police description had mentioned he spoke French. Now convinced beyond all doubt, Kendall ordered his Marconi operator, Mr L. Jones, to send that first telegram which was soon in the hands of Chief Inspector Dew.

Later, in his police statement, Commander Kendall would have no shame in seeking all the glory and the gain for himself: 'I am solely responsible for sending the Marconi message and no one whatever called my attention to these people, and it was entirely from my own observations that I suspected them as being the people wanted, and I therefore consider that I am entitled to the reward offered, as I recognised them from the full and complete description given by the police.'

Some days after the telegram was sent, the *Daily Mail* would publish an article by the deputy manager of the Marconi Wireless Telegraph Company, Mr W.W. Bradfield, which gave a vivid account of how the ship-board wireless worked, under the headline, 'Pursuit By Wireless, The Long Arm of the Law':

Each ship has on its upper decks a little cabin for the operator, a tiny square erection wherein two young men take turns by day and night waiting and watching for any word that may come rushing to them from unseen sources behind the horizon. The little cabin, crowded with apparatus, is like an Aladdin's cave. All kinds of appliances are stacked within it . . .

The operator on duty is wearing a telephone headgear with receivers over his ears. Suddenly there comes to him a low musical note. It is the first indication of a morse code message. It begins with two or three letters signifying the identity of the ship which is calling. He signals back the letter 'K', which means that he is ready to take the communication. As he replies, the cabin is transformed. A vivid electrical spark throws a weird blueish light over the operator and his machinery. The young man on duty with a pencil writes out slowly the message as it arrives . . .

A vessel such as the *Montrose* throws out her wireless message in a circle all around her, 150 miles in every direction. Should a wireless station on land be within 150 miles of her the message can be transmitted direct. But should the distance be greater, say 500 miles, the *Montrose* or any similar ship would have to wait until some part of her 150-mile radius struck that of another ship equipped with a 'wireless'. The higher the mast on a ship, the greater its radius for transmitting.

Soon, it seemed that everyone knew what was happening and they found the use of the latest technology fascinating, the narrative it had created enthralling. It was not even yet commonplace for ships to be fitted with wireless, so the *Montrose* really was at the forefront of modernity. Newspapers ran maps with dotted lines and arrows depicting shipping routes across the Atlantic, with graphics of ships and concentric circles showing how the signal had been sent. It must have been the thoughts of the two suspects, isolated in the middle of the Atlantic, unaware that the world was watching them sail to their doom, that particularly appealed. Real life had rarely been more thrilling.

It was the first time the wireless was being used to catch a murderer. Or murderers. Submarine cable had been used in 1864 to capture a killer named Franz Muller, who was already on a boat bound for America when his crime was discovered. He too had been defeated by the police overtaking him on a faster ship. More recently a man named Tawell had committed a murder near Slough and then boarded a train to London. The police had telegraphed his description to Paddington and he had been arrested on arrival. But that was just plain, old telegraph, not the crackling, electric blue of the wireless.

Such a firework display made the wireless room an object of interest to most passengers on the ships where it was fitted. Kendall said Crippen would sit on deck and watch the mast and listen to the sound of the sparks. 'What a wonderful invention it is,' Crippen said.

Kendall evidently could not stop watching and assessing his two suspects – no doubt they were a welcome diversion from the usual monotony of an Atlantic crossing. He said he saw no point in arresting them but still had to keep a close watch because if they smelt a rat they might try and do something rash, though he had not noticed a revolver in Crippen's hip pocket.

He chalked out Crippen's moustache in a press photograph and cut a hole in a piece of card which he fitted around the face of Ethel's photograph, so that he could compare it with Master Robinson. When they left their hats outside the restaurant while dining, he looked inside and found that Crippen's was labelled 'Jackson, Boulevard le Nord', while Ethel's had no label but had been stuffed with paper inside the rim to make it fit. He soon saw the split in the back of Ethel's pants, noting how tightly they fitted around her hips, and how they had been secured with large safety pins.

He was more discreet about this, not blurting it out in one of his long bulletins to the newspapers, but he must have poked around in their cabin too, and would make the ungallant report that Ethel was using a torn fragment of a woman's undergarment as a face flannel. This had unpleasant echoes of the discoveries in the cellar.

Kendall sounded as though he was a little taken with Ethel, describing her as having the manner and appearance of a very refined, modest girl who did not speak much but always wore a pleasant smile. She seemed thoroughly under Crippen's thumb and he would not leave her side for a moment. She followed him everywhere and, though she never showed signs of distress and was perhaps ignorant of the crime, she seemed to Kendall to be a girl with a very weak will. Whenever Crippen looked at her she gave him an endearing smile, as though she were under his hypnotic influence.

But, once or twice, as if playing a game with them, Kendall called out for Crippen by his assumed name Mr Robinson, while they were walking on deck. Crippen took no notice and it was Ethel who, Kendall said, showed presence of mind, in nudging him to turn around. Crippen apologised, saying the cold weather had made him deaf.

He invited them to dine at his table and saw how ladylike were the supposed boy's table manners, handling his knife and fork delicately, taking fruit from dishes with two fingers. Crippen cracked nuts for her and gave her half his salad, always being very attentive. Kendall told a joke, just to see Crippen open his mouth and laugh so that he could confirm the presence of false teeth, as described by the police.

One night, in mid-voyage, Crippen and Ethel sat in the saloon and listened to the songs and music. The next morning Crippen told Kendall how much his boy had enjoyed the evening and how heartily the boy had laughed when they were back in their room. One song, 'We All Walked into the Shop', had been drumming in Crippen's head all night. Crippen spoke about American drinks and said Selfridge's was the only decent place in London where you could find them.

Another time they missed the saloon concert and Crippen apologised to Kendall the next day, saying he had wanted to come but the young fellow did not feel well and would not let him go as he did not like to be left alone.

From their talks Kendall noted that Crippen knew Toronto, Detroit and California. One day in the captain's cabin they had a long discussion about all things American, especially about San Francisco which Crippen supposed he would not know now, having not been there since he was eighteen, but he loved California and thought of settling down on a fruit farm there. As usual, during this conversation, Ethel never spoke once but gave her now familiar laugh at anything funny and looked, to Kendall anyway, as though she would like to give vent to her feelings.

Crippen said he was taking his boy to California for his health. He would go via Detroit and hoped to get to Detroit by boat if he could as he preferred it. He often studied the track chart which showed the ship's position and counted the number of days to the end of the voyage. One day he told Kendall that, at their present rate of steaming, he ought to be in Detroit by Tuesday, 2 August.

Most of the time, Crippen sat on deck reading, or, as Kendall imagined it, pretending to read. He worked through Dickens's *Pickwick Papers*, *Nebo The Nailer*, a 1902 novel by Sabine Baring-Gould, *The Metropolis*, a 1908 novel by Upton Sinclair, *A Name to Conjure With*, a 1900 novel by John Strange Winter and *The Four Just men*, an Edgar Wallace thriller from 1905 about a London murder with a £1,000 reward.

Kendall and his chief officer had gone round the ship collecting any newspaper they could find with coverage of the North London Cellar Murder.

Ethel would say in her life story that they suspected nothing and it never entered her head that her disguise had been discovered. There were few other English passengers and they were mostly foreign emigrants hoping, like them, to begin life again in the New World. The cabin was quite cosy and the Captain kept her supplied with novels and magazines and detective stories. Naturally, Ethel would say, she kept aloof from the other passengers but felt she spoke freely to the officers if they spoke to her, never feeling in the least embarrassed. They were always courteous and often asked her how she was. She became chummy with an English boy and they talked football together. Crippen teased her, saying, 'How nicely you are getting along.'

Kendall's amusing stories kept them in good humour at meal times but Ethel was often on her own in the cabin or wrapped up in a rug in a corner of the lounge reading fanciful adventures. It was cold out there in mid-Atlantic and she did not have a coat or anything bar the suit, which was beginning to seem a bit thin for the climate.

Ethel thought of her sister Nina and her promise to write to her as soon as she was settled: 'I thought that she would be wondering what had become of me. As I touched land I promised myself that I would write her a long letter – oh! Such a letter! I had been saving up all my little adventures in Rotterdam and Brussels. How she would laugh at my boyish escapade. How she would marvel at my impudence! Alas! That letter was never written.'

Captain Kendall thought he detected some anxiety in Crippen as they neared land, sighting Belle Isle at the beginning of the approach to the Gulf of St Lawrence and Pointe au Père – Father Point – where they would pick up the pilot. Crippen asked Kendall many questions about how the pilot would come aboard, where they would stop and how long it would then take, up the St Lawrence river to Quebec. He said he would be glad when they arrived and was anxious to be moving on to Detroit.

His change of mood was also picked up by Ethel, who said he became very serious, coming down to the cabin and returning to her the money she had given him to look after, about £15, before they left London.

'My dear,' she recalled him saying, 'I think you had better take charge of these.'

'Why?' she asked. 'I have nowhere to put them except in these pockets. You can keep them, can't you, until you get to Quebec?'

'Well,' said Crippen, hesitantly. 'I may have to leave you.'

'Leave me?!' Ethel was astounded. It seemed incredible to have come all this way only to be left alone.

'Listen, dear,' he said. 'When you get to Quebec you had better go on to Toronto. It is a nice place and I know it fairly well. You have not forgotten your typewriting, have you, and you have got your millinery at your fingers' ends?' Ethel described how it occurred to her that he meant to go ahead and prospect the country so that they might settle down in peace in some out-of-the-way spot. (No mention, here in her life story, of any quest to find Belle or the person who had sent the cable informing the doctor of Belle's death. That was all forgotten.)

Feeling easier now, she could say, 'But how about these clothes?'

'Are you tired of being a boy?'

'Well, I am rather. I used to imagine I would make a good boy, but now I do not think I fit the part. I want to get into girl's clothes as quickly as I can.'

'Very well, you can buy them when you land.'

'But I cannot do that. It would be absurd for me to go into a shop dressed as a boy to buy women's garments. You will have to get them.'

'Ah, I hadn't thought about that.' Ethel wrote that Crippen thought a while and then said, 'Immediately on landing we must go to an hotel. I will go out and get some clothes for you, and you will have to do a quick change. Then you will leave and I will follow you out.'

Ethel said she agreed to this and carried on reading. She seems to have told this story to counter claims that, as she puts it, the pair of them formed a plot to commit suicide. This was not so, she writes, because she had no great trouble and looked forward with keen delight to an adventurous life in Canada. She had not the faintest suspicion that they were being pursued.

There was a suspicion, afterwards, that suicide was planned, but not by both of them, only by Crippen. On board, following the arrests, Dew found a batch of business cards in a valise in their cabin: 'P. Robinson and Co., Detroit, Mich., presented by Mr John Robinson.' Crippen had two of the cards with him and they both had handwritten messages on the back. One was obviously intended for Ethel: 'I cannot stand the horror I go through every night any longer, and as I see nothing bright ahead, and money is coming to an end, I have made up my mind to jump overboard tonight. I know I have spoil [sic] your life, but I-I [sic] hope some day you can learn to forgive me. Last words of love. – Your, H.'

Dew would point out the spelling mistake of 'spoil' and the double 'I' and also suggest the 's' was missing from 'Yours, H'. More likely, Crippen was signing off from Ethel as 'your hub'. On the face of it, the card was a suicide note and an admission of guilt, the very personal use of hub suggesting the note was meant for Ethel only, and not for the benefit of the police. If it had been written for the police he would surely have made a clear expression of Ethel's innocence.

What confused the position was the second card which said, 'Shall we wait until tonight, about ten or eleven? If not, what time?'

Crippen would be cross-examined on these cards at his trial – the apparent admission was important evidence – and would say that the second card was written to a member of the ship's crew, a quartermaster who had warned Crippen he was about to be arrested and offered to help him escape. The first card was intended to mislead the authorities into believing he had drowned himself. The problem with this story was that, like so much of Crippen's eventual defence and evidence in court, it was unsubstantiated. He could not name the quartermaster – there were four on the *Montrose* – or help identify him.

He said that two days before they were due to arrive he was sitting by the wheelhouse when the quartermaster came up and said he had a letter he wanted to give him. Crippen went back at 3 pm as arranged and the quartermaster gave him the note which said that the captain knew who they were and they were going to be arrested at Quebec. The quartermaster proposed to hide him on the ship. He said that Crippen should leave a note saying he had jumped overboard. The quartermaster would make a splash in the night and go and tell the captain that Crippen had gone. He said there was no charge against Ethel so it was not necessary for her to hide too. He even had an address in the United States where she could write to Crippen and eventually join him.

(Of course, there was a charge against Ethel. At this stage she was still charged with murder, like Crippen.)

Crippen said they were going to enact the plan that night but somebody came along and stopped him going into hiding. So he had written the short note to the quartermaster, 'Shall we wait until tonight . . . ?' to give to him the next morning. He proposed to leave the other note on Ethel's pillow in the cabin. He did not say whether the note had been left that night, when the plan was abandoned. Nor did he say whether Ethel was in on the plan.

At his trial Crippen would say the quartermaster was taller than him, thickset with dark hair and a moustache. He said all four quartermasters had moustaches. He denied that his suicide note was true, saying the horrors were purely imaginary and money was hardly at an end as he had 70 dollars and jewellery worth £90, so that was imaginative too. It was all a pretence.

Dew believed Crippen really had intended to kill himself, and that does seem the most likely explanation. It would make sense that he had nightly horrors which he found hard to live with. The human remains that had been found made clear that he must have been through a terrible ordeal, albeit of his own making. Perhaps he felt he could leave Ethel now that he had led her to the safety of Canada. Killing himself would draw the guilt and leave her free to begin a new life. He may have reasoned she would be better off without him. Or he may have been thinking of himself above all else, finding the burden of guilt and the prospect of being hanged unbearable. He certainly attempted suicide later, just before his execution, and there was some evidence of another attempt too.

Maybe that was behind the conversation she described in her life story: Crippen preparing Ethel to manage without him. Even if he didn't know the precise details of the police chase, he must have guessed that they might be waiting for him when the ship reached Quebec. Still, the other card with the supposed note to the quartermaster doesn't sit easily with the theory of suicide. If he had planned to live and be reunited with Ethel in the States he must have been confident that she was tough enough to withstand the inevitable interrogations on her own.

Ethel later recalled that 'fateful Sunday morning', 31 July 1910, when the doctor pressed her to go on deck with him after breakfast and she said, 'I don't think I will, it's very wretched up there and I would rather stay down here and finish this book before lunch.' The doctor 'went away quietly' and Ethel settled down in Cabin 5 with her copy of the 1896 novel *Audrey's Recompense* by Mrs Georgie Sheldon.

Presently, as Mrs Georgie Sheldon might have written, there came a gentle tap at the cabin door.

THIRTEEN

On 30 July 1974, exactly sixty-four years to the day since they had been sent, an anonymous buyer paid £1,600 at Bonham's auction house in Knightsbridge for the thirteen telegrams that passed between Chief Inspector Dew and Commander Kendall. 'Will board you Father Point,' Dew wrote. 'Please keep any information till I arrive there strictly confidential.' 'What the devil do you think I've been doing?' replied Kendall. 'Advise you to come off in small boat with pilot, disguised as one if possible,' he then suggested.

Dew's ship, the *Laurentic*, had overtaken the *Montrose* some two-thirds of the way across the Atlantic, still not passing near enough to enable communication. As it happened, the *Montrose* had already picked up transmission of a Marconigram intended for the detective and so Kendall knew what was happening. But Dew was unaware of this and so must have been relieved, arriving at Father Point a full day ahead of the *Montrose*, when he finally began 'speaking' to Kendall on 30 July 1910.

Bundled with the auctioned messages were some fifty others the *Montrose* received from reporters. The *Laurentic* too was deluged by inquiries after a *Montreal Star* reporter who was on board received a telegram from his office, tipping him off to Dew's hitherto undetected presence. The reporter on the *Laurentic* attempted to telegraph a story of his own, but Dew persuaded the captain to refuse transmission.

Back home in London the Crippen case, as it was now called, continued to dominate the news, despite the ongoing fascination with the Anderson/Atherstone murder and the lengthy accounts from the High Court of a father seeking to overturn his son's dismissal from naval college, claiming that he had been falsely accused of stealing a five-shilling postal order. The boy was George Archer-Shee, and his case would eventually form the basis of the play *The Winslow Boy*, by Terence Rattigan. There were reports too of the 'suffragists' seeking votes for women, who had descended in great numbers on Hyde Park for a rally after two processions from Shepherds Bush and the Embankment.

Having been away for the last week, Dew was surprised to find some thirty reporters and photographers on board the small boat, *Eureka*, that came to collect him from the ship at Father Point. The press had been gathering there for days. Father Point was a lonely place, no more than a dozen cottages and a telegraph station all in, and the press had been frustrated at being stuck there, waiting and not knowing what was happening. Reduced to writing about themselves, the *Toronto Star*, in particular, had provided a graphic picture of 'half a hundred pressmen', impotent, kicking their heels with nothing better to do than watch the tide go in and out and search for smoke on the horizon.

No wonder then, that Dew was mobbed with questions and a great deal of shouting and cameras thrust in his face. It was disgraceful, he would later write to Scotland Yard, and he became fearful lest the success of his mission should be marred.

Dew then discovered that most of the reporters had bought tickets for the twelve-hour onward journey aboard the *Montrose* from Father Point to Quebec and so were legitimately entitled to board the ship with him when he went to make the arrests. Again, Kendall seems to have provided the solution in a telegram. Dew could come ahead in a tugboat and the press could wait nearby on the steamer, the *Eureka*: 'Tell the captain of pilot steamer to steam with reporters to Big Island ... until I hoist a Canadian ensign at mainmast, indicating you have made the arrest.' Dew replied, 'Thanks will speak you later operator here will make arrangements. Meantime suggest suspects kept under discreet observation to prevent suicide.'

You can tell by the tone of his subsequent note to Scotland Yard that Dew was eager to reclaim his reputation and impress his superiors with his cautious and well-planned conduct of operations. He did not tell them that Kendall had suggested the plot, leaving himself to take the credit: 'I procured the loan of a pilot's uniform and made a really good disguise.'

The *Toronto Star* reported the disappointment of the press at Dew's silent approach to his dealings with them, and complained when he banned them from boarding the *Montrose* with him. Then he came ashore, booked out all the rooms at Madame Lavoie's lodging house, and went to sleep. Dew said he heard that some of the press tried to thwart him with a plan to get on to the *Montrose* first by going out on to the river, then drifting, pretending to be shipwrecked mariners so that the *Montrose* would be obliged to take them on board.

But he was first out next morning, on the tug at 8.30 am, alongside the *Montrose*, boarding the ship with two Canadian police officers, MacCarthy and Denis, crossing the deck to the captain's cabin, then seeing Crippen pacing back and forth just a couple of yards away. He sent the Canadian officers to bring Crippen to him and, as he entered, said, 'Good morning, Doctor Crippen,' and Crippen replied, apparently without betraying any shock or distress, 'Good morning,' making no attempt to disguise his true identity and making no reply when the charge was read.

Leaving Crippen to be searched by the Canadian officers, Dew went downstairs with a ship's stewardess to Cabin 5, and tapped on the door before entering, where Ethel was lying down reading her Georgie Sheldon novel. Dew saw that she recognised him straight away and as soon as he read the charge to her she fainted – 'swooned', she would later say – without speaking a word. Dew saw that she was comfortable and left the stewardess to find some women's clothes for Ethel to wear. Seeing her disguise for the first time Dew found it difficult to believe that anyone with an average amount of intelligence could ever have believed her to be a boy.

Crippen said afterwards that when Dew left him with the

Canadian officers one of them said to him, 'Now we deal very differently with people in Canada when we arrest them, to what they do in England. We tell them that they must not say anything. Now don't you say a word on anything. Cut your tongue out. Have nothing to say.'

It was good advice, but Crippen couldn't quite keep to it. When Dew came to take him downstairs – to a separate cabin from Ethel, now – Crippen said he was not sorry as the anxiety had been too much. When Crippen was searched, the cards relating to the real or fake suicide were found and Dew said he would have to handcuff him in case he jumped overboard, and Crippen said he would not, he was more than satisfied because the anxiety had been too awful. He asked how Miss Le Neve was and Dew said she was agitated but he was doing all he could for her. Crippen said, 'It is only fair to say she knows nothing about it. I never told her anything.' He did not say what the anxiety was about or what 'it' was that Ethel knew nothing about. But they sounded very much like the instinctive statements of a guilty man.

Dew found four rings stitched inside Crippen's underwear, along with the 'frequently described' rising sun diamond brooch and another diamond brooch. He only had ten dollars on him, but Ethel had sixty dollars, though no hidden jewellery. Crippen would later say he had a powder or formula taken from him, a medical remedy of his own creation which he had called Sans Peine. But there is no official record of this.

When Dew went with Captain Kendall to see Ethel the captain said he would do all he could for her and asked, did you not see the letter from your father in the papers? Ethel, echoing Crippen's words, said she knew nothing about it and if she had known anything about it she would have communicated at once. 'I assure you, Mr Dew, I know nothing about it. I intended to write to my sister when I got to Quebec.' In her life story, Ethel would say that when Dew told her about the remains being found in the cellar she was mystified and could only stare at him in amazement.

Now that the drama was over and the suspects were secured

in cabins, the *Eureka*, described as bobbing quietly in the morning mist, was informed with three blasts of the horn, and moved in so that the reporters huddled together on its deck, straining to see what was happening, could come aboard. They promptly swarmed all over the ship, peering through cracks in walls and doors and, as Dew said, adopting the most extraordinary tactics to gain information, subjecting Dew to the utmost annoyance.

The absence of reportable facts did not interfere with thrilling accounts of the arrests appearing in the newspapers. Crippen had drawn a gun and thrown it through a porthole into the sea. Ethel had produced a white pill and tried to swallow it. Dew had confronted Crippen on the deck of the ship, in full view of everyone. Dew was said to have told the press he believed Ethel was innocent. Crippen was said to have made a full confession. Dew, of course, had to tell Scotland Yard that these were purely imaginary and 'lying reports'.

Back in Quebec, said Dew, his refusal to talk to the press had made him many enemies. He was constantly followed and questioned in the most shameful manner, his every movement watched, the reporters invading his hotel and intruding on his meals. He had received the most fabulous offers of money for interviews or photographs of the subjects, especially of Le Neve as a boy (Ethel herself would take advantage of similar offers later).

When they reached Quebec Crippen went to prison, where he was said by Dew to be a 'gluttonous reader'. Like a grateful hotel guest, he signed a copy of Trollope's *Barchester Towers* to one of his warders, 'with compliments and in appreciation of many courtesies'. Ethel was too ill to go to prison and so, unusually, was held at the home of one of the two Canadian officers, MacCarthy, and looked after with great kindness by his wife and daughter. She did not even have to go to court for the routine of extradition, but instead there was an informal hearing at MacCarthy's home. She was later transferred to the infirmary.

Here, already, were the beginnings of the two great myths

of the case: Crippen as the decent, considerate, courteous little man (somehow overlooking his apparently methodical dismembering of his dead wife) and Ethel as the naïve, innocent, harmless young woman who knew nothing of what had happened (overlooking her proximity to the crime and her many lies and deceptions even to those she most loved).

Ethel's mother sent her a cable (which was reprinted in the newspapers almost immediately): 'My darling daughter, I implore you to tell the police everything you know and to let nothing count more than the establishment of your innocence. However great may be your affection for your husband [husband?!] do not, dear, let it be more to you than the duty you owe yourself, your mother and your brothers [note, no mention of the duty she owes her father]. Be brave, little girl, and have no fear. We are confident of your innocence.' It was signed 'Lottie Le Neve'.

Crippen received his own cable, from the London solicitor Arthur Newton, who said that friends of the doctor had instructed him to represent Crippen. Poor Crippen did not seem to have any friends, except those from the music hall who were certainly not his friends any more. Eddie Marr, the remedy man, knew Newton, so perhaps it was him. More likely, it was just Newton seizing an opportunity, knowing that Crippen's story was eminently marketable in the newspapers. There was no Legal Aid in those days and lawyers' fees had to be found from somewhere. The Poor Person's Defence Committee, a precursor to the Legal Aid system, was yet to be established.

Sergeant Mitchell travelled out to Quebec from London with extradition papers and two female prison warders from Holloway, Misses Martin and Foster, who would look after Ethel on the journey home. In the event, the papers were not needed as Crippen and Ethel waived their right to full hearings, seemingly so that they could leave for England as soon as possible.

The party finally left Quebec for Liverpool on 20 August, travelling under assumed names in first-class berths on the

Megantic, which Dew had wanted as it was the sister ship of the *Laurentic* and he knew the layout and how best to protect the suspects during the voyage. Mitchell had brought with him a letter from the Police Commissioner, Sir Edward Henry, which in turn contained a personal request from the Home Secretary, Winston Churchill, that the prisoners be shown courtesy and consideration at all times and be spared annoyance from the press. Dew had replied that he was grateful to know he had so fully anticipated the Secretary of State's wishes.

He would write in his memoirs that he often chatted with Crippen on the journey home and 'the more I saw of this remarkable little man the more he amazed me'. When they neared the Irish coast the sea became rough and Ethel, predictably, became seasick. When Crippen heard about it he told Dew that she should drink some champagne and lie flat. Dew promised to consider the cure if she did not improve and ended up buying a small bottle of champagne for her. When Crippen heard 'he was like a dog in his gratitude'.

Dew had Crippen on deck for exercise one day and Crippen said he wanted to ask a favour but would leave it until Friday and Dew said, 'Tell me what it is now and I can answer as well now as on Friday.' Crippen said that when he was taken off the *Montrose* he had not seen Miss Le Neve and he did not know how things would go. They might go all right or they might go all wrong with him and he might never see her again. He wanted to ask Dew if he would let him see Miss Le Neve. He promised not to speak to her. She had been his only comfort these last three years. Dew said it was a delicate matter but he would discuss it with Miss Le Neve.

There were reports that this meeting took place on the train from Liverpool to London, but Dew's memoirs place it on the boat. He said he was touched by Crippen's request and so brought them both to the door of their cabins where they stood staring at each other for a minute or two. He felt like an interloper, he said, there was no sound between them, only a slight motion of the hand from one to the other.

They docked at Liverpool on Saturday, 27 August, two days before the summer bank holiday, which was then known as the Festival of the People. A crowd of many hundreds had gathered to meet the suspects, and when Crippen saw them from the boat he said he couldn't face it. Dew loaned him his heavy Ulster overcoat which, Dew being a taller man, covered Crippen from head to toe. This would become one of the enduring images of the case: Crippen, completely hidden inside the coat and a hat being led down the gangway of the ship by Dew. Other photographs would show the massive number of people who jostled and booed and jeered as Crippen and Ethel were led through the crowd to the boat train to London. It was a chaotic scene, with a military band almost lost in the mêlée, playing a greeting to Canadian troops who had also arrived on the *Megantic*. The troops had to help hold back the crowds for Dew. Sightseers even lined the route of the train as it left Liverpool with Crippen and Ethel on board and were waiting in force at Euston, again providing a noisy and unpleasant chorus as the party got into waiting cabs to go to Bow Street police station.

That evening, after they had both been formally charged with murder and Ethel, in addition, with being an accessory to the murder, Ethel was allowed a visit from her sister, Nina, who described how Ethel came to her arms and lay there a minute or two while they kissed each other. Ethel looked pale and white, her cheeks had sunk since they had last seen each other at the beginning of July. 'I had her goddaughter, my little girl, in my arms and Ethel was overjoyed to see the child, for whom she has great affection.'

Next morning came the ordeal of the first public hearing, the remand at Bow Street Police Court, Bow Street itself choked with people hoping to see the suspects. They were now side by side together in the dock, so they could exchange whispers, though Ethel was on Crippen's left and he was slightly deaf in that ear so communication was still a challenge.

They were secretly photographed that morning in the dock, Ethel in her thick serge suit, her taut, drawn face largely hidden behind a large bonnet draped with a veil, gloved hands in her lap, eyes apparently cast down, while Crippen appears alert and attentive, already growing back his moustache, the alleged bulge of his eyes just perceptible. The pictures were apparently taken by a camera hidden in a hat. They have been attributed to Madame Tussaud's grandson, Jack, but they were more likely taken by a press photographer, James Jarche, who was then aged nineteen and in the early stages of what would become a distinguished career. Photographs in court, though disapproved of and discouraged, were not actually made illegal until 1925.

The *Daily Mirror* said that no more dramatic story had ever been told in a criminal case than that which was revealed that morning. It commented on Crippen's fish eyes and said his face could not be termed handsome. Ethel looked so inexpressibly sad and forlorn as to compel everyone's compassion.

Dew was the only witness and outlined the facts. It was clear that there was already a change of heart about Ethel, with the prosecuting barrister, Travers Humphreys, intimating that the murder charge against her was likely to be withdrawn, the evidence rather pointing to her having been an accessory after the fact.

When Crippen and Le Neve had left the dock, Ethel's father went into the witness box and asked for permission to see his daughter. His serial in the periodical *Answers* had just begun. There had already been some trouble over his appointment of a solicitor to represent Ethel at an earlier inquest hearing, without her knowledge. Ethel had her own lawyer now but was about to sack him as well and join Crippen with Arthur Newton.

Ethel's lawyer told the magistrate that he did not think Ethel wished to see her father. The magistrate told Walter that the lawyer was defending Ethel. Walter said he didn't care who the man was, surely the father came first? He stood before the man, whoever he might be. The lawyer said he didn't wish it to be thought for a moment that he was opposed to the interview. Dew was asked his view and said he didn't think Ethel wished to see her father either but he would go and find out. He returned saying Ethel did not mind seeing her father, so long as it was only to ask her how she was and on the distinct understanding that he make no reference to the charge in any shape or form. If he was going to do that she would not see him. Walter said that he did not want to talk about the case. He was glad to know she didn't want to discuss it. He too was fed up with it. He left the court with his other daughter, Nina.

Later a hostile crowd of around 500 people was reported to have gathered around two unnamed relatives of Ethel as they attempted to walk from the court down to the Strand. It must have been Walter and Nina. They were rescued by thirty constables and took refuge in a public house for some time until a taxi could be called. They still had to struggle through the crowd to enter the taxi. The crowd regrouped outside the court and stayed there until late in the afternoon, hoping to see Crippen and Ethel, but they went unexpectedly from a side door, one after the other, several hours after the hearing.

Ethel went to Holloway and Crippen was remanded to Brixton, to the prison infirmary where, after a long debate by Home Office and Prison Commission officials, it had been decided he ought to be held with a unique guard of two additional warders. There were complaints about the cost and precedent of this extra protection which was criticised as an unnecessary extravagance. Prison officials said murder case suspects were always held at the hospital, partly on suicide watch and partly because they often mounted a defence of insanity and this could be answered if they had been carefully and constantly scrutinised in the hospital. Prison Commission files contain a single reference to an attempt to convey poison to Crippen while he was at Brixton. There is no further information about who was involved or how it was discovered. Evidently, the attempt was unsuccessful.

A Brixton medical officer said the hospital was the wrong place to put him because there was daily traffic in and out of the hospital and information could be conveyed to the public.

The Times could not help complaining in a leader about the vulgar curiosity of the public as a besetting sin of the age: Where once people gossiped only about their own village, now they could gossip about the whole world. But when we gossiped about people we had never seen and didn't know it was easy to forget they were human beings and to regard them as mere spectacles for our amusement. To this public the Crippen case was a godsend. People would wait for hours to catch a glimpse of the accused and 'they will add to the excitement of the spectacle by hissing and groaning'. Their cruelty showed a lack of imagination. 'They flock to see a murderer because murder is a crime that appals them, because they have a human interest in the extremes of human nature. But their imagination, like their curiosity, is passive not active . . . and so the noblest of human faculties is perverted into a kind of intellectual prurience more repulsive than the indifference of animals, as "lilies" that fester smell far worse than weeds.'

Not for the first time, nor the last, there was more than a whiff of hypocrisy in this leader, *The Times* having devoted two full columns to the police court proceedings a day or so earlier and, altogether, providing full coverage of the case for all those hissers and groaners among the better-bred lilies. Whole pages of *The Times* would be devoted almost daily to Crippen's trial.

The murder charge against Ethel was formally withdrawn the following week when the two defendants were brought back to Bow Street for the committal proceedings that would test the evidence and decide whether they would be sent for trial at the Old Bailey. Once again there was a big crowd, people climbing on to the roof to watch through the skylight, from where they would have seen the guests in the small court room, who included the dramatist and magistrate W.S. Gilbert, the director of public prosecutions Sir Charles Matthews and the founder of London policing Sir Robert Peel. There was also, the *Daily Mail* reported, 'a grave and turbaned hindu' who was perhaps, if wearing a turban, a sikh.

Bizarrely, while the committal was in progress over the next couple of weeks, the inquest also resumed in the lecture hall of the Central Library on Holloway Road in Islington, with considerable overlapping of witnesses and testimony, so that a kind of Crippen-fatigue set in among the readers and their newspapers who were covering the case with all its repetitions. The inquest had outgrown its original location at the coroner's court but now the room was so big that the lawyers complained they couldn't hear the evidence.

Arthur Robinson, the mortuary-keeper who had covered Belle's remains with lining paper, caused some amusement when he said he could no longer produce the roll of lining paper because he had used it to wrap his children's sandwiches.

The foreman of the inquest jury wanted to know how the police had failed to stop Crippen going away and Dew, who was there, said he wanted to answer because so many attacks had been made upon him, but the coroner wouldn't let him, saying it was outside the scope of the hearing.

At Bow Street, the committal had to be adjourned one afternoon while a juvenile was being tried in the court next door, as no adult could then be tried at the same time in the same building as a juvenile. Halfway through the hearing Ethel went over to Arthur Newton, who then tried and failed to get the accessory charge against her dismissed. He was obviously acting with his clients' approval when he began sending a clerk to Brixton, supposedly for legal briefings with Crippen but in fact to take down notes for Crippen's own life story, which he proposed to sell to pay for his fees.

The ruse was discovered when the clerk told prison warders what he was doing. The prison governor asked for guidance. The Prison Commission and Churchill were furious with Newton: Such life stories were objectionable, even though the prisoner had the right to raise money to pay for his lawyer's fees. On the other hand, said Churchill, it was hardly possible to aggravate the publicity and sensationalism which already surrounded the case and, while the misuse of powers by the solicitor were grounds for censure, they could not silence the accused on grounds of taste.

It was clear from this and many other exchanges that Churchill was fascinated by the case and was happy to involve himself in the details. Maybe he wanted to read Crippen's life story too. The governor was told to censure Newton and extract from him an undertaking to use his professional visits for professional purposes only.

The governor had to seek guidance again when a woman, Mrs Adele Cook, wrote to Crippen at Brixton asking if he would prescribe a remedy for her illness. Crippen was allowed to see her letter and offer a reply.

Newton must also have been raising funds for himself when he organised, on Crippen's behalf, an auction sale of furniture from 39 Hilldrop Crescent. There were no personal items in the sale but, still, every one of a thousand printed catalogues was sold by the auctioneers Tooth & Tooth of Oxford Street. The sale raised £150, the most expensive single item being a small piano billed as a 'cottage pianoforte' which went for £15. Some of the money went to pay Crippen's outstanding rent.

The committal ended with both defendants, as expected, committed to stand trial at the Old Bailey. The inquest returned a verdict of wilful murder.

Now that the case was going ahead, the police asked the American detective agency Pinkerton's to locate and arrange the passage to England of two key witnesses, Bruce Miller and Belle's sister, Theresa Hunn. The sister was easy to find and willing to travel for modest remuneration, but Miller was less pliable. The Pinkerton's detective went first to Miller's agent at the Western Vaudeville Company in Chicago, who looked carefully back through his bookings' log before confirming that Miller had not had any bookings since 1904. Miller was now a partner in his own real estate business, Smith Miller, on the east side of the city. The detective found him there, friendly and helpful, apparently prosperous and settled with his wife and two children. He was a man of good standing, his wife a member of the church, and he was much embarrassed by the notoriety caused by articles on the case. He told the detective he was not keen to leave his business to go to London – but that seems to have been a negotiating ploy.

Miller wrote personally to the now famous Chief Inspector Dew and told him he was willing to face Crippen in any attempt to defame Belle's character on Miller's account. Miller proposed the terms on which he was prepared to be a witness, and must have been pleasantly surprised to have them accepted. He and Belle's sister went on the same ship, SS *Deutschland*, Theresa Hunn in a second-class berth, with a per diem of $10 a day and a $100 advance. Miller travelled first class, in a berth twice the cost of Hunn's. He got a $400 advance against $25 a day with an agreed minimum of thirty days and an extra $5 a day while he was in London. They arrived six days before the trial, on 12 October, and stayed at the Craven Hotel in the Strand.

The Director of Public Prosecutions, Sir Charles Matthews, had asked Treasury Counsel Richard Muir to lead the case against Crippen, with Travers Humphreys and a barrister from Muir's own chambers, S. Ingleby Oddie, who said he was given the junior brief to his great joy.

Muir was then in his fifties and already among the most eminent criminal lawyers of his day. He would be knighted after the First World War. He had been born in Scotland, the son of a ship-broker and had been a parliamentary reporter for *The Times* before turning to the law and becoming a barrister. Oddie said Muir's work was his life and he had no other amusements and no relaxation. Throughout the Crippen case there would be consultations every night in his chambers, organised by him and including the police officers in the case. The conferences would go on until late with only a pause for dinner at 7.30 pm. Muir's biographer Sidney Felstead would write that everyone involved would curse the name Crippen before the case was over. Perhaps they cursed the name Muir, as well, or instead.

Early on, apparently, Muir became extremely dissatisfied

with the manner in which the police had carried out their work. He believed that the suspicions about Crippen should have been sufficient grounds for arrest when Dew first interviewed him. He did not think Dew was doing enough preparation and complained to his lawyer colleagues that Dew was suffering from 'sleepy sickness'.

Travers Humphreys felt the same way too. On a visit to the scene of the crime he was surprised to find all Belle's furs still in the house. The fact that her furs had been left behind when she disappeared were good evidence to counter any defence that Belle was still alive and had left the house of her own free will. What woman, after all, would run off without her furs? Humphreys challenged Dew about the oversight and thought his answers unsatisfactory. Dew was sent back to sort out the furs and went to the house twice in September at the lawyers' bidding and collected a number of furs, many from a large trunk in the back room on the first floor, including muffs, gloves, an ermine jacket and a white fur jacket.

These would be entered as exhibits in the trial where, it must be said, they did not seem to have significant impact. Perhaps there was an element of snobbery in the lawyers' disapproval of Dew. It was gentlemen and players, professionals and tradesmen, and there was no doubting Dew's position in the social order.

There would be more significance in the pyjama fragment labelled 'Jones Brothers, Holloway, Limited' that had been found in the remains, which Muir had hoped to try and date with some accuracy, to answer any defence that the remains were not Belle's and so must already have been buried there when the Crippens moved into the house five years earlier. He pressed Dew to collect more information but, again, was unhappy that the work was not being done so finally wrote out a list of questions himself to put to Jones Brothers, the department store that had sold the pyjamas. It was not until the trial had begun that the information finally came through.

All along, it had been planned to try Crippen and Ethel together, side by side. Theirs had been a kind of joint enterprise, after all, even if they were now charged with different aspects of it. On 6 October, with the trial due to begin on the 18th, Muir and Humphreys had one of their late-night conferences and decided that the defendants ought to be tried separately. The decision was recorded in a memo, now in a case file at the National Archives.

The two lawyers reasoned that because Ethel's conviction as an accessory would be dependent on Crippen's conviction for murder, her barrister would be entitled to cross-examine all the witnesses produced against Crippen. Even if only one of the jurymen was so influenced by the appeal on behalf of Ethel that he delined to convict Crippen, that disagreement would be disastrous. From the prosecution's point of view it was better to simplify the case as much as possible, and putting Le Neve on the same indictment would confuse it and make the prosecution more difficult.

When concern was raised that this would mean two trials, one after the other, and that this prolonging of the whole case was not desirable, Muir said he did not think there would be two trials. When he opened the case against Ethel the judge would be bound to ask him what evidence he relied on to support the charge that she had been an accessory after the fact of the murder. He would be bound to say he had no sufficient evidence in support of that charge. So Muir was saying that the case against Ethel would be dismissed and there would be no second trial.

The signature on the memo is not clear. It appears to have been written to the Director of Public Prosecutions by another senior member of his office. The writer of the memo says he is strongly disposed to agree with Muir and Humphreys, 'on the ground that the great point was to secure a conviction of Crippen, and that the result of the proceedings against Le Neve was of little importance, especially as it appeared to be improbable that two trials would in fact be held'.

In the end, there was a full trial in Ethel's case but the prosecution so obviously lacked commitment that it seems they too were as determined as her own barrister that she should be acquitted. You wonder why the case against her went ahead after all. The DPP's answer to the memo is unrecorded, but perhaps he felt the public interest demanded a full hearing. More intriguing is the question of why the case against her was considered so unimportant in the first place. Maybe there was something unspoken behind this memo, a feeling that public sympathy would not stand for seeing her convicted and this in turn would create even more sympathy for Crippen and make it harder to execute him. If that was the case then it was political expediency that acquitted Ethel. It seems otherwise unthinkable that a case against her could not have been proved. Her many lies, her proximity to the crime, seem to have been erased from the official record of the case, as if they never existed. Even when Crippen says in evidence in court that Ethel stayed at Hilldrop the night after Belle disappeared, no one appears to bother to follow this up or make a note to mention it at the next trial, the trial of Ethel.

Travers Humphreys, in one of his numerous memoirs, says that F.E. Smith, Lord Birkenhead, later Lord Chancellor, Attorney General and Secretary of State for India, but already then a glamorous young politician and criminal barrister, was offered Crippen's defence but declined it in favour of Ethel's. Humphreys seems to think that Smith took Ethel's case because it would be easier to win than Crippen's and so would more readily add to his lustre.

Newton's first choice to defend Crippen must have been Edward Marshall Hall, who was then the leading defence lawyer in the country. Their partnership had already achieved some notable acquittals, including the case of the so-called Camden Town murder in 1907, when they defended Robert Wood who was accused of killing a young prostitute, Phyllis Wood, who had been found with her throat cut. It was said to have been Marshall Hall's skilful cross-examination and eloquent closing speech that had won the case.

The *Daily Mail* actually reported that Hall would represent Crippen at his trial, on 27 September. There are various anecdotal accounts of how he lost or missed or refused the brief. In one version he declined it because Newton had anticipated the defence at the committal proceedings and Hall had already formed his own views of how the case could be won. But this doesn't sound very convincing. Most arguments could be changed before, and even during, a trial if it was really necessary. According to Hall's clerk, A.E. Bowker, he was responsible for refusing the case, having argued with Newton over Hall's fee, when Newton brought the brief to him while Hall was on holiday. Bowker wanted some money up front and Newton said he was still negotiating with newspapers. Bowker was adamant that he would not accept the brief for Hall without an advance payment. Newton lost his temper, and left Hall's chambers and went straight to the nearby chambers of Sir Alfred Tobin, who accepted the brief instead.

No one could say that Tobin had exactly dazzled the judge or jury or anyone else in his conduct of Crippen's defence. On the other hand, he probably did the best he could with what was available, which does not seem to have been very much. The real damage, however, seems to have been done by Newton, who appears to have tricked at least one medical expert into giving evidence he did not really believe in. From this distance it looks as if Newton spent more time selling Crippen than he did defending him, even if he was a lost cause.

Crippen's defence was not helped by the decision to bury Belle at 3.15 pm in the afternoon, exactly one week before the trial started. Given that one of the key parts of Crippen's defence would be that the remains were not demonstrably Belle's or even a woman's, it was surely more than a little prejudicial to have a public funeral of those remains in Belle's name, undermining any argument to the contrary. It is surprising that this was not raised by the defence at Crippen's trial and mystifying that it was not part of his subsequent appeal.

Theresa Hunn had apparently asked the Ladies Guild to

arrange the funeral, which makes the timing doubly peculiar because she arrived the next day by boat so they could have waited until she could attend in person. They could in fact have waited until after the trial. Maybe the Guild also knew it would be prejudicial, and that was the intention – to do Crippen in. Maybe waiting a day or two longer for Hunn would have been pushing their luck with the law.

A hearse and three mourning coaches departed from Leverton's the undertakers on York Road and went to the St Pancras Roman Catholic Cemetery at Finchley, where Belle was buried. Her coffin had on its lid a large brass crucifix and a plaque with the inscription, 'Cora Crippen, died 1910 aged 35 years'. It was reported that Paul Martinetti was too ill to attend, but there were many floral tributes including a large cross from the Guild with an attached note: 'In loving remembrance of our dear departed colleague.'

A predictably large crowd gathered at Leverton's, and again at the gates of the cemetery where there were street vendors selling memorial cards and a full turnout of the press. One journalist, Joseph Meaney, would write in his memoirs, which he called *Scribble Street*, about how he put one over on his colleagues and gate-crashed the funeral by hovering outside the undertakers dressed in black and climbing aboard one of the coaches with all the Guild ladies. He had kept as a souvenir the small leatherette-bound copy of the burial service in Latin and English which had been handed to him as he walked into the chapel, with its shorthand notes in pencil which he had scribbled discreetly on the flyleaf.

He sounded disappointed when he wrote that there had been no scene at the graveside, the music-hall artistes conducting themselves with what Joe Meaney called their customary 'deep reverence'.

Outside the cemetery he had stood in a phone box, reading over his copy to his newspaper, aware that the colleagues he had earlier thwarted were gathered around the phone box and also taking down every word he was saying. He claimed that he stood in the phone box for an extra fifteen minutes to stop them phoning over their own stories and so protect his exclusive.

FOURTEEN

In 1910, the Central Criminal Court was still the new Old Bailey, having only recently been rebuilt and reopened in 1907. The ceremony was led by King Edward VII, who had marked the occasion by knighting the future Director of Public Prosecutions, Charles Matthews, with the only available sword, which was the ceremonial Sword of Justice that had hung over the judge's chair in the original court house. Matthews was the leading prosecutor of his time.

The original court had been part of Newgate Prison, which had been on the site for nearly a thousand years. Condemned men would go from the court to the prison down a covered path known as Dead Man's Walk (or, more decorously, Birdcage Walk on account of its latticed iron roof). Initials scratched into the stone walls marked the burial places of those who had been executed. The condemned cell had been situated at the end of the corridor and prisoners would go back down the walk to their execution, passing the place where they would shortly be buried.

Until the 1860s convicts were publicly hanged in the street right outside what was now the main entrance of the court. Fees were charged for entry to the public gallery at trials, and executions were also a bonus to owners of properties with windows overlooking the gallows, who sold seats and even rented out rooms, in an early form of corporate hospitality, in which champagne and fine food were provided for guests at 'hanging breakfasts'. One governor of Newgate regularly held such festivals, employing his daughter as a hostess, his breakfasts being held in the prison dining hall immediately after the hanging. Guests would then return to view the cutting down of the dead body, which had been left dangling during the feast, the body in the meantime likely to have been stoned or pelted with rotten fruit and vegetables by the mob – not invited to any breakfast – which usually gathered in the street and often responded to a hanging with riotous behaviour of its own. In 1807, twenty-eight people were crushed to death in front of the gallows, during surges by the crowd.

Around the time of the Crippen case, the father of the writer Victor Pritchett had offices on the opposite side of the road to the Old Bailey where he carried on his business as an 'art needlework manufacturer'. Victor and his brother were taken by their father to the office, from where they could look beyond the dirty balcony to the street below where crowds queued outside the courts for the murder trials and 'on the wood blocked streets, scavenger boys in white coats dashed in and out of the traffic with brushes and wide pans to sweep up the horse manure. My brother and I envied their dangerous and busy life and their wide-brimmed hats'.

Victor's grandfather, his Granda, kept on year after year about murder and made Victor study the Crippen case thoroughly, even though Victor was only nine or ten years old. Granda drew a plan of the house and the 'bloody cellar' for him to reflect on. Granda 'had a dramatic mind'.

On the morning of the first day of the trial of Hawley Harvey Crippen, 18 October 1910, the *Daily Mail* published a plan of the court, showing who would sit where. Photographs of the street scene outside the Old Bailey, taken early that day, showed hundreds and hundreds of people milling around outside the entrance to the court where those public executions had formerly been conducted. It was reported that nearly 5,000 applications had been received for seats in the public gallery. *The Times* said the authorities had 'set their faces' against the admission of women. The Corporation of London officials who managed the court had decided to divide the day in two and issue red tickets for the morning session and blue tickets for the afternoon session. All during the trial the cries would be heard: Red tickets over here! Blue tickets this way!

The jury would be sequestered for the duration at the nearby Manchester Hotel. The jury were all male. Women jurors were not allowed, and would not be allowed until January 1921. It was men's work, evidently, judging your peers, even when they were women. Crippen's trial was very much a men-only affair, with just a few witnesses who were women and the occasional distinguished guest among those celebrated figures who had not needed to apply for a ticket but had their own reserved seating area in the well of the court. Even that area would be so crowded sometimes that there was no space.

One day that week a twenty-year-old actress, Phyllis Dare, who was starring as Gonda Van Der Loo in *The Girl in the Train* at the Vaudeville Theatre, sat right next to the judge on his raised platform, known as the bench, during the afternoon proceedings, thus more than usually blurring the divisions between the court of criminal law and the theatre. Naturally, this would later provoke comment in *The Times*. The writer Arthur Conan Doyle and the actor-manager Sir John Hare were among the other notable visitors who sat in the regular posh seats.

That first day of the trial was certainly ill-starred for Crippen, as it was also the day of the failure of the Charing Cross Bank, where he and Belle still had £600 on deposit. So far as I can tell there were early expectations that some of this money would eventually be repaid, but it never was. No doubt the failure was unconnected to the trial, but it was an odd coincidence that the last of the sixteen witnesses who were called that afternoon was Edgar Brett, the assistant manager of the Bank's Bedford Street branch, who was testifying to the Crippens' substantial deposits, even as the bank was losing them.

Melinda May, the Guild secretary, also gave evidence on the opening day, obliged to bear witness to the sequence of events that had involved her. She had additionally been asked to see if she could identify some of Belle's jewellery, clothes and the hair fragments that had been found among the remains and were now in specimen jars. May later said that the very sight of those things had made her ill. Her nerves had been shattered and she had never been the same afterwards.

In his opening speech, outlining the case against Crippen, Muir made it clear that the Crown was ascribing two motives for the murder. Firstly, 'the prisoner' was pressed for money and Belle was an obstacle because some of the deposits were held in her name alone and she had property that could be converted into money. Secondly, his affection was fixed upon Ethel Le Neve and he was 'desirous of establishing closer relations with that young woman'. Here too, his wife was an obstacle, and if she died both these obstacles would be removed.

Muir could not at this stage say much about the pyjama jacket and the significance of the label, but he could emphasise his medical experts' views that the remains were those of a woman, based on the hair and the Hindes curlers and the fragments of women's underwear found with them. These things were matched to Belle, as was the identification of the mark on a piece of skin from the abdomen as a scar, which was like the scar seen on Belle after her operation.

Then too, there was the hyoscine, the poison which Crippen had purchased in January and which had been discovered in the remains found in the cellar. The traces had been identified from tests conducted by Dr William Henry Willcox, a Home Office forensic scientist who lectured on forensic medicine at St Mary's. The police had given him a series of jars containing body samples back in July, a week after the remains were found. He had begun his tests straight away, dismissing the traces of arsenic and carbonic acid he had found as coming from the disinfectant which had been sloshed around in the cellar. The test for alkaloid poisons took two to three weeks and had found evidence of that type of poison in weighted samples of the stomach, intestines, kidney and liver.

Willcox had then tried to narrow the search, testing for and failing to find common alkaloid poisons such as morphia, strychnine and cocaine. He had found instead a mydriatic poison, which he had demonstrated by conducting an infallible test – if you put a drop of the solution into an animal's eye and it enlarged and dilated, that was a mydriatic alkaloid poison. He had tried this out on a hospital cat – administering the drop and then exposing the cat's eye to a very powerful light.

There were animal and vegetable forms of this alkaloid and Willcox had needed to make further tests to prove it was vegetable. This was important because the other form, the animal type, could be naturally produced by putrefying bodies. By 20 August, Willcox had satisfied himself that of the three types of mydriatic vegetable alkaloid, known as atropine, hyoscyamin and hyoscine, the traces in Belle's remains were definitely hyoscine. This was not a naturally produced alkaloid – it was a poison that had been administered. Cocaine was also this type of alkaloid, but differed from other three in that, when tested, it caused a pupil to contract, rather than dilate. Atropine came from the belladonna plant, whose common name was deadly nightshade. Both hyoscyamin and hyoscine came from the plant henbane. Until recently these three had been thought indistinguishable, and had the same chemical formula. Hyoscine now had the unique formula $C_{17}H_{21}NO_4$.

Willcox gave evidence that the poison was not commonly used but invariably came in the form of a salt, hydrobromide of hyoscine. It was a powerful narcotic and anything upwards of a quarter of a grain could be fatal. He had found more than half a grain in the samples.

It could cause delirium and excitement at first, then the pupils became paralysed, the mouth and throat became dry, the 'patient' would become drowsy and probably become unconscious within an hour. They would be completely paralysed and would die within twelve hours.

Hyoscine was sometimes used medically as a sedative, typically administered by injection, for the treatment of delirium, mania and meningitis. Sometimes it was used to treat insomnia and could be mixed with morphia to make a different sedative. The accepted dose was between 1/100th and 2/100ths of a grain. Hyoscine was not, so far as Dr Willcox could establish, a homoeopathic treatment.

In Belle's case, Willcox was sure it had been taken by mouth and not by injection (he was not asked to explain why, when giving evidence). It was salty and bitter to taste but could be disguised in any strong-flavoured drink such as stout or beer or sweetened coffee or tea, or it could be given with spirits. Anything sweet would hide the bitterness. He was certain that hyoscine had killed Belle and that she had lived for anywhere between one and twelve hours after it had been taken.

The defence clearly wanted to argue that Willcox's tests might have been flawed and that he had mistaken hyoscine for the naturally produced animal form of mydriatic alkaloids. Tobin pressed him on these details in cross-examination but Willcox seemed authoritative and sure of his ground and did not waver.

Still, the defence appeared to have produced an ace when they called Dr Alexander Wynter Blyth, who was himself highly qualified and had written a book called *Poisons: their Effects and Detection*. In his evidence in chief he disputed the findings of Willcox's tests and said he had been unable to reproduce them with the same results.

When cross-examined by Muir, Blyth was immediately accused of speculating, a charge he denied. He tried to insist that it was possible to mistake vegetable alkaloids for animal alkaloids. Muir then quoted Blyth's own book back at him, in which he had said that there was no known animal alkaloid 'which so closely resembles a vegetable poison as to be likely in skilled hands to cause confusion'. This of course was the direct opposite of what he was saying in evidence.

Blyth said he had altered his opinion since he had written that, and had not yet had the chance of publishing his new opinion. He had changed his mind while reading papers – foreign papers. He admitted that he had changed his opinion for the purposes of this case. He said he had read some Italian scientists who had shown you could mistake one for the other.

Muir said Willcox had read the Italians too, and had been unable to find that comment.

Blyth was rattled. 'Well, I cannot help that. I have not searched for it; I have not had time.'

Here was the whole story of the trial and, especially, of the flawed medical evidence presented by the defence. The remains were so obviously those of Belle, the point was unarguable, but Crippen's legal team would clutch at any straw.

The Crown had three doctors all claiming that the mark on the piece of skin was a scar. They had the two who had carried out the post-mortem, Marshall and Pepper, and a young pathologist called Bernard Spilsbury, who was something of a protégé of his senior colleagues at St Mary's, Pepper and Willcox. It was the first big case of Spilsbury's career, his first time giving evidence at the Old Bailey. He would go on to become the leading criminal pathologist of the next thirty or more years, until he killed himself with gas in his own laboratory at University College in Gower Street at the end of 1947. He had suffered a series of strokes and was troubled with insomnia.

In July 1910 Spilsbury was thirty-three years old and already, it was said, was arousing professional jealousy outside St Mary's by virtue of his growing reputation. This could have motivated the experts who appeared for the defence – to cut Spilsbury and/or St Mary's down to size. Spilsbury had been intended to take a supporting role in the case, carrying out microscopic work on the scar to prove its composition in fine detail.

It was Dr Pepper who gave the main evidence about the remains in general and the scar in particular. During his cross-examination by Tobin it quickly became apparent that the defence thought it could disprove the presence of the scar and attribute it, instead, to a fold in the skin which had occurred while the remains were buried. Pepper acknowledged that there was a fold next to the scar and that the scar and the fold together formed a 'horseshoe depression' in the skin. But he maintained that you could clearly tell one from the other.

There was one oddity about the fragment of skin which showed the scar, in that it was clearly from the lower abdomen, but there was no navel there, and there ought to be. Willcox said the navel could have been removed during Belle's original operation – it was a common enough procedure – or could have been just outside the skin fragment. Although there were witnesses who could testify to the presence of Belle's scar, they were not consistent in recalling her navel. Crippen said she did have a navel. But he would say that, wouldn't he.

Tobin suggested that the 'scar' could actually be the ribbing marks of the underwear Belle had been wearing. He pointed out that there were no stitching scars that you might expect to see where the original operation wound had been sewn up. Pepper disputed that you could mistake a scar for underwear indentations and said stitching did not always leave scars. These ribbing marks were evident elsewhere on the skin but Pepper still insisted that the scar was a scar.

It was Spilsbury's turn the following day and he backed up the findings of Dr Pepper, saying that under the microscope you could see where glands and hair follicles were missing on the scar but clearly present on the skin around it.

Many years later, Spilsbury would disclose that he had been contacted before the trial by a pathologist he had known at Oxford who was now a highly qualified director of the Pathological Institute at the London Hospital. Dr Gilbert Turnbull said he had been at a bridge party when Arthur Newton, Crippen's solicitor, had asked him if he would like to take a look at the medical exhibits in the case and express an opinion.

Newton had said he was asking him to have a look purely as a matter of interest and he would not, of course, have to give evidence. Turnbull had subsequently signed a report saying that he thought the scar was not a scar, but a fold. He had then been told that he would have to give evidence and, realising he had been tricked into becoming a witness in the biggest criminal trial ever held in Britain, called Spilsbury to ask his advice. Spilsbury said he ought to withdraw his statement before he got into the witness box. But Turnbull had decided to stand by his original report.

You can tell by the tone of his evidence that Turnbull had opted to come out fighting. Perhaps he was nervous. That's human. Unfortunately, his obstreperous manner only heightened his eventual humiliation. He first said it could not possibly be a scar, that hair follicles and the corresponding glands were plainly present on the area of skin. It was just a fold, and the skin had dried out. It also bore the markings from pressure of material, those markings being clearly visible to the naked eye.

Barristers who are cross-examining witnesses generally never hesitate to resort to sarcasm, but usually only after some time has passed and the poor witness is proving particularly obstinate or awkward. Muir was there straight away, asking Turnbull if his 'great experience' told him the skin fragment came from the lower part of the abdomen. Turnbull agreed that it did.

He was then obliged to concede that he had first signed a report saying it was not from the lower abdomen. He said he had been promised he would not be called at all as a witness. His first examination of the skin had lasted twenty minutes, he said, which must have sounded embarrassingly inadequate to Turnbull even as he said it, and hopeless to the jury, who had already heard the Crown doctors describing their many hours of repeated examinations.

After a second inspection Turnbull had altered his opinions considerably. He had first said he didn't even think the skin came from the abdomen but now he had changed his mind, though he still said he could not see some of the characteristics that confirmed the skin to be abdominal.

Muir invited Spilsbury to come forward and point out the abdominal tendon to Turnbull. Even then, Turnbull said it was in the wrong place. The judge intervened. The Lord Chief Justice, Lord Alverstone, had kept the Crippen case for himself, as was his right. He tried several times to get Turnbull to elaborate and appeared to become irritated at the doctor's refusal to give a straight answer:

> LCJ: Please answer this one way or the other, it is most important. Do you find that tendon there or not?
> TURNBULL: Yes . . .
> MUIR: Have you any doubt that this skin is part of the abdomen?
> TURNBULL: Yes.
> MUIR: You have?
> TURNBULL: Yes.
> LCJ: Do listen, Dr Turnbull.
> MUIR: What part of the body do you suggest it comes from if not from the abdomen?
> TURNBULL: I have told you, and I do not think you could have a better explanation.
> MUIR: What part does it come from, if not the abdomen?
> TURNBULL: From the upper part of the thigh.

Muir suggested that Turnbull could have confused some other cells for the presence of hair follicles and glands. Turnbull in turn said that someone unaccustomed to using the microscope might be mistaken.

'We are not talking about people unaccustomed to the microscope,' said Muir, 'we are talking about people like Mr Spilsbury.'

Muir again tried to get Turnbull to admit his error, seeing follicles and glands where they didn't exist in an old scar:

> TURNBULL: Not in an old scar, no. I do not think you understand.
> MUIR: I think I do. Pray give me the credit for understanding it.
> LCJ: Do not get into controversy with Mr Muir; do not suggest that he does not know what he is putting. You say not hair follicles?

TURNBULL: No.

The judge could not keep himself out of the exchanges and weighed in again, apparently to try and bring some clarity to the evidence. Now Dr Pepper was called forward alongside Turnbull to point out to him the clear shape of the scar on the piece of skin, which was sitting openly on a plate in the courtroom. Pepper marked the shape with three pins and the plate was passed around the jury. None of this made any difference to Turnbull, who disputed that this was clearly the shape of the scar from an ovariotomy operation.

Turnbull's evidence was given some support by his own London Hospital colleague, Dr Reginald Wall, who had also been part of the first twenty-minute inspection. He now said he thought the skin 'probably' did come from the abdominal wall. But he definitely did not think the scar was a scar. He thought it was a fold, though did not sound very convincing as he tried to show how the skin could have been turned in on itself not once but twice, to explain the presence of two distinct folds (one of which, according to the Crown experts, was a scar). The judge sounded incredulous.

LCJ: Twice?
WALL: Well, if we throw a cloth into a basket it will roll over a good many times.
LCJ: You think it could have been rolled over twice by something?
WALL: I think it is very easy to explain it in that way.

Wall said he and Turnbull had asked to see the skin a second time after reading the depositions of the Crown experts. It was only then that he had decided the skin probably came from the abdomen after all. He had followed the Crown expert's earlier trial evidence from reading the *Daily Mail*. He was still not absolutely sure about the abdomen but was unable to say where the skin could have come from, if it came from elsewhere on the body.

Wall and Turnbull must both have been glad to get away from court. It must have taken both men a while to recover from the very public – and professional – disgrace of giving evidence. They had obviously been suckered, perhaps flattered too, by Newton into taking part. Maybe they were temporarily blinded by their own vanity.

They had one last scene to perform, at the end of all the expert evidence when the jury went into the next-door court with the judge and Tobin and Pepper, Spilsbury, Turnbull and Wall so that the jurors could be shown the miscroscopic slides that Spilsbury had produced of the scar tissue. No reporters went with them, so this episode was played out in private. Then, in his summing-up of the evidence, the judge would remind the jury that Pepper had pointed out, under the magnifying glass, what he said was the irregular line through the scar where the knife had cut for the original operation. As the judge said, if it was a knife mark it was conclusive proof of the scar.

The case for the defence that Tobin had outlined in his opening speech was slowly crumbling around Crippen. Tobin had promised to undo the Crown's evidence about the scar and the poison, instead of which he had ended up making the Crown's position seem stronger. He had promised too that there would be expert evidence questioning how long the remains had been in the ground, clearly pointing to the possibility that the body was that of someone else entirely, perhaps buried there before the Crippens had moved in five years earlier. In the event, he had not even broached that subject with his witnesses, which could only mean they had been unwilling to dissent from the evidence of Dr Pepper and Dr Marshall that the remains had been there for between four and eight months. They had said that some of the remains seemed so fresh they might not even have been there that long.

Tobin had asked all the Crown witnesses who knew Crippen what they thought of him, and they had all said what a decent man he was, amiable, kind-hearted, good-hearted, good-tempered and so on. And yet, he said, the jury were being asked to believe he had become a fiend incarnate. He emphasised the practical difficulties that would have faced Crippen in disposing of his wife's body between 1.30 am, when the Martinettis had left, and the next morning when he went to work. What murderer, he said, would run the risk of leaving the body behind like that? And where was the evidence? The knives he had used, the bloodstains?

After challenging Bruce Miller in his cross-examination, pressing him repeatedly for an admission that Miller refused to give of his affair with Belle, Tobin still felt free to say there was an illicit intimacy between them, as there had been between Crippen and Le Neve. And the latter could have been another reason for Belle's departure.

Tobin's rhetoric was flying. Where was she now? Where had she gone? She had gone because she had long disliked Crippen and her dislike had turned to hate. Who knew where Belle Elmore was? Who knew whether it was Belle Elmore's flesh that was buried in the cellar? Who knew for a certainty whether Belle Elmore was alive today or not? Who knew for certain whether she was abroad, whether she was ill or well, alive or dead?

He reminded the jury that they needed to be sure, beyond all reasonable doubt. It was a matter of life and death. He said the remains could be those of a man and (having his cake and eating it), even though the defence disputed it was a scar, if it was a scar, it could be the scar of a man's operation.

When he called Crippen to give evidence the case was reaching its climax. Until 1898 a defendant had not even been allowed to speak for himself in court. A change in the law had ensured that this was invariably now the dramatic peak in any trial. The reporters had already observed Crippen's apparent detachment as he watched in idle curiosity while bits of his wife were passed around the court on plates. Many people in the courtroom had felt revulsion, but Crippen had not seemed at all bothered. All eyes were on him, always, and now he was taking the stand.

Being led through his evidence in chief by Tobin's second, Huntly Jenkins, Crippen had tried to dispense with the inconvenient idea that he had been about to kill himself on the *Montrose*, when he was arrested. As he spoke about the quartermaster's role, the judge interjected and asked if the quartermaster was or was not coming to court. He was told no, and at first said he didn't think they could have the evidence without the witness, then relented and allowed it anyway.

(The *Evening News* would get into trouble just before the end of the trial, for some reason running a story which was not even loosely associated with the truth, to the effect that the quartermaster was in London and had spent an evening in conference with Richard Muir. This was a serious contempt, implying that the Crown was withholding a witness, when in fact no one even knew who the quartermaster was.)

Crippen conceded that his wife had a scar – and a navel – but said it was a small scar, in other words smaller than the 'scar' produced in evidence, because only the ovaries had been removed. He had no idea, he said, whose remains had been found at his home. He had known nothing about them until he got back to England.

It is possible that the opening exchanges of Muir's cross-examination of Crippen, at the start of the fourth day of the trial, Friday, 21 October, are the moments that determined his fate, if his fate had ever been in doubt. It was a devastating and brilliant beginning:

MUIR: On the early morning of the 1st February you were left alone in your house with your wife?

CRIPPEN: Yes.

MUIR: She was alive?

CRIPPEN: Yes.

MUIR: Do you know of any person in the world who has seen her alive since?

CRIPPEN: I do not.

MUIR: Do you know of any person in the world who can prove any fact showing that she ever left that house alive?

CRIPPEN: Absolutely not. I have told Mr Dew exactly all the facts.

MUIR: At what hour did you last see her on the 1st February?

CRIPPEN: I think it would be about between two and three some time that we retired; that would be the last I saw her . . .

MUIR: Where did you think your wife had gone?

CRIPPEN: I supposed, as she had always been talking about Bruce Miller to me, that she had gone there. That was the only thing I could make.

MUIR: That is to America?

CRIPPEN: To America.

MUIR: Have you made inquiries?

CRIPPEN: No.

MUIR: As to what steamers were going to America on or about that date?

CRIPPEN: No, I have not.

MUIR: At no time?

CRIPPEN: At no time.

MUIR: Not since your arrest?

CRIPPEN: Not at all.

MUIR: What?

CRIPPEN: Not at any time . . .

MUIR: It would be most important for your defence in this case on the charge of murder if any person could be found who saw your wife alive after the Martinettis saw her alive. You realise that?

CRIPPEN: I do.

MUIR: And you have made no inquiries at all?

CRIPPEN: I have not conducted my own defence.

Muir questioned Crippen about his finances and asked why he had been in such a hurry to pawn his wife's jewellery. He said he had wanted the money to pay for advertising a new scheme he already had in mind. He did not think he was lying when he told Dew that he had not pawned any of Belle's jewellery, because he did not think of the jewellery as his wife's.

It was when Muir moved on through the sequence of events following his wife's disappearance that Crippen made the unexpected disclosure that Ethel had slept at Hilldrop for the first time on 2 February. The trial transcript suggests that even the Lord Chief Justice was surprised to hear this. 'You must press him upon that,' the judge told Muir, 'for a particular reason.' Muir did press Crippen, who repeated that he was sure of the date. I wonder what the judge had in mind as the particular reason for being sure of the date. Was he thinking about the disposal of the body and Ethel's role, or otherwise?

The following exchanges must have been painful, even for such an apparently dissociated character as Crippen – being reminded of the various letters he had sent about Belle's death, Muir emphasising his lies.

> MUIR: And had you to play the role of the bereaved husband?
> CRIPPEN: Yes.
> MUIR: Did you do it well?
> CRIPPEN: I am sure I could not tell you that . . .
> MUIR: And the letter [to John and Maud Burroughs] in keeping with your role of bereaved husband?
> CRIPPEN: Yes.
> MUIR: [after reading the letter out, just to drive the point home]: Sheer hypocrisy?
> CRIPPEN: It is already admitted, sir.
> MUIR: Sheer hypocrisy?
> CRIPPEN: I am not denying any of this.

When it came to the remains Crippen said it was possible, if not probable, that they could have been put there during his tenancy, while he and his wife were not in the house. This led conveniently to the pyjamas. Muir by now had the additional evidence he had wanted, but if he attempted to introduce it 'cold' into the trial halfway through, the defence could object and he might not be allowed to put it to the jury. If, on the other hand, Crippen gave evidence about the pyjamas Muir would be free to introduce additional evidence to counter or disprove what Crippen had said, though he would still be vulnerable to the accusation that he had set a trap for the defence.

Crippen was shown the two complete sets of pyjamas that Dew had found in the box under the bed. He said he thought he had bought those himself at Jones Brothers in September 1909. He usually bought three pairs at a time. Then he was shown the odd pair of trousers (the ones that matched the fragments of the jacket found in the remains). He said they were from an old pair, the last of the previous purchase of three sets, which had been after he moved to Hilldrop Crescent as it was only then that he began to wear pyjamas. He could not say what happened to the jacket.

No, his wife had not bought the recent pairs, not, as Muir put it to him very specifically, at a winter sale on 5 January 1909. He started to backpeddle then. Well, maybe she had bought some pyjamas for him. He wouldn't say for certain that she hadn't. Muir then produced the fragments from the remains and Crippen had to agree that the pattern looked similar to the pattern on the lone trousers.

Now Muir played his hand, saying that all three pairs – including the incomplete set – had been made of cloth that only became available in November 1908. There was nothing Crippen could say to that. His own barrister, Tobin, stood up and suggested that the judge should stop the line of questioning. Muir had done enough now, anyway – effectively enabling him to bring the evidence that would prove his point about the date of the pyjama fragments.

He asked Crippen about when and why he decided to leave London, and Crippen said he thought he might be held in jail for months and months on suspicion. He could not, or would not say, what it was he thought he might be suspected of. He was pressed and pressed and the best he could say was that he might be suspected of being 'concerned in her disappearance'. He would not say kill or murder or any word like it.

Finally, Crippen was questioned about the hyoscine which he claimed had mostly been used to make up 'pillules' used to treat 'nervous diseases, coughs of a septic character and asthmatic complaints'. He said the unused hyoscine had been left in a cupboard at Albion House but he had done nothing to find it. He said there was a book which referred to hyoscine as a homoeopathic cure, '*The Dictionary of Homoeopathic Materia Medica*,' he thought. The book was never produced in court. Nor were the names of any patients he could prove he had treated with his supposed hyoscine 'pillules'.

After some legal argument about whether he could do it or not, Muir was allowed to call his Jones Brothers' witness, a buyer named William Chilvers. He had the receipt – the sale duplicate, he called it – for the purchase that Belle had made at the store on 5 January 1909. She had bought three pairs of pyjamas, costing 17s 9d, and two other items, costing £2 9s 4d. Everything had been sent to Hilldrop Crescent as cash on delivery. Chilvers could not say whether they had been sent by the usual cart or by special messenger.

He could tell by the material that the pyjamas had been made for Jones Brothers shortly before December 1908; he could not be exact but it would have been about a month or three weeks beforehand. He confirmed that the trousers matched the jacket fragments from the remains. The label on the jacket, Jones Brothers, Holloway, Limited, was further evidence of timing, as the store had only been a limited company since 1906.

In his final speech, Tobin did his best to improve Crippen's position. No wonder, he said, that he hadn't made inquiries after Belle left. They had been unhappy together and it would be idle to suppose he would be other than relieved at her departure. He had his mistress there and did not want his wife back, so why make inquiries? It was not surprising that the quartermaster wasn't in court – he was hardly likely to come forward and confess his planned role in impeding officers of the law.

Tobin must have had little hope, by this stage, that there was much doubt left in the jurors' minds about the identity of the remains. Still, he had to argue the case: could they be sure that the flesh was the flesh of a woman, and of Belle? Was she really dead? Strange things, he said, were recorded in our legal history. There were cases where men had been hanged and, afterwards, the supposed victim had appeared alive again. He went through it all, one more time: the weak motives, the lack of Crippen's surgical skills, that he was too nice to kill. The body could have been there for a long time, the mystery of the missing navel, was the scar really a scar? A man's life or death depended on it, so the jury had better be sure.

There was one factor, said Tobin finally, that dominated everything, and that was that Crippen had carried on as normal, after his wife's disappearance, without anyone who knew him ever seeing a strange look in him or any sign of fright or agitation. Was it conceivable that such a murderer could go to work next morning without a trace of terror in his eyes?

(Apparently, it was.)

In his response to Tobin, Muir said the jury should not be frightened by the ancient bogey of a returning corpse. It was out of place to try and frighten them as if they were little children in the nursery. He reminded them that Crippen was not nearly as nice as Tobin had tried to paint him, having lived a life of studied hypocrisy, regardless of the pain he had been inflicting on the friends and family of his wife. The jury had watched him during the trial and they would be the judges of whether the prisoner had the nerve to conceal his feelings.

According to Crippen, Belle was a living lie. She was the unfaithful, bad-tempered wife and he was the kind-hearted, considerate husband. Would Bruce Miller have travelled across the ocean to give evidence in court if he really was an adulterer? Their accuser was the one carrying on the intrigue, with Ethel Le Neve.

'No motive?' said Muir. Love, if they dignified it by that name; lust, if they gave it its true appellation – one of the most powerful motives actuating the thoughts of men. Money to gratify that lust. Immediately, on 2 February the wife's jewels were pawned, £80 was raised, and it was suggested that there was no motive!

Muir went on at some length about the sorry spectacle of the defence experts. The two men (Turnbull and Wall) who did not scruple to give a report, after a twenty-minute examination and had been forced to admit the grossest carelessness and rashness. Muir itemised the numerous errors Turnbull had made and said he had never heard anything more extraordinary in his life, than Wall's testimony. He reminded the jury that they were in court to do their duty, to perform a difficult and painful task. 'From that duty a jury of the City of London will not shrink.'

It was nearly over now, as the Lord Chief Justice began his summary of the case for the jury, reminding them to disregard anything they might have read or heard outside the court during this 'great and important' case. There were two key issues, he said. Were the remains those of Cora Crippen and, if they were, 'was her death occasioned by the wilful act of the defendant Crippen?'

Alverstone said that this was not a court of morals but a court of law. The fact that Mrs Crippen, or Belle Elmore, was an immoral woman at some time, the fact that the man was confessedly a very immoral man, and had been living under improper circumstances with Ethel Le Neve, was a matter the jury might regret in their own minds but was no reason to acquit or convict. He looked as though he was getting ready to criticise Belle in more detail when he began to describe her as a woman with a past. But he went on to speak of her in more even terms, saying that she was always beautifully dressed, spick and span, and was in a position that many women of that rank of life would aspire to have. If she went away, why didn't she take her clothes or her jewels?

Whatever the truth of the case, the jury might think

Crippen was an extraordinary man. If he was guilty he had committed a ghastly crime and covered it up, or endeavoured to, in a ghastly way, behaving afterwards with the most brutal and callous indifference. If he was innocent it was impossible to fathom his mind and character, since he again seemed indifferent to the charge against him, having not taken any step of any sort or kind to prove his innocence. Time and again, the judge would point out that there was no evidence called in support of Crippen's position. He had said he lied to cover up a scandal, at Belle's request. What the scandal was, said the judge, was difficult to see.

He emphasised the importance of the pyjamas in dating how long the remains had been in the cellar. He clearly did not think much of the defence experts and told the jury they should treat with some reserve the statements of someone who had been positive about something and then changed their mind. He asked the jury directly, as if the answer was obvious, have you any doubt that that is the body of Cora Crippen?

Judges claiming neutrality in their case summaries often cannot help trying to tell the jury what they ought to be thinking. It was the same with Alverstone, who seemed to be looking ahead to the next trial when he said, 'You will not think, probably, that there was more than one person mixed up in this, and probably you will be of the opinion that examining the question of who killed her answers the question of who buried her.'

The gentlemen of the jury went out at 2.15 on Saturday afternoon, the fifth day of the trial. They came back twenty-seven minutes later at 2.42.

CLERK OF THE COURT: Gentlemen, have you agreed upon your verdict?
FOREMAN OF THE JURY: We have.
CLERK: Do you find the prisoner guilty or not guilty of wilful murder?
FOREMAN: We find the prisoner guilty of wilful murder.
CLERK: And that is the verdict of you all?

FOREMAN: Yes.

CLERK: Prisoner at the bar, you stand convicted of the crime of wilful murder; have you anything to say why the court should not give you the judgement of death according to law?

CRIPPEN: I am innocent.

CLERK: Do you wish to say anything?

CRIPPEN: I still protest my innocence.

The usher called for silence in the court. A chaplain came and stood by the Lord Chief Justice, who now had a black cloth placed over his wig as he delivered the sentence:

Hawley Harvey Crippen, you have been convicted, upon evidence which could leave no doubt on the minds of any reasonable man, that you cruelly poisoned your wife, that you concealed your crime, you mutilated her body, and disposed piece-meal of her remains; you possessed yourself of her property and used it for your own purposes. It was further established that as soon as suspicion was aroused you fled from justice and took every measure to conceal your flight. On the ghastly and wicked nature of the crime I will not dwell.

I only tell you that you must entertain no expectation or hope that you will escape the consequences of your crime and I implore you to make your peace with Almighty God. I have now to pass upon you the sentence of the court, which is that you be taken from hence to a lawful prison and from thence to a place of execution, and that you be there hanged by the neck until you are dead, and that your body be buried in the precincts of the prison where you shall have last been confined after your conviction.

And may the Lord have mercy on your soul.

'Amen,' said the chaplain.

FIFTEEN

Crippen's composure was frightening. He had not once seemed shaken or discomfited during cross-examination and he never broke down at the verdict, according to his junior barrister, Ingleby Oddie. There would be some evidence, afterwards, that he showed distress following his arrival at Pentonville Prison, where he was now transferred, directly from the Old Bailey, as this was the prison where he was to be hanged.

The Lord Chief Justice wrote to the Home Secretary, Churchill, that same afternoon, to give him formal notice of the conviction, saying that there was no doubt as to the facts. He thought it right to add that he could conceive of no grounds which should prevent the death sentence being carried into effect.

The governor of Brixton, having lost his prisoner, was in need of reassurance that justice had been done. He wanted to know what had happened to the letter he had forwarded to the Prison Commissioners. The letter had arrived at Brixton during the second day of the trial and claimed to come from Mrs Crippen. The Commissioners told him they had forwarded the letter to Churchill. The judge had received some similar letters and there would be several more sent to the Home Office or to Churchill personally, over the next month. Hoaxes, all of them, obviously.

The Commissioners wrote to the governor at Pentonville, asking him to take care during all visits to Crippen, as they had reason to believe there had been an attempt to convey poison to him while he was at Brixton.

In the next edition of *The Times*, that Monday morning, the leader returned to one of its favoured themes – the turpitude

IPPEN & MISS LE NI

Ethel's parents, Walter and Charlotte Neave, with their youngest son, Sidney, pose for a newspaper photograph, *Weekly Dispatch*, August 1910.

Ethel's sister Adine True Neave with her husband, Horace Brock, around the time of their marriage in July 1903.

Ethel Le Neve in *Lloyd's Weekly News*, 6 November 1910. The locket almost certainly contains a miniature photograph of Crippen. The likeness between the two sisters is remarkable.

Adine Brock being treated for tuberculosis in a sanatorium, shortly before her death in 1918, aged 34.

ABOVE, LEFT & RIGHT
Adine's children: Ronald George
Brock during the Second World War
and Ivy Ethel Brock at her marriage
to Jack Palmer in 1936.

Ivy and Jack Palmer with their son
Roger, born February 1945.

Ethel Smith (wearing glasses) with her friends Rex and Ada Manning not long before her death in 1967, aged 84.

The American Waltham pocket watch, once owned by Crippen, later worn by Ethel's husband, Stanley, who was unware of its previous owner and died without ever knowing his wife had once been Ethel Le Neve. After Stanley's death Ethel presented the watch to her friend Rex Manning. It was later bought for £10,000 at a Christie's auction for the benefit of charity (now in the possession of David Gainsborough Roberts).

Family photograph, circa 1949.
Back row, from the left, Bob Smith, son of Ethel (standing); Bernard Neave, son of Sidney; Stan Gray, husband of Iris; Iris Gray, daughter of Sidney; Sidney Neave holding Linda Gray, daughter of Iris and Stan; Front row, from left, Amy Neave, wife of Bernard; Doris Neave, wife of Sidney; Ethel Smith (Ethel Le Neve as was) in hat and pearls; Nina Smith, daughter of Ethel.

Crippen prescribing for a patient of the Drouet Institute in November 1904 and a follow-up letter to the same patient – clearly soliciting further business – signed 'E Le N', in March 1905. The two letters were bought at auction for just under £300 in May 2005 and are now in the collection of David Gainsborough Roberts.

sweeping through modern British society, as seen, on this occasion, in the Crippen trial: 'Only one feature of the trial is to be regretted . . . A criminal court is not a show room, nor is such a trial of the nature of a matinee; the Old Bailey is not a place to which fashionable ladies may fitly go in search of the latest sensation, where actors may hope to pick up suggestions as to a striking gesture or a novel expression, and where descriptive writers may go in search of good copy . . . This trial is a warning of the danger of an increase in accessories which are wholly inconsistent with the atmosphere of a Court of Justice; and it is to be hoped that in future there will be less readiness to gratify obtrusive and not altogether harmless curiosity.'

The commentary had not gone far enough for some readers. W.E. Cameron from Middle Temple Lane, EC, wrote complimenting the paper on its forcible if restrained leader. He had been in court himself and, referring to the ticketing arrangements, said the 'two-houses-a-day system' had meant that all the appurtenances of popular music-hall were present. 'Is it not an incongruous thing that while a man is being tried for his life there should sit on the Bench on the right hand of the Judge a famous musical or comedy actress? The lady is, I am sure, charming and delightful and as worthy of the position as any other of her sex, but her name is associated with lighter things of life than a murder trial and her presence, I insist, detracted from the solemnity of the occasion.'

Cameron moved on to complain of the 'hideous trappings and archaic formalities' that accompanied a death sentence, such as the black-clad chaplain, 'upstanding like the dread figure of doom'. 'I write as one who has had experience of four death sentences and who has been so profoundly moved and horrified by that of the Crippen trial that he will not rest until these disgraceful incidents to the most solemn function of the law are got rid of for ever.'

There were some further letters in response. One asked, why not a comedy actress? And what did it matter, what the ladies were wearing? The writer saw nothing wrong in the ritual surrounding the delivery of the death sentence. Another correspondent was sure that everyone in court had taken away a lasting impression of the dignity of British justice. He had sat next to a celebrated actress one day at the trial and she had not only been well dressed but also actively interested in criminology and the various questions of prison reform. This, she had said of the court, is our real dramatic school.

It had not been a very long trial. These days, it would most likely have run for weeks; the volume of scientific evidence alone would have taken days. The crime scene – the whole house, probably – would have been microscopically examined. The defence would have spent hours challenging and arguing the points, finding every possible opportunity to suggest that evidence had been harmed, lost or contaminated by clumsy, careless or corrupt officers. Dew would have been taken mercilessly through the wringer.

Aspects that barely even featured in the actual trial would have been scrutinised. Where, when and how had Crippen disposed of Belle? What knives had he used, had he taken them from his kitchen or his medical kit or had he bought them, if so from where, and what had he done with them afterwards? Modern forensic science would probably have made the house yield its secrets. Invisible blood spatters would have been brought to light. The remains would have been readily identifiable by DNA. Perhaps, too, the police would have considered what happened to Crippen's first wife. They might have wondered what traces of what poisons, if any, they would find in her body.

Still, Crippen's trial, such as it was, certainly lasted longer than Ethel's, which began in the morning of 25 October and was over by 4.15, Ethel walking free from the dock.

There was no application to stop Ethel's trial proceeding, and no mention of anything that related to the memorandum in which Muir was recorded as saying there was unlikely to be a trial. Churchill had kept away from the Old Bailey during Crippen's case but attended for some of Ethel's. Ethel herself did not give evidence. It was said that the Lord Chief Justice had subsequently told her barrister, F.E. Smith, that he thought Smith ought to have put her in the box. Smith, supposedly, had replied, 'No, I knew what she would say, you did not.' Why the judge would have said this to Smith, after he had won the case anyway, is hard to figure. Particularly when the judge and all the lawyers who shared that close-knit, incestuous world of the bar, must have known that the trial was little more than a formality, a going through the motions, a charade even, with no real intent by the Crown to seek a guilty verdict. They had their man, in Crippen, and that was all that seemed to matter.

Richard Muir again led the prosecution, such as it was, and said Crippen had flown from justice accompanied by the prisoner at the bar, she assisting him to evade justice by disguising herself. He said that for some reason – it mattered not what – it was decided that Crippen was not to fly alone and, she being a source of danger to him unless she disguised herself, she made the sacrifices involved. She cut off her hair, dressed as a boy and passed as his son, with a false name, flying to a foreign country by a circuitous route. All these things for what reason? For no reason that she offered at all, and Muir submitted that, unless and until the jury received from her, or from somebody else, an explanation, the only interpretation they could put upon these acts was the interpretation that she knew of Crippen's crime and she assisted Crippen to escape.

Chief Inspector Dew was there, of course, and gave a truncated account of his role. He was asked by Smith about Ethel's background and, for no apparent reason, asked her father's position in life. Dew said Walter was 'of the lower middle classes', a canvasser for coal orders.

Ironically, the chief witness against Ethel was her landlady/ surrogate mother, Emily Jackson, the main point of her evidence being the date when Ethel had suffered the fit of hysteria – was it before or after Belle's disappearance? F.E. Smith's son, in his biography of his father – *Birkenhead by Birkenhead* – would describe Smith putting Jackson through a 'racking' cross-examination. But that was hardly necessary and not the case at all. After an inquest, a committal hearing, numerous police statements, various press interviews and the trial of Crippen, poor Mrs Jackson's mind must have been so befuddled she probably would have said anything to please.

Here was that 'racking' exchange. Note that Smith plucks the date of 25 January from nowhere, from the air:

SMITH: How did you fix the date of this occasion on which you say she was very ill? You told my learned friend (Muir) it was during January – towards the latter part. Would you be prepared to say on oath that it may have been as far back as 25 January?

JACKSON: I could not fix a date.

LCJ [YES, HIM AGAIN]: It may have been as early as that?

JACKSON: It may.

SMITH: You have stated that she came home one night more pleasant than you had seen her and said that somebody had gone to America. If it is correct that she came back and said this at the beginning of February, it would suggest the other conversation when she was so agitated would be about 25 January?

JACKSON: Somewhere about that.

SMITH: You mean she was in high spirits at the beginning of February when you say she came back pleasant?

JACKSON: Yes.

SMITH: No trace of anxiety, no depression, no sign of physical ill-health?

JACKSON: No.

Smith was happy with this; it gave him all he needed. Ethel's hysteria was not because she had been involved in, or had just found out about, a murder. It was before that. In fact, she could not have been told about the murder, or been a party to it, because she came home happy, instead.

Smith was lucky that his defence could turn on such a simplistic position, given the complex sequence of events. Had

Ethel known about Crippen buying the hyoscine on the 19th? Had she been distressed because she and Crippen had sat in Frascati's planning a murder, in mid-January? Had Ethel been pressing Crippen to leave Belle or otherwise resolve his relationship with her? Could she have pushed him to do what he now planned? Could she even have suggested it? Or, at the very least, guessed it in advance? What was going through her mind when she told her friends the two Lydia Roses that she was engaged, at her birthday party. Her birthday being 22 January three days after the hyoscine had been collected.

Not calling his defendant to give evidence, nor indeed calling any witnesses for the defence, left Smith with the freedom to make a long, somewhat repetitious speech. Reading between the lines, it seems his oration – for which he was duly famed in Parliament – might have caused some amusement on the prosecution bench. Ingleby Oddie described in his memoirs how he saw that Smith had the whole thing written out and watched him turning through it, page by page. Oddie said it was a fine if lengthy speech. Perhaps the joke was that he had already won the case but felt the need to make a long speech anyway.

In fact, Smith's defence is fascinating for its deployment of class and morality, and makes plain his motive in asking Dew about her father's place in life. In Smith's hands, in his appeal to the decent gentlemen of the jury, Ethel quickly becomes a luckless Dickensian heroine. Little Eth perhaps:

> We know, for instance, that ten or eleven years ago, at the age of sixteen or seventeen, an age when I need hardly remind you young girls in happier circumstances are going to a finishing governess, it became necessary for her to earn her own living as a typist.
>
> You know what are the temptations to which, under normal conditions and with normal employers, a young and attractive girl is exposed going to the city as a typist . . . [Le Neve] had the extreme misfortune to come across the path, at the age of seventeen, of one of the most dangerous and

remarkable men who have lived in this century; a man to whom in the whole history of the psychology of crime a high place must be given as a compelling and masterful personality.

Smith said that there was no reason to suppose the 'intrigue' between Crippen and Ethel had lasted more than three years, and there was no reason to suppose she had been anything other than chaste during the earlier seven years of his influence. He asked the jurors to think of the lives they gave their own daughters and contrast them with those seven years and Ethel's drab and dreary toil by day as a typist and her nightly return to a gloomy lodging-house. 'And this in the very dawn of womanhood.'

He invoked a biblical comparison, likening Crippen and Le Neve's relative positions to those of the Centurion who had told his servant, 'do this and he doeth it'.

In his view the idea that Crippen could have told Ethel of the crime in all its hideous and filthy detail was a monstrous and stupid suggestion. 'In other words he gave this enormous hostage to fortune – he told a woman he had killed his wife. If the teachings of human psychology have any value, the odds are prodigious that any young woman not belonging to the criminal classes having this horrible statement made to her would receive it with aversion, revulsion and disgust.' Could anyone believe she went back to live at Hilldrop Crescent knowing that its last tenant had been killed by the man she was going to live with? 'Was woman ever known, so wicked and abandoned?'

A defenceless child, Smith continued, she had maintained herself at the age of seventeen in the struggle for life without any indication of moral obliquity.

The prosecution might have asked for an explanation from Ethel but Smith said he took full responsibility for not submitting her to deadly cross-examination, knowing that she was a young and inexperienced woman, without any knowledge of the world, that she was dazed and shattered. He asked the jurors to judge her in her hour of agony with the same consideration they would wish shown to a daughter of their own if she were placed in the same position.

As he had in the Crippen trial, the Lord Chief Justice told the jury that they were in a court of law not a court of morals. They were not to judge Ethel Le Neve because she was Crippen's mistress. They were not to judge the woman because she was fallen. It would not be right for anyone to judge the woman from the standard of morality.

The judge seemed keen to point to an acquittal, telling the jury that the earliest Ethel could have known of Belle's disappearance was 2 February, when Crippen left the note and letters for the Guild on her desk. In reality she could have known much earlier. He was then happy to turn a maybe into a certainty and, on Mrs Jackson's evidence, put Ethel's hysteria back into January, well before the disappearance. The judge referred to Crippen as a scoundrel twice during his summary of the evidence and warned the jury to take care in judging Ethel, as she appeared to have been very much under his control.

The jury went out at 3.52 pm and came back with their not guilty verdict at 4.12 pm. The *Daily Mail* said that on hearing the verdict Ethel slumped back in her seat and appeared to need reminding by a wardress that she had not been convicted. The judge said, 'Discharged,' and no more.

Richard Muir later said privately, maybe to his wife, that full justice in the case had not yet been done. This could only mean he believed Ethel was guilty too. Of something.

Ethel was now free to visit Crippen. Once again, Churchill was personally involved, signing a note that she was not to be refused access to Pentonville. The visit turned sour when people discovered she was inside the prison, with her sister Nina, and a hostile group of about 500 people gathered. The police had to force a way through the crowd so that Ethel and Nina could reach a waiting taxi. Ethel was asked to make her subsequent visits at night and Churchill asked officials to ensure that Ethel was secured from future molestation.

Almost immediately after her acquittal, Ethel fell in with the two journalists who were to ghost her life story for *Lloyd's Weekly News*. Both men, Philip Gibbs and J.P. Eddy, had already been covering the case as reporters for the *News*'s sister publication, the *Daily Chronicle*. Eddy would go on to become a QC and a High Court Judge. Gibbs would be knighted for his work as an author and war correspondent.

Eddy made several trips to Pentonville and waited outside while Ethel visited Crippen. He would recall that she always came away very subdued and anxious that he should, if at all possible, escape the gallows. He said she showed no bitterness at the ordeal Crippen had put her through. Eddy felt he got to know her quite well and had no shadow of doubt as to her innocence. It seemed inconceivable to him that she could have left the country with a man she knew to be a murderer. He ended his chapter about Ethel in his memoirs – written fifty years later – with the comment that if she happened to read them she would know that his faith in her innocence never faltered.

Gibbs's memoirs described how Ethel spent weeks – would it really have been that long? – being looked after at the expense of the newspaper group's proprietor. (The late owner of both papers had been Edward Lloyd, who was famed as a pioneer of sensational weekly serials known as Penny Dreadfuls.) 'They provided her with a furnished flat, under an assumed name, and for weeks the *Daily Chronicle* office was swarming with her sister's family, while office boys fetched the milk for the baby, and sub-editors paid the outstanding debts of the brother-in-law, in order that Ethel Le Neve should reserve her tale exclusively to the nice, kind paper! Such is the dignity of modern journalism, desperate for a "scoop".'

Gibbs seems to have retained a healthier scepticism about Ethel, though he describes his colleague Eddy cross-examining her, artfully and persistently, during their interviews without ever trapping her into an admission. To Gibbs she was just a little Cockney girl (well, Norfolk actually) of humble class and means, but she had astonishing and unusual qualities.

She told him, glibly, that she had known, while they were on the run in Brussels, that Crippen was wanted by the police for 'some old thing or other' and that right up until her arrest she had regarded the whole episode as a great 'lark'.

> She admitted to me that, putting two and two together, little incidents that had seemed trivial at the time, and remembering queer words spoken by Crippen – 'the doctor' as she called him – she had no doubt now of his guilt. But, as she also admitted, that made no difference to her love for him. 'He was mad when he did it,' she said, 'and he was mad for me.' That was the extraordinary thing – that deep, sincere and passionate love between the little weak-eyed, middle-aged quack doctor, and this common, pretty little Cockney girl.

Ethel, I bet, would have hated being described as common. If Gibbs is telling the truth, this was the only time she ever acknowledged Crippen's guilt. Her public position, in so far as she had one, was always to maintain his innocence.

Gibbs said he sat with Ethel day after day in a Soho restaurant, while all the journalists of England were searching for her. Many times she was so gay that it was impossible to believe she had escaped the hangman's knot by no great distance and that her lover was a little bleary-eyed man lying under sentence of death. Yet that gaiety of hers was not affected or forced but bubbled out of her because of a quick and childish sense of humour which had not been killed by the frightful thing that overshadowed her. She wept sometimes, but never for long.

Ethel asked Gibbs to have a photograph of the doctor made into a miniature locket which she 'could wear concealed upon her breast'. He recalled that she put on black for the morning of his execution and wished she could have died with him on the scaffold. Though he was glad to see the back of her, because this was not the kind of journalism that appealed to his instincts or ideals and he sickened at the squalor of the whole story, Gibbs could not help feeling some pity for Ethel and was certain of her innocence, even though he felt she was as careless of the crime as any Borgia woman might have been. He thought the secret could be in the history of Ethel's family name, Le Neve. No doubt he imagined the name harked back to a turbulent past. Gibbs was wrong about that, in one way, because of course it wasn't her name. But surely her involvement with Crippen was associated with the same social ambition and determination that Ethel had invested in the assumption of that grand-sounding surname.

In addition to telling Ethel's story, Gibbs also had access to the series of letters that Crippen wrote to her – 'immensely long letters, written on prison paper in a neat little writing, without a blot or a fault'. They had surprised Gibbs with their good style and their beauty of expression.

They too, must have been sold to the newspaper, along with Ethel's story. The terms of the deal were not recorded, though it seems likely that Arthur Newton was involved. Crippen would also be reminding Ethel, in those letters read by Gibbs, to try and ensure her financial security. At this stage, however, he was still daring to hope they might yet have a life together:

Friday, 28 October 1910
     You can imagine what my feelings are to have before me your dear handwriting again. I have longed so passionately for a letter from you to sustain me through the long and weary separation, and, although I have been able to subdue my nerves and preserve my outward control, my heart has been bursting and throbbing with the pain of longing for you and even for a few written words from my ever-loving darling. I knew my darling's heart and love for me would never waver in the slightest, and hope sustained me, and that our union has not only been for life but for all eternity.
     But, dear wifie, do not yet despair. There is yet the appeal, and friends are coming forward to help. One here in England tells my solicitor he does not consider I

had a fair trial, and offers to pay all expenses ... [that must have been the rogue parliamentarian and owner of the weekly *John Bull*, Horatio Bottomley, whose contribution to the Crippen defence fund was not without cost] ... and, just think, Munyon has awakened to his old friendship for me and cabled he will spend £12,000 for me if necessary ... [it was reported that Crippen's old employer, 'Prof.' Munyon, had offered a reward to anyone who could find Belle, following the reported sighting of her in Chicago] ... I had also a letter from Lady Henry Somerset telling me you were to come to live with her today, but for fear that was not certain I am sending this care of Horace to be forwarded to you.

I do not of course know if you are keeping your name where you are staying, but I strongly advise you not to do so, and, wifie dear, it would please me so much if you would take my first name or my second Christian name, which you prefer – probably you prefer Hawley – and add Mrs to it, as you will wear my (or our) ring as before. So tell me in your next how and where to address you, which will save delay.

My good things all came at once today. Your visit was a surprise. I have just returned from it, and sat down to my letter again. I nearly broke down, but struggled to be composed and not upset you. My own dear heart, how I longed even to touch your hand. To hold you in my arms would have been paradise, but we must look forward to that.

To return to what was taken from my pockets at Quebec, be sure you get the prescription for 'Sans Peine'. I have written to my solicitor to see that it is returned; but this will be your authority to demand it from him, and I want you to keep it safely until I tell you, darling, what to do with it. It may be of great value to us.

Write me fully, wifie dear, and tell me everything, but

don't arrange anything finally until my appeal is over, because I shall want you with me at once to comfort me and help me to regain my nerve, which is beginning to break down. If all goes well, as please God, I hope you will come to me at once, won't you, darling? After this I shall try and write often, and hope to have good letters from you. Dear wifie, greatest love of my heart and soul, God protect you and keep you safe.

Earlier that week, the governor had withheld from Crippen a letter sent by the same Lady Henry Somerset, as mentioned in the letter above, on the grounds that her letter appeared peculiar and seemed to contain a hidden meaning. Lady Isabel (1851–1921) was the estranged wife of Lord Henry Somerset and the sister-in-law of Lord Arthur Somerset, who had moved abroad to try and live down the notoriety of his association with the so-called Cleveland Street scandal, in which he had been caught visiting a male brothel. His solicitor had been Arthur Newton. Lady Isabel was well known as a philanthropist, particularly for her involvement with the temperance movement. There seems to have been something not altogether philanthropic about her interest in Crippen and Ethel. Perhaps it is the connection with Arthur Newton that tells its own story.

Ethel must have been referring to her, when she later published an additional statement in *Lloyd's Weekly News* which contained the following: 'A lady whom Dr Crippen and myself were led to believe was a philanthropist did visit him and me earlier in the case, but when we discovered her real identity we refused to have anything to do with her.' It seems likely that she was a Trojan Horse from Fleet Street – or Arthur Newton sent her to extract a confession. Crippen, at least, appears to have died without discovering how outrageous Newton's conduct of his case had been.

When she wrote to Crippen a day or so later Lady Henry appeared to be trying to get Ethel to go and stay with her, and also appeared to have aroused Crippen's anxiety with a proposal to make some information about Crippen public, ostensibly to help his case. Crippen had to get special permission to write an extra letter to her, asking her to keep the confidences he had shared and not publish any of the letters he had written to her. He reassured her that Ethel was well cared for at present (by the *Lloyd's* reporters, presumably) and said they would see about her future later.

Crippen had been told he could write no more than once a day to Ethel. She had obviously taken note of his request to start using one of his forenames as her 'married name'. The governor of Pentonville makes mention of him now writing to Mrs Ethel Hawley. Later still, she would become Miss Harvey.

Sunday, 30 October 1910

I had a letter from my solicitor saying the appeal might be heard on Thursday, and let us hope God will be good to us and bring me safely through in spite of it all.

My solicitor writes me he gave you £5, and says he will make great efforts with regard to what I want from him to you. I have replied to remind him of his promise and insisted as plainly as possible in his allowing you 30s a week as an advance until the Charing Cross Bank affairs are settled. I told him he ought to do it, as such a small weekly sum would not amount to much against the dividend that the bank is sure to pay out of £600, after some months. I write all this so you will know how to talk to him.

I have also told him I decidedly object to anything on the stage for you, darling . . . [one music-hall wife was clearly enough for one lifetime; Ethel had evidently received a, perhaps flippant, offer of a vaudeville tour in America, in a sketch, 'Caught by Wireless'] . . . My dinner is just waiting, and I must eat it while it is hot. Have just had a nice dinner – roast mutton, vegetables, soup, and fruit – and now back to my wifie again.

I have also told him that perhaps the friend who has come forward to pay the expenses of my appeal would be willing to advance the 30s per week I want for you (if my solicitor will not do it). Do not forget though, my own wifie, your promise to me to keep your money for yourself. If God helps us through safely, I myself, with you at my side to help me, will then help Horace to clear off all their debts as a little return for their great kindness. Please always when I write give my greatest love to them as I shall now only write to you for the present ... [The debts of Horace Brock, Ethel's brother-in-law, had also been referred to by Philip Gibbs in his account of ghosting Ethel's life story. Elsewhere in his letters Crippen would refer to the Brocks' misfortune. Perhaps Horace had started a business which had failed. Their misfortune would quadruple soon enough, during the First World War, when Nina became ill with tuberculosis] ...

I am glad you arranged the newspaper matter as you did. Remember you owe my solicitor nothing, as I myself arranged to pay all the expenses of the trial for you from the first. I am coming to the end of my letter, darling, and have not said half I want with regard to business, but must say this, there was £100 advanced by Mr Harvey (Mr Hamilton, he says) ... [this must be Eddie Marr, the quack remedy man] ... £114 odd realised from the sale of our furniture, and £500 for my memoirs.

Crippen's reference to his memoirs was evidently the tale he had been telling to Arthur Newton's clerk while he was still held at Brixton Prison. There was apparently an offer from a New York paper to publish the story, so perhaps that was the £500 offer. In the event, so far as I can establish, the story was published in *Lloyd's Weekly News* instead, and probably not for £500.

Crippen's letters betray his obsession with 'putting by' for

the future, whether his or Ethel's, or hers alone. He returned
to the theme of the memoirs the next day:

Monday, 31 October, 1910

My solicitor distinctly told me a friend had come
forward and guaranteed payment of the expenses of the
appeal with the understanding I would, in return, do
certain things that were not to be unreasonable, among
which I might be asked to open business in America . . .
[Eddie Marr, again] . . . Of course that would suit both
of us, would it not, darling wifie? So you see, as the
matter stands now, so far as I know – and my solicitor
has not written to me otherwise – the expenses of the
appeal are provided for, and, besides, he has Munyon's
offer.

I saw the two letters you enclosed about 'Lady S.' . . .
[Lady Henry Somerset] . . . I did not intend to write her
again, but today I had a letter from her asking about
you and saying she thought of publishing something
which she thought would help my appeal, so I had to
get permission to write and forbid her to do any such
thing.

Oh! Darling, there is so much I want to tell you and
so little time and space. I told my solicitor to notify
Scotland Yard that all property outside your own was to
be sent to his office, and that no one has a claim on it
but myself. This is to keep off those 'harpies' you
mention . . . [Harpies? Who could Ethel have been
describing? Surely not Belle's grieving sisters, or the
Music Hall ladies. That would have been in very poor
taste.]

. . . Legally no matter what happens, all comes to me,
and then I have instructed my solicitor you must be
allowed to select what you want, and the balance is to
be sold for you. As to Char. X Bank, they must pay
some dividend, and if only $\frac{1}{2}$d, that would mean a good
sum. My greatest grief has been the disappointment in

not being able to put all in your hands at once without all this trouble and made you independent of all.

One more thing on business, dearest. While at Brixton I wrote an account [twelve foolscap pages finely written] of my experiences of seven weeks, and my solicitor has this, yet unpublished. I am going to ask him to give it to you to be rewritten, as, with your experiences, you can enlarge on it, and then sell it as a help to my own dear wifie.

Do not forget to insist on having at once the trunk of silver, and sell it to best advantage for present needs, and get the MSS I have written, but get a good sum for it.

There was an anonymous letter to the prison governor: Belle had been seen entering a house in Upper Rathmines, Dublin with a tall man, last Thursday. Another letter to 'Mr Winston Churchill, Home Office, London' from Switzerland, enclosing a newspaper cutting from Canada which stated that Belle was alive in Alberta and had fainted on being told her husband was to hang.

There were letters pleading for mercy, in spite of the evidence, a letter from Belle herself, with a postmark London, SW: 'For the past four months I have been confined in a lovely house here. I am free tomorrow and will come to London and startle the world.' Another, from the same author perhaps: 'Don't hang my husband. He is innocent. I am alive in London but under restraint so cannot appear at present.' There was an abusive letter to Churchill threatening his life, the life of the judge and of the jury if Crippen hanged. It was signed, 'the black hand gang' and 'the unknown gang society'. It had been posted in Putney.

Tuesday, 1 November, 1910

Your visit last evening was precious indeed to me, but I am afraid I did all the talking, darling, and you had no time to explain much. Probably you did not have time to write to me last night, as I have had no letter yet.

Perhaps it may come later when the Governor comes in to see me.

In the meantime, wifie, I must content myself with those you have sent me up to now – four of them, and all treasured more than diamonds. I read them over and over again, and get great comfort from your loving words and the thought that, though we are separated, your love is all mine for always, as my love is yours to eternity. It is so precious a thought to me to tell you are always and ever my wifie, and that not even death can come between us. My heart rejoices in the promise that you will always bear the name you have taken, no matter what comes.

I suppose I am downhearted today because I have a letter from my solicitor saying the chance of anything from the Char. X Bank is most remote. I had looked forward to being able to provide wifie dearest the means of my own to keep you in comfort for a long time, and the bitterness of this terrible disappointment would be worse to me than death itself.

Pray God to help us in the appeal, that I may be spared to protect you again and keep you, darling, as I have always hoped. My only thoughts now are that you shall be kept from all harm in life, as I would keep you. We have been so long one in heart, soul, thought and deed that, wifie darling, nothing can separate our inward consciousness and spirit.

I had notice this morning that the appeal will be heard Thursday. Well, the sooner the better, if only my counsel and solicitor are prepared to fight.

Crippen seems so prosaic and undemonstrative in his character that these eloquent communications of his love and care for Ethel almost appear to emanate from a different person. But they are his letters and they must reflect his desperate situation, sitting in a condemned cell with nothing else but his words to draw Ethel to him; as death closes in he becomes increasingly uninhibited in his language, as if freed from the conventional restraints.

In his influential introduction to the case in the 1920 *Trial of H.H. Crippen*, one of the Notable Trials series, the journalist Filson Young describes Crippen as having been, at the end, looked upon by all, not only with respect but something like admiration. The very crime, says Young, brought out in Crippen high human qualities. Young is profoundly critical of Belle and seems determined to paint the case in black and white terms. There is nothing admirable or 'high human' in chopping up your wife – certainly not because she was, as Young would have it, extravagant and demanding and kept her kitchen filthy.

Still, in these letters, there is another Crippen, open-hearted and almost poetic in his turns of phrase and expressions of feeling. The only nagging worry is that he apparently had to murder someone to bring these feelings to the surface. Knowing her lover and his crime, Ethel might have wondered – as anyone surely would – if Crippen had once written to Belle in the same honeyed, and occasionally just a little mawkish, tones.

Wednesday, 2 November 1910
    You will find at Whitefriars Street safely today, I hope, the letter I wrote you yesterday ... [Whitefriars was just off Fleet Street, so must have been either the offices of the *Daily Chronicle* and *Lloyd's Weekly News* or the flat where Ethel was being kept] ... As I write I jot down the facts that come into my mind which I want you to know.
    Do not forget the prescription for 'Sans Peine', and that you add to the solution as made up from the presc. Five drops to each ounce of Adrenaline (Parke, Davis & Co.). You may be able to make a valuable deal with someone to put it on the market for you, either buying it outright or paying you a percentage on the sales, so much royalty per bottle. Then there is Ohrsorb – you

know the basis – and to this, to 14lbs goes 1 oz 1 od., resub., $\frac{1}{2}$ oz, Acid Sul., and 1 oz Sod. Brom. I believe Munyon would take it up for America, and perhaps pay you well to manage it, as you know so well our method of handling the correspondence.

You see, hub's darling, I am trying my best to see that you may be independent and not be led into any false step through obligation to anyone. I want my wifie's life to be a happy and comfortable one. That is the greatest desire of my heart. I had indeed hoped there would be enough left to let you establish yourself of some business, when you could order your life as you wished it, without being put into a position where another's will might force you to submit to anything opposed to your wishes.

I quite understand what people say, and even at the trial the prosecution deliberately misrepresented our relations to each other for their own ends. But I know there are many who can understand what we are to each other, truly husband and wife, sacredly so; no more sacred relations to each other such as ours could ever exist ... [what is this sacred pact of which Crippen makes so much? Is it simply that they have had sex, made love? Or could it be that he is making discreet reference to the secret of the murder that is shared between them?]

May God bless us again and restore us to each other, darling, and may God protect you and always keep you safe from harm. Every time I write you I find there is more to be said before I finish, and oh! How I long for our hopes to be realised that letters soon may no longer be necessary.

There was time for just one more letter, full of wishes, before the appeal was heard.

Friday, 4 November 1910

I hope you will find no trouble with my MS. As soon
as you have it look it over, and during one of your visits
tell me anything you do not understand. I expect they
will want to make a copy of the plans of the buildings I
have drawn, as they serve to illustrate ... [the drawings,
whatever they are, were never published and so far as I
know, have long since been lost. Perhaps they were the
homes of his early life. Or a plan of Hilldrop Crescent)
... I hope you can obtain a good price for it, to add to
what your clever little business has secured for your own
work ... [this must be a reference to Ethel's ghosted life
story, for which she must have told Crippen she had
earned enough to live on for the next couple of years, as
he went on to write ...] Yes, it is a comfort to me to
know you have secured for yourself sufficient to carry
you over two years, and if you do well with my MSS
and in the sale of the furs, etc., I shall feel satisfied you
will be well cared for.

I have had so many disappointments, I dare not even
hope tomorrow will bring release, but oh! how I pray to
be spared to take care of my own wifie and make her
happy again.

Three judges sat for the Court of Criminal Appeal on
Saturday, 5 November 1910. The appeal had originally been
scheduled for the Thursday, two days earlier, and Crippen's
barrister Tobin, perhaps genuinely already committed elsewhere, or possibly trying to wash his hands of Newton and the
case, had 'returned the brief', claiming a prior obligation in
Liverpool. His second, Huntly Jenkins had asked for an
adjournment to give himself time to prepare. The Appeal
Court judges had apparently insisted on Tobin's presence. So
on Saturday Tobin was there after all, and the first thing he
did was apologise for his mistake.

At least the delay had one beneficial effect, for Crippen. His execution had first been set for next Tuesday, 8 November, but would now have to be put back.

Tobin initially appealed on a single point, that a juror had fallen ill during the trial and had been separated from the other jurors. The jury ought to be kept together at all times. The juror had actually fainted during medical evidence, on the second day of the trial. A bevy of doctors – including Dr Willcox who was in the witness box at the time – had been on hand to attend to him and the juror had been taken from court, leaving his eleven colleagues still sitting there. The trial had eventually been adjourned for a couple of hours, to give him time to recover. Tobin argued that there had been a procedural irregularity that warranted a retrial.

The judges dismissed this point after hearing evidence that the juror had not discussed the case, nor had anyone spoken to him about it, while he was separated from the rest of the jury.

They also rejected Tobin's argument that the trial judge had been wrong to allow Muir's additional evidence about the pyjamas after the defence case had been concluded. According to him, this had been unfair to the defence, who might have marshalled their arguments differently, if they had known of the evidence beforehand. Tobin denied it, but the Appeal judges said surely he was complaining of a trap – Crippen having been led into a lie, which was promptly proved a lie. The Appeal judges said Crippen was bound to lie because the truth of the point was fatal.

Tobin was never going to succeed on his next point, that the remains were not proved to be those of a woman, or, if they were, that they were not proved to be those of Belle. The Appeal judges said the arguments for and against had been properly aired in court, for both sides, and the jury had been free to make their decision. There was plenty of evidence to support their verdict that the remains were Belle's.

The final complaint, that the Lord Chief Justice had betrayed bias in his summing-up, was also rejected.

The appeal was over.

Crippen had been brought to the Royal Courts of Justice in the Strand for the hearing, but was not in court at first. The judges had hoped to avoid the public spectacle of bringing him in, but when they decided to hear evidence about the fainting juror they decided that Crippen ought to be there to hear it too. He then remained for the rest of the hearing.

In an account of the appeal, in the next edition of the *Daily Mail*, signed 'By a barrister', Crippen was described coming into court:

> It was a very pitiable sight. A great deal has been written about the man's coolness and imperturbability. He was certainly neither at his first appearance on Saturday. His nervousness was painful to see . . . Thackeray wrote a paper once upon 'going to see a man hanged' and in that way ended for ever public executions in England. Perhaps another Thackeray will arise to write about 'going to see a condemned man listening to his appeal' so as to end that sight for ever too. It was certainly a horrible sensation to everyone in that court; so horrible that it is probably no exaggeration to say that few could take more than a furtive glance at him.

Remarkably, the Appeal Court was still less than forty years old. It was the first time the appellant had been present, in a capital case. 'A barrister' hoped it would be the last time, too.

SIXTEEN

Saturday, 5 November, 1910

The appeal has decided against us. Hope has completely gone, and your hub's heart is broken. No more can he hold his wifie in his arms, and the life he planned to devote to making your life comfortable is rapidly drawing to its end. Death has no terror for me. I fear not at all the passing from this life, but oh! wifie, my love, my own, the bitterness of the thought that I must leave you alone, without me in the world, to those who can never, I am sure, love you, cherish you, and protect you as I would have done hereafter as in the past.

These years past that we have been all in all to each other I was always looking forward to our happy life, to years together in a paradise of our own, like that we have always enjoyed since we have been everything to each other. I did not intend to write so mournfully, but my heart overflows in spite of all my efforts and opens itself to wifie, all I have in the world and all I ever wanted.

Your letter came after I had gone this morning, but I had it tonight, also another one, and one from Nina. Please tell Nina and Horace, although I cannot repay their great kindness to me, I shall pray God to help them through their troubles and make their life smoother and easier than in the past, and give them all my kindest love.

Your letters are such a comfort to me, my own wifie. I just feel your love surrounding me, and those dear, sweet words of your love shall lie on my heart at the last.

I hope you will have no trouble, now the appeal is finished, in getting everything from Scotland Yard through my solicitor. A new date will be fixed in place of 8 Nov., so I hope I shall be here long enough to know that you have everything all right. You see, I want you to have all my personal property, my watch ... chain, plain-band ring, clothes etc., as my gift to you now, so that there will be no question of these things being included in the property to be taken in under the proving of the will. Also, as my gift to you in the same way, of all the baskets of things taken from the house. There are two suits of clothes here and some other things which I want you to have, and any of my clothes you do not wish to keep please give to Horace.

About the diamonds, I want you to have them to wear as long as you can afford to keep them and to sell to help you anytime you need money. I shall on Monday write my solicitor to hand all those things over to you.

Today the Governor has written to the Home Office for permission for me to make a new will, explaining that I wish to cancel the one signed at Brixton, and also asking permission for the prison authorities to be witnesses. Now I do not want any mistake made in the wording of this will, so please on Monday have your solicitor on my authority draw up the will in proper form for signing and bring it with you on Monday night. I have had a talk with the Governor since I came back from the court, and he has been most kind in saying he will send permit for Monday in this.

I shall feel bereft of everything indeed if I cannot give you at least one good-bye kiss, but oh! wifie dear, I am fearful it may not be permitted. Still, when I know what day our last farewell must be, I shall beg the Home Office to grant us that favour ... [Crippen was pre-empting a debate that would shortly be taking place between the Home Office and the Prison Commissioners.]

It is comfort to my anguished heart to know you will always keep my image in your heart ... [perhaps Ethel has told him about the locket Gibbs had made for her] ... and believe, my darling, we shall meet again in another life. We have been always so entirely one in heart and soul, thought and deed ... [Deed? Another reference to the murder?] ...

even in flesh and spirit, I cannot believe otherwise but that we shall be together in that other life I am going to soon.

I am not so selfish, darling, as wish you not to marry again, but inasmuch as you have been the one woman who has had all my heart, so do I believe you will ever keep me in your heart.

If only I could have left you well provided for I would have wished our little one had lived that you might have had what would have been part of both of us. But like other things it was not to be ... [here is the reference to the miscarried pregnancy Ethel had suffered in 1908. This one reference to one lost child runs counter to the possibility that Ethel had a second pregnancy, and gave that baby up to her sister, as Ivy, in September 1909. Unless, somehow, though it seems improbable, Crippen never knew about it.]

To return to the will, tell your solicitor to draw it up by my authority, that it will not be necessary to come and see me. You can bring it and leave it with the Governor or leave it with the Chief Warder to give him. If you can I should like to know your plans for the future before I am gone; it would be a comfort to me indeed to know how wifie, my own darling, is to be provided for. If you have time on Monday try and get those notes from my solicitor, so that I can know soon if they will be of any value. No one shall get any statement, or anything else, except through wifie's hands.

I have not been able to keep the tears back tonight, the bitter news of the disappointment has been so terrible, and my longings for my wifie have been so intense, but I shall soon be brave again and keep up to the end. Were it possible I would wish to be cremated, and wish wifie then to dispose of my ashes as she desires. Please, darling, when you think of something to suggest or ask me, put it down on a memo to write me about or to ask me when you see me. The time is short, and we must try and think of everything for wifie's benefit and get all settled for you that I can accomplish.

Today at the appeal I realised more and more that the medical evidence for my defence was so mismanaged that it told against me rather than for me. This I saw at the Old Bailey in the judge's summing up and again today in the summing up of the Appeal. I am powerless now, and can do nothing more, but bow to the inevitable.

SEVENTEEN

The actor Seymour Hicks claimed that he was visiting a detective-friend at Bow Street Police Station on the day of Crippen's appeal. His friend said, 'Who do you think was here a moment ago? It was Ethel Le Neve. She wanted to know if she could "borrow" the pair of trousers she had worn when she had been arrested disguised as a boy.' She had been offered money to be photographed wearing them – which was true, there was a series of studio portraits of her in a man's suit, looking very androgynous, one of which appeared in the *Daily Mirror* and another that illustrated Crippen's 'farewell message' in *Lloyd's Weekly News*, three days before his execution. As Ethel and the police officer had been discussing this, Hicks was told, the news had come through of the failed appeal. 'Oh,' Ethel had said.

Chief Inspector Dew had also waited for the appeal before handing in his resignation, apparently giving a month's notice that he would leave on 5 December, when he would begin receiving his police pension. His motive in resigning was never disclosed. All he would say in his autobiography was that he had 'special private reasons'. He was reported to have made the decision before the Crippen case and then stayed on to see it through.

Ethel's life story began its serialisation that Sunday, the day after the appeal, in *Lloyd's*. She was photographed for the front page in a high-buttoned blouse with a locket pinned to her left breast. This must have the one with the miniature Crippen inside it, a private message that he was still close to her heart, as she was to his, in the letter he wrote that very day, reflecting on Sundays past.

Sunday, 6 November 1910

All day I sit here by a table with my eyes on a book, and I suppose the guards believe me to be reading, but over and over again the words are only a blank before my eyes, and the book with pictures of ourselves together. I see ourselves in those days of courtship, having our dinner together after our day of work together was done, or sitting sometimes in our favourite corner in Frascati's by the stairway, all the evening listening to the music. The dinner too with Nina with us, in anticipation of her marriage; and ah! how even in those early days we began to realise how near and dear we were to become to each other.

One Sunday, how early I came for you – six years ago last summer it was – and we had a whole day together, which meant so much to us then. A rainy day indeed, but how happy we were together with all sunshine in our hearts. It is good to think, darling wifie, that even in those early days before our wedding came that we were always in perfect harmony with each other. Even without being wedded.

Then came those days when hub felt, and wifie too so earnestly felt, it was impossible to live on and not be all in all to each other, and from our wedding day . . . [this just must be, cannot possibly be anything other than, the day they had sex for the first time] . . . all has been a perfect honeymoon of four years to 6 Dec. next.

That Monday, a man appeared before Cambridge Borough Magistrates to volunteer himself as a substitute for Crippen at his hanging. No doctor, he said, should be permitted to suffer the most extreme penalty of the law and he was ready to die instead. The man was an old soldier, known locally for his eccentric habits. The magistrates told him he would have to make his application in London, where Dr Crippen would probably not object. The man thanked the court and withdrew.

The execution was re-scheduled for 23 November. Crippen's solicitor told reporters that he had sent a petition of

2,500 signatures to the King, apparently seeking a royal pardon, based on the contention that the remains were not proved to be Belle's. Newton immediately started a new petition for a reprieve, taking signatures at his luxuriously appointed offices in Great Marlborough Street.

The Lord Chief Justice must have been asked his views about the prospect of a reprieve and wrote, as he had after the trial, that he could see no grounds. 'Crippen's motive for the murder was probably a mixed one,' he said, 'desire to establish closer relations with Le Neve and to possess himself of the jewels and money.' It had been a cold-blooded and deliberate crime carried out and concealed with horrible ingenuity. There could be no question of a reprieve. He noted that the medical evidence for the defence had been badly shaken in cross-examination.

Someone wrote to the Home Office complaining that Ethel was being allowed to visit Crippen when another convicted killer who had recently been hanged, John Dickman, had been denied the opportunity to see and kiss his own children good-bye. Dickman had been hanged in Newcastle for the robbery and murder of a colliery pay clerk, John Nisbit, on a train. He too had protested his innocence.

The note was sent to Churchill, with a memo from a Home Office official pointing out that Dickman had been allowed to see his wife and children constantly before his execution. It was, however, not improbable that Ethel would ask to be allowed to kiss Crippen at their final interview: 'It is kinder to the parties themselves to keep such interviews as formal and unemotional as possible. Shall the governor be so instructed?' Churchill did not agree. 'I see no reason for any such instruction,' he said. 'Every precaution must however be taken against the prisoner becoming possessed of poison.'

Though they had at least waited for the outcome of the appeal, you might have thought that Madame Tussaud's would have allowed a decent interval after the execution, before putting Crippen on display. But they were already advertising his presence in *The Times of* 8 November: 'Madame Tussaud's

Exhibition. In the Extra Rooms. Lifelike Portrait Model of Hawley Harvey Crippen. Open from 10 am till 10 pm. Now on view.'

There was no mention of Ethel, but she ended up there too. They were together, side by side in the Chamber of Horrors, as they had been photographed in the dock at Bow Street, those photographs apparently the basis for the tableau. Crowds gathered to see Crippen there at the next bank holiday. *The Times* was asked to scotch the rumour – an urban myth, in all but name – that Tussaud's was willing to pay a large sum of money, variously stated as being from £100 up to £1,000, to anyone who would spend the night in the Chamber of Horrors. Tussaud's clerical staff, said *The Times*, were quite unable to cope with the number of applications from volunteers. Crippen has been in the waxworks ever since. He is still there now. Ethel was removed in 1996. Her head was pulped.

Crippen wrote some letters to Ethel that did not survive or find their way into the newspapers. A couple are mentioned in Home Office memos, where the Governor of Pentonville Prison, Major Mytton-Davies, conscientiously referred them up the bureaucratic chain, when he thought they might contain contentious comments. Ethel herself told the readers of *Lloyd's* that his daily letter had been to her and not once had he made an exception. That would be some thirty letters from conviction to execution and nothing like that number entered the public domain. She claimed that she would always keep his letters, but I don't think she did.

The Governor seems to have allowed Crippen to read the first instalment of Ethel's *Lloyd's* saga. The date of this letter from him is unknown, but it must have been some time that week.

What a nice long letter from you this morning, and what comfort do I indeed derive from wifie's loving words. I was anxious to read what you had written in my defence, and you have, my wifie dear, most ably set forth important facts that must tell with great weight in the minds of the unprejudiced. Well, we must wait patiently the end, whatever God wills it to be.

Should it be that I must die, I have no fear of that, sure of my wifie's comfort to the end and of being with her in spirit after, until we are united where there is no more separation. Should I be spared, we must look forward to time to prove my conviction unjust, with your help, to drag out the evidence that someday must be found.

I have never intended to wound you, wifie dear, with suggesting I might become a burden to you, but I know my wifie understands I could not bear to think my love might be so selfish as to ask of you an unreasonable sacrifice. Darling, my own wifie dear, you can see, I am sure, that my love for you has become so great, so absorbing that I was afraid I should ask of you, in my longings to be all in all to you, what would be unreasonable. But no, dearest, I shall only think now that as I would have been ready any time and at all times to lay down my life and soul to make you happy, so you too are mine forever.

I am glad the photo in the *Mirror* brought you a few more pounds, and I thoroughly appreciate the joke on them. The papers have treated us so shamefully they all owe us a great reparation, which we shall never get. It is impossible to deny that everyone was prejudiced by the newspaper lies.

The joke on the *Mirror* could perhaps have been Ethel, unable to get the actual suit she had worn, borrowing or buying a different suit and claiming to them it was the original. Crippen was evidently overlooking the not so shameful generosity of *Lloyd's* in providing temporary shelter for his beloved wifie and enough money that she would be able to look after herself over the next couple of years. If Ethel was shameless enough to have dealings with them, he could hardly complain of the newspapers' shamefulness.

With next Wednesday's execution now only six days away, Newton had collected 15,000 signatures for his petition to reprieve. Newton took the petition round to the Home Office in a taxi, pausing only to tell reporters that this was a measure of the spontaneous nature of Crippen's support and suggesting that, whatever the suspicions of the case might be, the case had not been proved and Crippen was entitled to the benefit of the doubt.

There was no great public appetite for a hanging, and some indication that Crippen was becoming a popular figure, on the grounds that he had been harshly judged in court and there was still uncertainty about the case against him. There was, I suspect, a sense that he did not seem like a murderer, that quiet little man.

Ethel had evidently been preparing an article to be published in Crippen's name on the eve of his execution. She appeared to have combined the text of some of his letters with some of the life story material that he had dictated to his solicitor's clerk at Brixton. When she took it to Pentonville, the Governor asked the Prison Commissioners what he was supposed to do with it. The statement had been prepared and amplified by Miss Le Neve, he told them, and she had asked that the prisoner be allowed to read, correct and sign it so that she could collect it when she came back later for her eight o'clock visit to Crippen. It was intended for publication that Sunday in *Lloyd's Weekly News*. The commissioners were not happy and said it was very undesirable that such a letter should be signed and published. The Governor was told to tell Ethel that it had been referred to the Home Office, where an official said it was bad enough for newspapers to be filled with statements made by notorious prisoners. That, perhaps, could not be helped. But there was no need to let Crippen put his name to sentiments attributed to him by another person, probably a journalist. In the end, Ethel was given back the statement, unread and unsigned by Crippen.

On Saturday evening, at about 9.15 pm, the Governor was called by the Home Office and told that the petition for a reprieve had been rejected. It was Churchill's decision, though he was not personally involved in the phone call or the formal letter that followed it. The Governor went straight away to the condemned cell and passed on the news to his prisoner. Crippen described it in his next letter to Ethel:

Monday, 21 November 1910

How can I find the strength and heart to struggle through this last letter? God, indeed, must hear our cry to Him for Divine help in this last farewell. How to control myself to write I hardly know, but pray God help us to be brave to face the end now so near.

The thoughts rush to my mind quicker than I can put them down. Time is so short now, and there is so much that I would say. There are less than two days left to us, only one more letter after this can I write you, and only two more visits, one tonight before you read this letter and one tomorrow.

When I wrote to you on Saturday, I had not heard any news of the petition, and though I never at any time dared hope, yet deep down in my heart was just a glimmer of trust that God might give us yet a chance to put me right before the world and let me have the passionate longing of my soul.

Your letter written early Saturday came to me late Saturday evening and soon after the Governor brought me the dreadful news about ten o'clock. He was so kind and considerate in telling me, in breaking the shock as gently as he could. He was most kind and left me at last with 'God bless you; good night', that I know you will ever remember him most kindly for his goodness.

When he had gone I first kissed your face in the photo, my faithful devoted companion in all this sorrow. Oh! how glad I was I had the photo. It was some consolation, although, in spite of all my greatest efforts, it was impossible to keep down a great sob and my heart's agonised cry.

How am I to endure to take my last look at your face; what agony must I go through at the last when you disappear for ever from my eyes! God help us to be brave then.

The latest edition of the weekly *John Bull* had published an open letter to Crippen, inviting him to unburden his soul and confess before he hanged. The editor of *John Bull*, Horatio Bottomley MP, a friend of Arthur Newton's, had forwarded the open letter to Pentonville and asked that it be passed to Crippen. The Governor sought advice and was told to ignore it: 'We do not allow even the chaplain to put pressure on a prisoner to confess. The present proposal is monstrous.'

Newton went to see Crippen that Monday. He must have been so used to seeing them that he completely forgot that there were the usual three warders sitting in on his interview. As the most senior of the warders, George Ball, later described it, in a deposition to the Law Society, Newton said to Crippen at some point that there was an open letter in *John Bull* to him. Ball had interrupted, saying, 'That will not do, sir.' Crippen had anyway said he knew nothing about it. Nothing more was said on the subject.

No letter had passed between Crippen and Newton, according to Ball, which was puzzling because the next edition of *John Bull* produced a letter amounting to a confession purporting to have been written and signed by Crippen in his death cell. Worse still, Newton would later write to the *Daily Chronicle* – at Bottomley's urging – saying that Crippen's confession letter had been forwarded to *John Bull* through him.

Crippen told *John Bull*, in the letter he had never written, that he was grateful for the interest taken in him and touched by some of the passages in *Bull*'s open letter. 'As to making any statement which could implicate anybody else in this terrible business that is altogether out of the question ... I am expecting to see an old friend tomorrow to whom I may possibly say more than I can now ... Mr Newton [he was the old friend] has my fullest confidence and I am leaving all my affairs in his hands. If, when it is all over, he cares to tell you more than I can say today I am sure you will treat the matter in the same broad and sympathetic spirit in which you have written me ... again thanking you ...' *John Bull* said below that it hoped to give the True Story of the Crime, which had never yet been told, the following week.

Newton later said that Bottomley had initially asked him to find out if Crippen had seen his open letter, and he could hardly refuse because Bottomley had assisted in a substantial way with the case. He told the Law Society that Bottomley had paid two sums of money to Crippen's defence, one of 50 guineas and one of £150. He explained his letter to the *Daily Chronicle* by saying that he had received the draft while he was at lunch and looked over it hurriedly before saying, 'I can't be bothered now' and rushing to catch a train.

The truth was that the Crippen confession letter had been cooked up in Bottomley's offices in Long Acre. Newton had gone there straight from his prison visit with Crippen and when he arrived there empty-handed, Bottomley called in a Mr Wray, one of his sub-editors, who took a shorthand note as first Bottomley and then Newton dictated the text of the letter. Wray said he had simply typed it up and added Crippen's signature.

Newton insisted to the Law Society that he had not seen or participated in writing any false letter. They didn't believe him.

Following a High Court hearing the next year, Newton was found guilty of professional misconduct and suspended for twelve months. The judges said Crippen's defence had not been conducted as it should have been, but largely for the purpose of making 'copy' for the newspapers. Newton had lied and abused the privilege of prison visits. Two years later he would be struck off altogether and go to prison on a two-year sentence, after being convicted of criminal fraud in a separate case. (The prosecutor would be Travers Humphreys.) Later still, Bottomley would also go to prison, for seven years, on a conviction for fraud.

Newton was lucky that the Law Society did not pursue his second, even more flagrant bogus confession, which was published on the day of the hanging in a London newspaper, the *Evening Times*, which was then new and trying to make a name for itself, and would not survive very long. It was said that Newton had received £500 for his part in the *Evening Times*'s confession exclusive. They even issued a statement the following day, after numerous official denials (including one from Newton) defending the truth of their story, though they well knew it was a lie. There had never been any confession.

The death of Crippen's father, Myron Augustus, aged eighty-three, was reported from Los Angeles around this time but, if he heard about it, Crippen never referred to the death in his published letters. It was suggested that Myron's end had been hastened by the worry of his son's arrest. He was said to have been suffering financially, too, since the regular payments Crippen used to send him had stopped. There was no other evidence, beyond this newspaper account, that Crippen took a role in caring for his father. They had not seen each other for at least a decade and probably much longer. Perhaps the two deaths, of father and son, so close together, were just an unhappy coincidence.

Though he had not been able to read or sign it beforehand, Crippen did at least get to read his own Farewell Message to the readers of *Lloyd's Weekly News*, the day after it was published. He told Ethel in his last letter, 'The Governor was so kind as to let me read yesterday afternoon your story [the second half had appeared in *Lloyd's* the week before] and my statement. I am indeed so grateful to have been permitted to do so at the last. I find though, in some way, they have omitted that part entirely in which I criticised the Crown's evidence on the scar and on the absence of a navel. My criticism on this point was important and I hope you can get it put in next Sunday.'

Thus, there was not one, but two farewell messages from

Crippen, the second appearing on the Sunday after the execution and making amends for the omission of the previous week, in addition to publishing much of his final two letters. He seemed, at the last, to have become fixated on the flaws in the case against him, as if he was an innocent man, unjustly going to the gallows. Ethel must have gone along with this, and there is some suggestion that she was seeking information from the hospital in Philadelphia where Belle's operation had been carried out, years earlier. The inquiries were soon forgotten, though, after he was gone.

I don't propose to reproduce his lengthy and repetitious complaints about the prosecution or his claims for Ethel's innocence in full. But here is an abridged version of the article he sat reading about himself, based on his own words, in his cell, just before his execution:

20 NOVEMBER 1910, *LLOYD'S WEEKLY NEWS*

DR CRIPPEN

✻

FAREWELL MESSAGE

THROUGH

'LLOYD'S NEWS'

We have received the following message from Dr Crippen, through Miss Le Neve, with the request that it should be published in *Lloyd's News*:

Pentonville Prison

This is my farewell letter to the world. After many days of anxious expectation that my innocence might be proved, after enduring the final agony of a long trial and the suspense of an appeal, and after the final endeavour of my friends to obtain a reprieve, I see that at last my doom is sealed and that in this life I have no more hope.

With all the courage I have I face another world and another Judge – from Whom I am sure of justice greater than that of this world and of mercy greater than that of men. I have no dread of death, no fear of the hereafter, only the dread and agony that one whom I love best may suffer when I have gone . . . But in this letter of farewell I desire to make a last appeal to the world not to think the worst of me, and to believe words now written from the condemned cell. I beg them to remember that I have been condemned on inconclusive evidence, and chiefly by evidence of expert witnesses who were contradicted by other experts upon the most vital point of the case – the scar found upon the remains in Hilldrop Crescent . . .

. . . In spite of my fate there is one working for me now in collecting fresh evidence, and it is still possible that after my death the real truth may be revealed.

Face to face with God, in Whose presence my soul shall soon stand for final judgement, I still maintain that I was wrongly convicted, and my belief that facts will yet be forthcoming to prove my innocence.

I solemnly state that I knew nothing of the remains discovered at Hilldrop Crescent until I was told of their discovery by my solicitor Mr Arthur Newton, on the next day after my arrival at Bow Street.

My conviction was obtained on purely circumstantial evidence, and I am positive that if I had at my disposal a sum equal to that spent by the Crown on the prosecution, the important points of that evidence would have been rebutted so decidedly that a conviction would have been impossible.

I possess no legal training or knowledge but I shall venture to analyse some points which are, to my mind, of the greatest importance . . .

. . . About my unhappy relations with Belle Elmore I will say nothing. We drifted apart in sympathy; she had her own friends and pleasures, and I was a rather lonely man and rather miserable. Then I obtained the affection and sympathy of Miss Ethel Le Neve.

I confess that according to the moral laws of Church and

State we were guilty, and I do not defend our position in that respect. But what I do say is that this love was not of a debased and degraded character.

It was – if I may say so to people who will not, perhaps, understand or believe, a good love. She comforted me in my melancholy condition. Her mind was beautiful to me. Her loyalty and courage and self-sacrifice were of a high-character. Whatever sin there was – and we broke the law – it was my sin, not hers . . .

. . . Facing my maker, very close to the hour of my death, I give my testimony to the absolute innocence of Ethel Le Neve . . . I believe she has told in full detail the story of her adventures in boy's clothes, and although I have not been permitted to read a line of her narrative, I know that every word is true, for she has the heart of truth. I feel sure, also, that she has said no unkind word about me . . .

. . . We were as man and wife together, with an absolute communion of spirit. Perhaps God will pardon us because we were like two children in the great unkind world, who clung to one another and gave each other courage . . .

. . . Oh! the bitterness of the thought that I must leave her alone to those who can never love her and protect her as I would have done! I had been looking forward to a happy life – to years together in a little paradise of our own. And now I have to face the great separation of death . . .

. . . During these last days I have sat with my eyes fastened upon a book, so that my warders may have imagined me to be reading. But the words have swum before my eyes, and I have been thinking all the time of the last letter and the letter to come, of the last visit and the hope of the next, from the woman who has been dear to me.

I have been thinking by day and by night of what little thing I might do, while wifie is still mine, to protect her interests, and to ensure, as far as may be, her future welfare. I am thankful that she has found good friends to help her and guard her, at least for a time, from people only too willing to take advantage of her helplessness, and I am still more thankful that she has steeled her heart, with splendid courage, to endure the tragedy of these black days.

I myself have endeavoured to be equally courageous, yet there have been times during her visits to me when an agony of intense longing has taken possession of me, when my very soul has cried out to clasp her hand and speak those things which are sacred between a man and woman who have loved.

Alas! We have been divided by the iron discipline of prison rules, and warders have been the witnesses of our grief.

Why do I tell these things to the world? Not to gain anything for myself – not even compassion. But because I desire the world to have pity on a woman who, however weak she may have seemed in their eyes, has been loyal in the midst of misery and to the very end of tragedy, and whose love had been self-sacrificing and strong.

These are my last words.

I belong no more to the world.

In the silence of my cell I pray that God may pity all weak hearts, all the poor children of life, and His poor servant, Hawley Harvey Crippen

Crippen was hanged at 9 am on Wednesday, 23, November 1910.

EIGHTEEN

The execution provoked a debate on the letters pages of *The Times*, which began with a rather magnificent declaration of disapproval by Arthur C. Benson, a noted poet and biographer, newly celebrated for writing the words of 'Land of Hope and Glory' to Elgar's music for King Edward's coronation.

Benson's long letter, written on 30 November after a respectable interval of one week, complained that it was 'horrible to reflect' that the case had given thousands of people the keenest excitement and even enjoyment. Excitement might be inevitable, given the pursuit of a suspect in such sensational circumstances, and he did not want to raise the rights and wrongs of capital punishment in general, but why did the whole frightful business have to take so long? The attendant publicity made it seem like a return to public executions.

> There seems to me something frightfully cold-blooded, in the midst of our boasted humaneness and our ordered civilisation, in allowing the perpetration of so sickening a drama to continue as the execution which has just taken place. A man at such a crisis of his fate is not a thing to exult and gloat over, whatever his crime may have been; and I believe that the solemn barbarity of the whole proceeding has an entirely debasing and degrading effect on the public mind.
>
> I confess that I found myself profoundly thankful when all was over, and I wish I could feel that the compassion and generosity and dignity of all just and kind English hearts would find such expression as would make it possible for a thing so inhuman, so disgraceful, and so ghastly to be

relegated once and for all to the class of horrors with which society has bravely and wholesomely dispensed.

The debate ran to fifteen letters in all, plus a leading article, and continued over Christmas. As Benson had perhaps intended, the discussion quickly became one about the value of capital punishment.

The most eloquent campaigner was the journalist Filson Young, who would go on to edit the account of *The Trial of H.H. Crippen* in the Notable Trials series. His arguments prefigured the case for abolition of the death penalty that was still being promoted over fifty years later, when the last hangings in Britain were carried out simultaneously, one in Liverpool, one in Manchester, at 8 am on 13 August 1964.

You could also trace, in Young's letter, that part of the discussion that still rages today about the difficulties of expressing compassion for both the perpetrator and the victim of a crime. And here, perhaps, were the origins of his sympathetic portrait of Crippen in his introduction to *The Trial*.

He said he had studied the whole business and routine and apparatus of executions and could assure Benson that the reality was incredibly more brutal, sordid and barbarous than anything which could be imagined from mere description or sketches. 'I do not think we have any right to "punish" people by killing them . . . But, it is argued by some, the excuse for the death penalty is that it acts as a deterrent to others. It is extremely hard to get any statistics on this point, but I am afraid that the balance of such information as is obtainable is in support of the theory. But what then is the logical application of that theory? It is that the criminal dies for the benefit of the State. His murder by the State is defended on the ground that it does other people good . . .'

Part of the carelessness of people with regard to a subject like this, according to Young, was because they insisted upon regarding the unfortunate people to whom these calamities happened as being of entirely different stuff from themselves. Nice people, people one knew, did not get hanged; those who did were unmitigated scoundrels, and probably deserved all they got ... It was really amazing that people continued to have the courage to decide what other people 'deserved' in the way of torture and punishment. 'It is nothing to them that half the people who become entangled in this ghastly machinery of death have all their lives been tortured and punished, not by whips and irons, but by miserable and squalid environment, lack of fit education, lack of beauty and brightness in their lives.'

Young said that it was not fair to imply, as *The Times* and several of its correspondents had, that because Mr Benson had pity for the victim of the scaffold he had no pity for the victim of the murderer. Of course, we all had pity for the murdered person, but the expression of it was no use; whereas the criminal was still, while he lived, in our charge and we were responsible for him. To be cruel to him could not benefit his victim; yet some of the correspondents had written as though any attempts to show human feeling for a man awaiting death by hanging amounted to a condonation of his crime; and as though any mitigation of his sufferings (which in the case of Crippen were infinitely greater than those of the murdered woman) were in some way robbing the victim of a benefit.

(On reading this, I wondered what miserable and squalid environment Filson Young had in mind for Crippen. The kitchen of his home, it must have been, which Belle had so carelessly failed to keep clean.)

Young's sentiments were broadly absolutely right, and some way ahead of their time. All the same, it would not be easy to defend the argument that Crippen's suffering – appalling though it must have been – was 'infinitely greater' than Belle's.

Contemporary newspapers confidently asserted that Ethel had chosen to emigrate on the day of the execution. She was said to have booked passage on the liner *Majestic*, which sailed from Southampton at midday on 23 November, for New York, and so was boarding at about the time Crippen was hanged. They said she had travelled under the name Miss Allen. This version of events has never been contested and appeared in the last and best book about the case, *Crippen the Mild Murderer*, by Tom Cullen, published twenty-eight years ago.

According to Cullen, after boarding the *Majestic* in her 'widow's weeds', Ethel went and lived in Toronto and did not return to England until 1916, when she came back to nurse her dying sister Nina and then used the name Ethel Nelson.

To all intents and purposes, Ethel vanished from public view on 23 November 1910 and, with one exception, remained hidden, even beyond her death in 1967 at the age of eighty-four. In her lifetime only one journalist ever found and spoke to her, and she only spoke to her briefly on two occasions in her fifty-seven remaining years.

It was true that there had been an Elsie Allen among the ten unaccompanied female passengers on board the *Majestic* when it left for New York, but *she was* Elsie Allen, not Ethel Le Neve. Ethel was still in England during 1911 and I have found proof that she was back in London in mid-1913.

I started to believe that she had never been to Canada at all, but then I spoke to her son Bob, who recalled a conversation with his mother from his own childhood in which she had described trying to start a new life in Canada, and not getting on very well. He recalled her mentioning Ontario and other places and had the impression that she had been travelling around by train. She had become ill and had no one to look after her. She had not found much warmth or friendship among the people she had met. Bob did not know exactly when she'd gone or when she'd returned, but he believed she returned to England in 1912.

It seems likely that she left London for a while, immediately after the execution. She never used the name of Nelson, to the best of my knowledge, but remained faithful to Crippen's request that she take his forenames as her surname and so somehow remain 'wedded' to him. She lived for three years in Battersea from 1913 and then moved to South Norwood and eventually to Croydon, where she lived out most of the rest of her life.

The single extraordinary thing about this next world of Ethel's, is that she married in 1915 and had two children, and never told her husband or her son or her daughter that she had once been Ethel Le Neve. They never knew. Ethel's husband even wore the fob watch that had been Crippen's, which he had left for her at his death. Ethel continued to socialise and engage with her siblings who grew up, married and had children of their own. Even though they, of course, knew her history, because they had lived through it, they somehow understood that it was not to be discussed and never brought it up with Ethel, or her husband or children.

It was as if Ethel led two quite separate lives, one as Miss Le Neve and another as the conveniently anonymous but perfectly genuine Mrs Smith, the wife of Stanley Smith. Ethel Le Neve had effectively died with Crippen. There was some occasional blurring of the division between these two lives, but not much. One relative – a niece of Ethel's who had found out about the crime on discovering a box of old cuttings hidden in the loft of her home – told me of her disappointment, on meeting Ethel for the first time, anticipating a glamorous, femme fatal-type character, and instead being confronted with a small, quiet, myopic woman who enjoyed embroidery. Her only concession to her racy past was her habit of smoking heavily.

'Weren't you bursting to ask your Aunt Ethel about her past life?' 'No,' said Iris Crawford, Ethel's niece, 'I wouldn't have dreamed of it. You just didn't talk about things in those days, did you?'

Still, I imagine those encounters with her siblings to have been uncomfortable for Ethel, knowing that her extended family knew her secret, while her immediate family did not. She must always have been on her guard, in case some remark should slip out and give the game away. Although, of course, you could never overestimate a family's capacity to keep its secrets.

Ivy, the daughter of Nina, who was born in 1909 after Ethel's seven-month disappearance from her London home of the time, also married and had a son and never told anyone she was related to Ethel Le Neve. She finally disclosed the family connection to her son Roger, as she faced death following a stroke in 1992. There was talk of insuring Ivy's rings and her husband was saying he would take charge of them. Ivy spoke privately to her son, and asked him to look after the rings instead. One of those rings had belonged to her aunt. Her aunt, she explained, had been Ethel Le Neve. She told Roger she had never told her husband, who survived her, and Roger never told his father either, so he died without ever knowing he had been married to Ethel's close relative.

Roger then recalled meeting Ethel once when he was just a boy, and after his mother's death was able to look back in her diaries and find that he had visited Ethel's home with his mother on 10 April 1956. Ethel would then have been seventy-three. He remembered that the ceiling was dirty, or in need of repair, and that Ethel could not have noticed because she had cataracts. He remembered too that he had played that day with Ethel's grandson, Vaugn, from her daughter, who was named Nina, surely in tribute to Ethel's sister, who had been Roger's grandmother.

Because Ivy had always told her son she was born in Diss, Norfolk, Roger was surprised to hear from me that in fact she had been registered as being born in Tottenham. He wondered if this was a way of dissociating herself from her relationship to Ethel's notoriety, as perhaps, her change of name had been – she was always known as Molly, not Ivy, and Roger could find no other rational explanation for the name change.

Roger sat graciously and listened to my theory about Ivy – his own mother – and the possibility, for that was all it was, that she was Ethel's child. 'So that would make me Crippen's grandson?' said Roger.

Was this something that could have been hidden, perhaps even from Ivy?

*

Cullen, and all the many other earlier authors of books about the case, did not have the benefit of access to the various files on the case which have since entered the public domain of the National Archives. They helped to clear up some of the errors and assumptions that had been perpetrated over the years. Here and there, the papers in the files offered faint clues to Ethel's whereabouts and much firmer evidence of her determination to claim her dues.

It was always written that Crippen had been buried with the letters he received from Ethel and the photograph of her, the single photograph he had been allowed to keep with him in his cell, which he described having kissed after hearing his reprieve had been denied. The unsourced version of events was that Crippen had been granted this final request by the Governor. Cullen said there were four letters from Ethel, but actually there must have been many more and it seems unlikely that a Governor who, in other respects was such a stickler for the rules, with his constant referrals to his superiors for their advice, could have overlooked the regulations for this request.

In fact, the files prove that Crippen had asked for something completely different, in relation to the photograph of Ethel. He had written a final private message to her on the back of it, and asked that it be returned to her.

On the very next day, after the execution, the Governor told his superiors that he had already received a written request from Ethel asking for all Crippen's belongings that were being kept at the prison, including his spectacles and the suit in which he had been hanged. Naturally, the Governor sought advice for this request, also pointing out that Crippen had 'desired that the photo of Miss Le Neve which he was allowed to have might be returned to her. He has written a farewell letter on the back of it, but there is nothing objectionable.'

One of Churchill's deputies told the Governor that the clothes should be destroyed and the spectacles should be kept at the prison in case a question over Crippen's suicide attempt should arise. Le Neve was to be told that the clothes had been destroyed, according to custom.

The Governor was unwilling to fall in with this. He produced 'a list of articles belonging to the prisoner' and asked if everything was to be destroyed, or only the things that Crippen had been wearing at his death. He enclosed the photo of Le Neve and said – somewhat disapprovingly – that as she was disposing of so much to the press, she might also dispose of these last words. Since the Governor had not given his permission to Crippen to write these words, he asked if he should retain the photo and not allow it to pass out of the prison. He said that the prisoner had expressed a wish that Miss Le Neve have all the things belonging to him, and so he would be glad of instructions as to what he might hand over.

9146 H.H. CRIPPEN
INVENTORY OF CLOTHING, ETC.

1 overcoat

1 coat

1 waistcoat

1 trousers

2 hats

4 shirts

pr. drawers

4 socks

5 handkerchiefs

1 handkerchief silk

10 collars

2 bows

1 pr gloves

6 books

1 gladstone bag

1 toothbrush

Cash 5s 4½d

1 pair of spectacles

For some reason, the photograph was not listed. Nor was

there any mention of Ethel's letters. Perhaps Crippen had returned them to her, before the execution. Perhaps they had been destroyed or perhaps they really were buried with him. There is no mention of the letters in any of the papers in the files. They vanished, along with those of Crippen's letters to Ethel which she did not 'dispose' of to the press. There is no mention either, in this list, of his rings or his fob watch, which definitely passed to Ethel.

At least two rings belonging to Ethel were later handed on to members of her extended family, one with the explanation that it had been given to her by Crippen. The only other item of his that I know she kept for most of the rest of her life was the fob watch. I can only assume that she later destroyed whatever else – letters, photographs, clothes – she may have collected or kept at the time. Perhaps the destruction had become a ritual of ending. Making way for the next life.

At the same time as this discussion was being batted back and forth between the prison and the Home Office, Belle's sister, Theresa Hunn, instructed solicitors in London to act for her in challenging the probate of Belle's estate. Belle had left no will and so, in ordinary circumstances, her estate would pass to the next of kin, her husband, who had willed his estate to Ethel, meaning that she would get everything of Belle's too. Hence the legal action from Hunn, who was represented by Harold Seyd, the lawyer for the Music Hall Ladies Guild. Perhaps the Guild had put Hunn up to the challenge.

The Governor was called by the Home Office and told that, since a caveat had been enforced against probate of the will, nothing was to be handed over to Miss Le Neve. The official was waiting for Churchill's authority to destroy the photograph with the message. Churchill finally saw the photograph for himself and read the message and decided it should go to Ethel. The Governor had obviously been reading the newspapers and told the Home Office he believed Ethel had left the country.

After her acquittal, the end of the criminal proceedings against her, Ethel had fired Arthur Newton and taken new representation from Hopwood & Sons, a firm of solicitors at 13 South Square, Gray's Inn. They had been acting for Ethel in her quest to obtain Crippen's effects. The Governor now wrote to them, asking where he should send the photograph and was told she was 'at present away in the country' (not 'out of the country' but 'in the country'), so he should send it to the lawyers.

There was one other clue to Ethel's whereabouts at this time. In his final letter to her (see the final chapter) Crippen had made two references to a Mrs H. The letter had been reproduced in his own handwriting in *Lloyd's* of 27 November, where he had said he would leave it to Ethel to decide whether to put on mourning after his death and he realised it might not be well for her to do it in going to Mrs H. He had later said he greatly hoped Ethel had heard favourably from Mrs H. and that she might soon go to her, where she would be comfortable and made more cheerful by the bright sunshine and be free entirely from the newspaper men and their lying tales.

Who was Mrs H.? There was only one Mrs H. I knew of among their network of acquaintances and that was Mrs Adelene Harrison, Belle's self-appointed biographer, and she had moved from Islington to Brixton, which was not exactly the country, nor associated with bright sunshine. She seemed an unlikely candidate to offer shelter to Ethel.

There was Lady Henry Somerset who could, colloquially, have been Mrs H. but Ethel and Crippen seemed to have fallen out with her. The wife of Hopwood the solicitor? If she was any kind of acquaintance at all, she would be a very new one. There was no one else and no other clue to Mrs H.'s identity. It could have been someone Ethel had met on remand in Holloway, or someone who had recently come forward to help her, or anyone from her past who had not otherwise featured in the case. Or it could have been a pseudonym for someone else entirely.

In February the following year, Ethel was granted probate of Crippen's estate with a net value of £268 6s 9d. The address for her on the letter of administration was 313 Hornsey Road, in north London, which was then the site of a tailor's shop owned by Charles Jeffrey and a flat above, where a George Frederick was registered as living. Neither of these names could be connected to Ethel. Perhaps it was just a forwarding address, but there was a reference in her life story to Crippen saying Ethel might make use of her skills as a milliner, so it was possible that she was working at the tailor's.

There was some support for this from the Ladies Guild secretary Melinda May, who said that on Easter Monday, March 1913, 'I had been staying at Eastbourne and had entered a compartment in a train for London Bridge. A young woman was sitting opposite me and to my amazement I recognised her as Neave. She saw me too and knew who I was and she hung her head. I could not take my eyes off her all the time we were on the journey.' May said that she too read the stories that Ethel had gone abroad but believed, as a matter of fact, that she had remained in London and was engaged in a dressmaking business.

It did not reflect well on Ethel that, having got Crippen's estate, she opposed the legal action which Belle's sister had begun. On the face of it, there was something obscene in the idea that a woman would seek the estate of the wife who had been murdered by her husband, the woman's lover. If Belle's estate passed to Crippen (even after he had been executed) then he (or Ethel as his beneficiary) had made good out of the murder he had committed.

The case went to a hearing at the Probate Division of the High Court, where Ethel's barrister argued that Crippen's conviction did not prove his guilt, in civil law, and was not even admissible as evidence that he had committed the crime. The judge did not accept this argument and said that it was clear in law that no person could obtain or enforce any rights resulting to them from their own crime. He said, 'The human mind revolts at the very idea that any other doctrine could be possible in our system of jurisprudence.'

Ethel lost the case and Hunn won Belle's estate, which

amounted to just under £160. Ethel's lawyer told the court after the judgement that he had been instructed to state that at no time had Miss Le Neve intended to touch any of the articles which had belonged to the deceased. Some of the articles in question, however, never did belong to the deceased. Miss Le Neve made no claim to certain furs and jewellery which had belonged to Mrs Crippen.

Even this did not much sound like graciousness in defeat. I wonder how she felt about the rising sun brooch, which had been taken by the police and was now part of Belle's estate – that brooch which Ethel had known she could prise from Crippen with a little persuasion.

The value of Belle's estate was boosted that September by the sale of the brooch and the rest of Belle's jewellery and then her clothes, over a two-day auction at Debenham, Storr & Sons in Covent Garden. The brooch was bought by a Liverpool dealer for £20, but it was not the most expensive item in the sale; that was a single-stone brilliant ring, sold to a Mr Harris of Houndsditch for £65. The following day's sale of clothes and other effects raised brought the total to around £200. Among the items sold were two framed certificates of thanks from the Mansion House Committee, dated 1902 (some four years before the launch of the Ladies Guild), when Belle and other performers had assisted at a dinner for the City of London poor.

Perhaps because the will had been settled, fresh rumours arose that Ethel had crossed the Atlantic. In late February, Canadian reporters searched in vain for her on board a ship, the *Royal Edward* arriving from Bristol. Ethel was said to be among 100 young women who were prospective – prospecting? – brides, heading for the Canadian north-west in search of husbands. In April she was said to be living in Montreal with a newborn baby. But she could not be found.

To the best of my knowledge, this was the last speculative reporting of Ethel's whereabouts in the press, until 1932, when she was 'found' living in the direst poverty under an assumed name in Perth, Australia where she was still protesting her innocence.

John Nash, the husband and manager of Lil Hawthorne, whose visit to Scotland Yard had finally prompted the police to take action, may have felt aggrieved that he did not benefit from the reward offered in the case, which appears to have gone in its entirety to Captain Kendall.

In February, when there was publicity about the legal action around the wills, Nash wrote to the Treasury Secretary, no less, rehearsing the role that he and his wife had played in the case. They had acted, he said, out of personal regard for their old friend Belle Elmore and in the interests of Justice. They had both sustained pecuniary loss through Lil's failure to carry out engagements due to the strain and anxiety of the case, which had rendered her unfit to properly discharge her duties on the variety stage. He hoped for a grant of compensation for services rendered.

The Treasury Secretary wrote and asked the Director of Public Prosecutions what he thought of the merit of Nash's claim. Sir Charles Matthews replied that he was of the opinion that these two people had rendered a 'signal service' to the cause of justice. He had spoken to both Inspector Froest and the Police Commissioner Sir Edward Henry and they supported the claim too. Froest (the Nashes' friend, a handy advocate in high places) had said that, without the Nashes' efforts, it was quite possible this grave crime might never have been discovered.

Nash was invited to submit a statement of losses and, following his return from a tour of the provinces, he forwarded an account showing the loss of three engagements, each of them a week long, in London, £20; Stockton, £40; and Glasgow, £60.

In April 1911, Nash wrote to Sir Charles to thank him for his great kindness in obtaining compension of £100 for their loss.

NINETEEN

Many local authorities have long since destroyed the hefty rate ledgers in which they meticulously recorded, by hand, the half-yearly payments they once collected from their residents.

At the Wandsworth Local History Service on Lavender Hill in Battersea, south London, they keep the surviving volumes of the Metropolitan Borough of Wandsworth General Rate ledgers, including a sequence beginning with the half year ending 30 September 1913 and concluding with the volume for the half year ending 31 March 1916. The covers were turning to dust and left traces on any surface they touched. The staff provided cushions on which to rest the books.

Miss Harvey's arrival at 19 Coalbrook Mansions, an apartment block which still stands on Bedford Hill in Balham, south-west London was recorded in a pencil entry in the first of those ledgers for 1 July 1913. The next volume shows that she moved from flat 19 to flat 13 on 1 February 1914, the fourth anniversary of Belle Elmore's death. In the volume for September 1915 some superstition has taken over and the flat number, 13, has been crossed out and 14a has been entered instead. Perhaps the superstition was Ethel's husband's, as her name has been crossed out too, and Stanley Smith's has been entered. The last available volume, March 1916, shows his name.

Ethel married Stanley Smith on 2 January 1915. The wedding certificate records the event as the marriage of Ethel Clare Harvey, aged thirty-one, no occupation given, of 14a Coalbrook Mansions, Balham, father Walter William Harvey, coal merchants' commercial traveller, and Stanley William Smith, aged twenty-four, a household furnishers' clerk of 45

Albert Road, South Norwood, father William Smith deceased, a fishmonger's manager. The ceremony took place at Wandsworth register office. The witnesses were C.E. Smith, G.M. Smith and Adine Brock.

Ethel's name had changed, even her father's name had changed, but Adine's presence proved the link with the past which Ethel was trying to erase. Stanley Smith worked at Hampton's, a prestigious furniture store of the age, right on Trafalgar Square. Ethel had got a job there and that was how they met. Their son later served his apprenticeship at Hampton's carpentry workshops, beneath its large depository on Queen's Road, Battersea.

She may have given up her job because she was already pregnant when she married, her son Stanley Robert Smith, always known as Bob, being born at home just six months after the wedding, on 9 July 1915. Ethel and Stanley's second and last child, their daughter Nina Margaret Smith, was born on 25 October 1920. By now the couple were living at 107 Harrington Road, South Norwood.

Even though he was little more than a toddler, Bob remembered his Aunt Nina/Adine, at their home in South Norwood, being cared for during her illness by his mother. He even remembered being told to look after her himself sometimes, while his parents were out.

Adine died, aged thirty-four, of pulmonary tuberculosis on 1 December 1918 at Croydon Union Infirmary, though her home address had been across London in Dalston. Adine's husband Horace had enlisted in the army in 1913, a year before the start of the First World War, and was still a sergeant in the 12th Bedford Regiment at the time of his wife's death. There is no record of who became the primary carer for Adine's two children Ronald and Ivy, who were still only thirteen and eight, respectively, when their mother died. They both grew up and married and, by chance it seems, ended up living quite near each other in Harrow, north London. They both had only one child, both of them sons. Ivy never spoke of her mother's death, or her life afterwards, to her son Roger.

Ethel and Stanley settled in Croydon, at 10 Parkview Road, where Ethel must have taken on the burden of looking after her father in his final years. Walter William Neave survived his wife Charlotte by three years and lived on until November 1941, when he died at the age of eighty-one, described on the death certificate as a retired insurance clerk of 10 Parkview Road, killed by myocardial degeneration and senility.

Bob recalled his grandfather staying with them, remembered going to meet him from the train sometimes so that he would be sure to come home and not be diverted to the pub. And then, some Sunday lunchtimes, being sent to retrieve him from the pub so that he would come home and eat. There was no poverty that Bob could recall, but not much spare money either, so that he could only remember one holiday, staying on the south coast with relatives.

Whatever ambitions Ethel had harboured had long since been thwarted. She had apparently settled comfortably in the very world she had once been determined to escape. Perhaps anonymity had become the highest prize.

In the mid-1950s, a journalist and author called Ursula Bloom, already then in her sixties, began work for the *Sunday Dispatch* on a new serial account of the case, to be called 'The Girl Who Loved Crippen'. She seems to have known Ethel was still around, but very little else, at the time her series of articles first appeared, despite the arduous research she claimed to have carried out.

In her memoir, *The Mightier Sword*, she says she had covered miles to get the story and was spending so much time in Camden Town it felt as though she was living there. She had written her story with deep sympathy for Crippen and the 'poor girl' who must have been uncommonly brave. The more she learned about Belle Elmore, however, the more disgusted she was with her. She wrote five instalments ahead of publication and her editor, Charles Eade, after reading them, told her she seemed to know a lot about murder. In total, the series ran for twelve weeks from April to June, 1954.

According to Ursula, immediately after the first episode was published she received a call from the *Dispatch* office to say that an irate relative of Ethel's had turned up, complaining loudly of the inaccuracies in the material. She told the office to send him round to her, and so he and his wife joined Ursula for sherry and she persuaded him to act as a go-between for correspondence between herself and Ethel.

Ursula claimed that she already knew how Ethel had left for Canada on the day of the execution, worked in a typing pool in Canada and returned in 1916 to nurse her dying sister. Now, Ursula said, 'I wrote to her from time to time, and she replied, our mutual friend posting the letters. He told me much.'

Apparently getting more information from the relative than from Ethel, Ursula said she concentrated on building up a picture of Ethel's husband and his commuter routines and then her editor hired a private detective who tried, without success, to find him and follow him home to discover Ethel's address. Finally, in one of her letters, Ethel told Ursula she had never got on with her relative and would prefer to use another intermediary; she supplied a different address which turned out, of course, to be her own. Ursula wrote and invited herself to tea, and Ethel agreed.

The relative was Ethel's little brother Sidney, who was by now in his late fifties and had married Doris May Salter in 1920. The couple had four sons, Bernard, Reginald, Alfred Raymond and Brian, and a daughter, Iris. They were living in Greenford, where Sidney worked in a bus company stores.

Iris, who turned eighty in 2005 and celebrated with a cruise in the Caribbean, remembers the contact between Sidney, her father and Ursula Bloom. She and her surviving siblings think that Sidney hoped to make a few pounds from the reporter's interest in his sister and did indeed go to the newspaper offices, probably not to complain but to offer his services as a source of more reliable information. It is possible that he actually supplied Ethel's address to Ursula Bloom, in return for money. That knowledge would have been the most valuable thing he had.

Sidney's daughter recalls him complaining that Ethel's notoriety had deprived him of his name – Le Neave, by registration – so perhaps this was why he felt able to betray her. It's not difficult to imagine that some of Ethel's family may have resented her lies and her scandalous conduct, perhaps blaming her for some of the troubles in their own lives.

There is no one alive who can now be sure what exactly happened between Ethel and Sidney and Ursula Bloom, but the incident caused a falling-out between Ethel and Sidney which lasted for quite some time. Ironically, apparently, Sidney would not have even known where Ethel was, but she had earlier contacted him, after a long silence, following the death of a relative who had left everyone in the family a share of some money. Sidney, who could be quick-tempered, had not been close to his father, Walter William, either. Sidney had not been notified when Walter died, while living at Ethel's in 1941.

Iris says her own daughter who was born in 1947 recalls seeing Bloom, who was memorably sporting an eye-patch, at Sidney's home one lunchtime, when she went there from school.

Bloom herself would later write more articles giving the impression of sustained contact with Ethel, but I have the evidence of contemporary letters which makes clear that it was very limited. Bloom appears to have traded for a long time on a couple of brief meetings, the first of which took place in 1954.

By the time of her death in 1984, Bloom had written over 400 books, most of them romantic fiction, under a variety of pen-names, such as Sheila Burns, Mary Essex and Lozania Prole. In the circumstances, it would not be surprising if the divisions between fact and fiction had become blurred in her creative imagination.

I have a copy of a handwritten letter, dated 14 June 1945,

which I believe to be genuine. The true date must be 1954, the mistake made by Ethel:

10 Parkview Road
Addiscombe, Croydon
Surrey
14/6/45

Dear Miss Bloom,
    Thank you for your letter received today.
    May I suggest that you come here, we shall be alone and can talk with ease – but could you possible make it 3.30 to 4 o'clock as I shall have two hungry men to feed at 6 o'clock.
    Of course, I don't know if you have a car, it could be used, there are plenty of cars in the Rd.
    Otherwise there are plenty of fast trains from Victoria to E. Croydon, just outside the station it is possible I believe to get a taxi here. It is only a short run.
    Now the day. For preference Tuesday would suit me best.
    Thanking you for your very kind letter,

Yours sincerely

Ethel Le Neve
PS The name is Mrs Smith.

The two hungry men would of course be Ethel's husband and her son, the two Stanleys. The writing is a clear match with other correspondence from Ethel.
    Bloom says that going to tea with Ethel was a mountain-top moment in her life. She described the ordinary house in the ordinary street with the extraordinary woman inside it: a small sitting-room with a three-piece suite, a tired piano, an overmantel, and a tea-cloth that Ethel herself had embroidered. Bloom agreed with Ethel that Crippen was innocent – in her memoir she dismisses the case against him in a few

quick paragraphs. Bloom says Ethel told her, 'he died because he loved me', though it's hard to follow the logic of that remark, if she really believed he was innocent.

It was surely testimony to the continuing fascination with the case, forty-four years after Belle's murder, that as well as meeting the real Ethel, Bloom also encountered a few bogus Ethels who had contacted her, or been reported to her newspaper, claiming to be the real thing. There was an old woman who lived in Hampshire, in an isolated house at the edge of a wood, where she told a visiting district nurse that she was really Ethel and began talking about the dear doctor she had known; a woman who visited Bloom at her Chelsea flat immersed in character as Ethel, until Bloom expressed disbelief, when she became angry and called Bloom a bitch. Best of all, there was a grey-haired elderly waitress in a Bexhill café who brought hot drinks to the customers' tables and then whispered in their ears, you have been served by Ethel Le Neve.

On 30 April 1997, Crippen's fob watch came up for sale at Christie's in South Kensington. It was expected to fetch between £1,000 and £1,500. The brochure described a 'gold filled hunting cased keyless lever pocket watch, Waltham Watch Co., circa 1900, white enamel dial signed American Waltham Watch Co., Roman numerals, outer Arabic five minutes, subsidiary seconds, frosted gilt movement, signed A.W.W. Co., Waltham, Mass, compensation balance, numbered 5818686, engine turned case with milled band, diameter 52mm'.

There were three main bidders at the auction, a restaurateur who apparently wanted to put it on display in a restaurant, a solicitor bidding by phone and a collector of crime, western and showbusiness memorabilia, David Gainsborough Roberts, who claimed a sentimental association with the Crippen case on the grounds that his mother Betty had been born 100 yards from Hilldrop Crescent. Gainsborough Roberts was a flamboyant character who now lived in Jersey but travelled regularly to the London auction houses, where he was well known to the staff.

The lot exceeded its reserve ten-fold and was secured by Gainsborough Roberts for £10,350. Along with the watch came two notes, a series of letters and two photographs that together disclosed considerably more of the story of Ethel's second life. They revealed that she *had* shared her secret – not with her husband or her children, nor ever discussed it with her family, but with a friend, Reginald Manning, known as Rex, whom Ethel had asked to help her when Ursula Bloom began writing to her again in the 1950s.

I have been unable to find the origins of the friendship between Rex and Ethel, but they must have been very close. Manning lived most of his married life in Sidcup, Kent but he was born in 1902 in Lulot Street, Highgate, which has since been renamed Lulot Gardens. He had just turned eight when Crippen was hanged.

The street is not far from the Hornsey Road address that was given for Ethel in 1911 when Crippen's will was probated. Rex was still living in that area when he married Ada Doris, who liked to be known as Doris, in 1931. It is possible that his connection with Ethel stems from that area. Perhaps she knew his family, while he was still a child.

There is one other possible link in that Rex, who worked as an auditor for the London Transport Passenger Board, was a keen amateur boxer and ran a boxing club in Addiscombe, the area of Croydon where Ethel and Stanley Smith lived.

Rex kept the letters he exchanged with Ethel in 1958, beginning in early January when she wrote to him enclosing a new letter she had received from Ursula Bloom. Three years earlier, in 1955, Bloom had published a hardback account of her earlier serial, *The Girl Who Loved Crippen*. It was described as a factual novel and it certainly would not have passed for journalism with its many careless errors and multiple inventions. In Bloom's book, to take a minor, recurring detail, Ethel said, 'Oh, Hawley!' a lot, though in life she had referred to him as Harvey or 'the doctor'.

Bloom had her own headed paper with a quill pen motif and the printed words 'From Ursula Bloom, Novelist'. With her address in Cranmer Court, Chelsea, the whole presentation was very grand. She had written to Dear Mrs Smith, expressing concern that she had not heard from her at Christmas and wondering if her eyes were bothering her again – Ethel suffered from cataracts – and offering the help of her own clever occulist. But this was a mere preliminary to the request for a meeting, which was what she really wanted: 'I would so like a little talk with you. Might I come to see you, or would you like to come here as last time? There is a scheme afoot which I think for your sake should be guarded against. It is not frightening. Don't be anxious, but it should be settled, and you can trust me as I hope you know . . .'

The scheme that was afoot was not described at this stage. It could have been any one of a number of projects that were then apparently being planned around the case.

Perhaps it was the early machinations of a stage musical, *Belle or The Ballad of Dr Crippen*, which was staged for six brief weeks of 1961 at the Strand Theatre, Aldwych. The show was heavily criticised, not least for its poor taste, on the grounds that one of the principals, Ethel, was still alive somewhere. Here is a sample of the lyrics which were written by Wolf Mankowitz: 'Funny little fellow, Ethel by his side, There in the Old Bailey, For murder they were tried, When the trial was over, The jury sad to tell, Found old Crippen guilty, Of killing poor old Belle.'

Or maybe it was the preparations for the black and white film that would eventually be released in 1962: *Dr Crippen* – 'the crime of the century! Was he really guilty?' – with Donald Pleasance in the title role, Coral Browne as Belle and Samantha Eggar as Ethel.

The letter shows that there had been a second meeting, at Bloom's home – 'would you like to come here as last time?' – which perhaps had taken place around the time of publication of Bloom's fanciful account of Ethel's life. I wonder why, if she had access to Ethel, the facts in her book are so few and far between. This can only mean that Ethel had not really wanted or intended to talk to her and, when they did meet, had very little to say.

Now Ethel wrote to Rex Manning, enclosing Ursula's letter, asking his advice about it. She had heard nothing from Ursula for ages, she wrote to Rex, not since the book had come out, so why Ursula should have expected to hear from her at Christmas, she really didn't know. She was certainly a very crafty woman, Ethel wrote, using the same trifles she had used before, namely the state of Ethel's eyes. Rex replied to 'My dear Eth.' telling her he would call in with a solution and, in the meantime, not to worry and keep smiling.

Ursula was getting impatient, awaiting a reply, and wrote again a few days later expressing her disappointment at not having heard from Ethel, asking her to get in touch as (now playing her hand) she was 'seriously disturbed about the film which is being planned' and thought Ethel ought to be told about it. Rex wrote to Ursula and proposed to come and see her but, by a coincidence, Ursula replied that she would be walking her dogs as usual on Saturday at the golf links near Rex's home and she would call on him instead. Ursula must have been encouraged by this meeting as she wrote promptly afterwards thanking Rex and Doris for their hospitality and saying she hoped something could be done to stymie the film. No doubt she had in mind something written by herself.

Rex wrote back, a formal typed letter, saying that Ethel was now seventy-five years of age and sought only to be left alone and in peace. She had, Rex explained, reiterated a profound dislike of, and desire to avoid publicity in any shape or form. She would never be a consenting party to any joint publicity effort, nor personally initiate any such activity. 'She is of the opinion that any "personal hurt" which the proposed film, or films may cause her by misrepresentation, etc. (which you consider a possibility) is a calculated risk to be taken until the film is, or films are publicly exhibited. Only then – can such damage be measured and, if necessary, dealt with appropriately. Only then – since, as you indicate, your proposed article will not stop the film or films. Indeed, might it not further boost it, or them despite all the good intentions.'

Ursula wrote back saying how disappointed she was. Still, she was very fond of Sidcup and her visit had been another of her pleasant associations with the place. And finally: 'What a case that was! I wonder what the answer is.'

In his reply Rex made it clear that Ethel would never change. 'I am sure that our actions are influenced (let's face it) by what we tell ourselves to be a most earnest endeavour to reach basic truth. So – we join in the seemingly never ending search for detail to close gaps which some may think still remain in this (that) fascinating human story . . .' Ethel wrote to Rex and Doris thanking them for all they had done for her and hoping she hadn't asked too much from them. How they must bless her, she wrote – too polite to say 'curse' – and she wouldn't blame them if they did.

Ursula Bloom's article, 'Crippen died to save her from scandal' appeared anyway, in the *Sunday Mirror* on 1 June 1958. The opening line was, 'All I want is peace, says the woman whom the world knew as Ethel le Neve.' The article explained that Ethel now had a husband and children who did not know her past. Her secret was safe with Ursula.

Bloom wrote one last time, to Rex, that October. 'I have heard no more about Mrs Smith. How is she? I am a little worried, for there is a new venture afoot . . .' He does not appear to have replied.

Stanley Smith, Ethel's husband, died in December 1960, in an ambulance on his way to St Thomas's Hospital, following a heart attack. He was sixty-nine years old and had collapsed on Waterloo Station, on his way home from work as a wages clerk for a building contractor. He had worked for Hampton's right up until his retirement at the age of sixty-five.

In February 1962, Ethel gave Rex Manning the fob watch and a plain band wedding ring. I have been unable to trace what happened to the ring but I later heard that Doris Manning, Rex's wife, hated the association with these items and was revolted by the thought of the crime. I wondered how such revulsion had made her feel about Ethel and whether this had caused any tension between her and Rex, as he had obviously always been so solicitous in his dealings with Ethel.

Ironically, Ethel's son Bob said the watch had first been given to him after his father's death. So far as he was concerned, the watch was not Crippen's but his father's. Knowing how fond his father had been of his grandchild, Nina's son Vaugn, Bob had suggested the watch be given to him instead. Next thing he knew, his mother had given it to Rex.

The Mannings did not have children and, after Rex's death, Doris put the fob watch in the loft with the letters, and refused to have anything to do with them. She asked a cousin, Leslie Andrews, to dispose of them when she was gone and he kept them a while after her death, in 1994, before deciding to put them up for auction. Not wanting any personal benefit from the notoriety, and knowing someone whose child had contracted leukaemia, he decided to donate the proceeds to the Leukaemia Research Fund. There had been a drawing of Ethel with the watch and the letters, but Christie's had declined to put the drawing in the sale. Andrews still had this in his own attic.

In his lifetime, Rex had worried over what he would do with the watch and the ring. He had added a short, handwritten letter of provenance for the watch, which he had signed, explaining that it had been given to him in friendship by the former Ethel Le Neve. He had also typed out, signed Anon., a longer explanation of the origins of the watch. It was a ruminative note which he had constructed as if it were a story and carefully corrected with longhand additions, crossing out and adding in words here and there, clearly trying to capture something of the importance of the watch and what it had symbolised for Ethel.

Rex must have been dying himself when he wrote the note. He contracted cancer of the colon and died in late November 1967. Ethel had died only a few weeks earlier on 9 August 1967 at Dulwich Hospital: Ethel Clare Smith, a female, aged eighty-four years. The primary cause of death was heart failure. She had left Parkview Road after her husband died and, at the time of her death, was living at 62 Burford Road, Lewisham.

In his note, Rex had described how the much-travelled watch and ring had found sanctuary in the tender and possessive care of their late owner's young mistress. This little lady had no part in the crime, as her own trial had proved. Yet all unknowingly she might have been its main motive force. 'In course of time and under another name, the little lady met and came to like and respect, as distinct from love, an honest to goodness and hard-working man of modest means and background. She became his wife, bore him children and was relatively content, albeit in her wisdom always withholding from them the secret of her former identity.'

According to Rex, Ethel's husband had often worn the ring and carried the watch in his pocket at family parties and other special occasions. He believed they were her family heirlooms, given to him in affection. But for Ethel, seeing them worn by another man served strangely to symbolise and stimulate a profound and enduring love still nurtured in her heart for the dead lover. 'Time passed, some forty years, in fact, when, in failing health, the good husband departed this life. Later still, so did his widow, the little lady. Before her passing, however, she presented the watch and the ring to me, a friend, who, knowing her identity, had faithfully respected her secret over the long years.'

Rex kept his 'revelation' for the last lines, disclosing that the original owner had been Crippen and the little lady, Ethel Le Neve: 'And over the years that followed she chose to preserve and treasure these relics as symbols of an undying love. For she loved Crippen devoutly to the end of her days.'

I like to think that Rex wrote the truth about Ethel and her marriage and her continuing love for Crippen, that he was describing Ethel's feelings as she had described them to him, her one confidant after Crippen's death. What no one knew, not even Rex, apparently, was the scale of the secret that Ethel kept tucked away. Not just her old self in another life, but what had gone on there, and how and why Belle Elmore had died, and who exactly had killed her and helped clean up afterwards.

Ethel had begun lying with Crippen and about Crippen. And she had never found a way to stop or to begin telling the truth. She had become Crippen's secret lover when she was twenty-three and so almost her entire adult life had been filled with secrets and lies of some enormity.

One can only try to imagine what it would be like, being her two children, and finding out, long after she was dead, that you had never seen below the surface of your own mother; that she had shielded herself from you and your father, for the whole of your lives, without even so much as a posthumous note to set you straight afterwards.

In December 1914, Churchill was First Lord of the Admiralty and ordered a number of ships to be sunk at the entrance to harbours, to defend against attacks from U boats. The SS *Montrose* was poised to be scuttled at Dover Harbour when a storm blew up and she broke moorings and foundered on Goodwin Sands. Her mast remained visible above the sea for forty-nine years, until it disappeared in June 1963. According to Captain Kendall, the last man to leave the ship when it was lost was a William Crippen.

No lives were lost when the *Montrose* went down, but Captain Kendall had not been so lucky earlier that same year, in May, when he was in command of the *Empress of Ireland*, making its way up the St Lawrence to Quebec in thick fog, when it collided with another ship and sank, killing over 1,000 passengers and crew. The accident occurred five miles east of the scene of Crippen's arrest at Father Point. Kendall survived and lived until 1965, when he died in a London nursing home at the age of ninety-one.

Eugene Stratton died in 1918, aged fifty-seven; Fred Ginnett died in 1921; both Lil Hawthorne and Paul Martinetti died in 1924. Martinetti died in a hotel in Algiers, north

Africa. He left all the accessories of his act, his music, props, scenery to his brother Alfred. His wife Clara Martinetti died in 1945. Arthur Newton, the solicitor, died in 1930, aged seventy; the journalist Filson Young died in 1938, aged sixty-one; Walter Dew, retired Chief Inspector, died in December 1947, aged eighty-four, at his home in Worthing which he had named 'the wee hoose'. Bernard Spilsbury, the pathologist, killed himself the following day. Horace Brock, the surviving husband of Adine, was seventy-seven when he died of a heart attack, at Hackney Hospital in 1948. He had been living at 5 Spurstowe Terrace, Hackney.

The Music Ladies Guild enjoyed Gracie Fields's patronage in the 1930s and she donated a building that became an orphanage, run by the Guild, which changed its name to the Variety Artistes Ladies Guild & Orphanage. When the orphanage was sold in the 1960s it became the Variety Artistes Ladies' and Children's Guild. The Guild last supplied accounts to the Charity Commission in 1992; the Commission tried to contact the Guild in 1997, without success.

A music hall performer, Sandy MacNab (possibly McNab) had briefly attempted to run 39 Hilldrop Crescent as a lodging house for theatricals, in the years following 1910. He had posed at the top of the steps for a photograph which was reproduced as a postcard. There is no evidence of his success, but some suggestion that it was not a popular place in which to board.

On the night of 8 September 1940, during the early stages of the Blitz, a German bomb landed in the back garden of 40 Hilldrop Crescent. The explosion demolished the rear walls of both 39 and 40. A subsequent air raid report of damage which was completed in duplicate by the 'assistant deputy to the controller' of ARP (Air Raid Precautions) described the bomb as HE (high explosive) and said it had also fractured the lower parts of the rear walls of 37 and 38 Hilldrop Crescent, but they remained standing. This suggests that numbers 39 and 40 did not remain standing.

All four houses from 37 to 40 were eventually demolished

and cleared. By 1951 it was a vacant site for development and within a couple of years building had begun on a four-storey apartment block which was called Margaret Bondfield House, named after Britain's first woman cabinet minister. In 1969 a plan to put a plaque on the wall of Margaret Bondfield House, commemorating the association with Crippen, was abandoned due to 'local opposition'.

TWENTY

Bob and Nina, Ethel's children, had known Rex, but had no idea that he knew more about their own mother than they did. Nor, indeed, did they know that their extended family knew more.

I have in front of me a group family photograph, a Sunday afternoon in a garden in Sunbury, west of London, from the late 1940s I think it must be, on a rare occasion when Ethel and her son and daughter were together with Ethel's brother Sidney and his wife and some of their family, including their daughter Iris. Sidney is holding Iris's daughter, who must be about eighteen months old. Sidney looks moon-faced and jolly, standing at the back with the baby. Ethel would be in her mid-sixties here and is sitting in the front in a dark dress, thick stockings and sensible shoes, with a string of pearls showing at her collar and a hat with a turned-up brim topped with a big bow. Sidney's wife, next to her, is grinning broadly and has placed her arm through Ethel's, but Ethel has kept her hands clasped in her own lap and is showing a hesitant smile. Ethel's daughter Nina is sitting next to her mother and her son Stanley, who is known as Bob, is standing with his hands in the pockets of his baggy trousers and has a pipe clamped between his teeth. He already looks older than his years, which can only be mid-thirties.

How ordinary Ethel has become in this photograph, blending in. How extraordinary, the story that lies behind her faint smile, the untold secrets, the things she knows and does not say, will never say, not even to her own children who pose alongside her in blissful ignorance of their mother's past. Were they to look at this photograph now, they would surely see a different person from the woman they believed their mother to be when it was taken.

'I thought you knew,' Iris told her cousin Bob, Ethel's son, when she got back in touch with him in the mid-1980s. She read about him in a newspaper after a journalist tracked down Bob and Nina and disclosed to them for the first time that their mother had been Ethel Le Neve. 'We didn't know anything about it, Iris,' said Bob. 'We never knew.'

Bob later told me that at first he thought it was a joke, when he opened the letter from the journalist, Jonathan Goodman, which referred to his mother as Ethel Le Neve. It was also clear to Bob that Goodman had assumed he knew, and could not at first believe he didn't know. As Bob said, was still saying twenty years on, it was unbelievable.

He could not say he had felt angry and betrayed by his mother when he found out, and had obviously tried to rationalise her conduct to himself, imagining that she had not wanted her children to know for fear they might have blurted it out in the school playground. But of course, that did not explain why she had not told her husband, or her children when they were older.

He and Nina knew their mother had been in Canada once – well, twice, as it now transpired – but that was about it, in terms of the connection they could make to the case. There did not seem to have been any mystery about her life. If she was ever evasive they hadn't noticed. They couldn't be sure, now, Bob told me, but presumed their father hadn't known either. (He hadn't, not according to Rex Manning's note.)

Having since seen the photographs of Ethel in her veil at Bow Street, Bob felt sure that the veil had been around in their time and that Nina had played dressing up with it as a little girl.

Bob was kind of fascinated with the story too and wished he could go back and ask his mother some questions. He was obviously confident of her innocence of the crime, but still there were things he would have liked to know. Things it must have been hard, not knowing.

During their telephone conversation, Iris and Bob had discussed the lost years and the times they had been out of contact, and Bob said the family was always like that, always falling out, having arguments over something or other. Perhaps that was not surprising, when you had an elephant in the living-room and were trying to pretend it wasn't there.

It seemed remarkable, how everyone in the family had known not to talk about it, without anyone actually saying, 'Don't mention Crippen!' In the absence of any discussion, and without really giving it any great thought, Iris had simply assumed that Bob and Nina knew too.

I also wondered how Ethel had explained to her husband the presence of all those relatives whose surname was not Harvey but Neave. A cousin, Roy Neave, the son of Ethel's brother Monty, had actually lived with them for a while. Had she renamed them all Harvey, for her husband's benefit, as she had on her wedding certificate? Or had she constantly been on her guard to prevent any contact between her husband and that tricky surname, though at least it was Neave and not Le Neve.

Bob believed that his mother had actually told two of her brothers, Claude and Monty, not to say anything. They too had lived in Croydon and been a presence in Bob and Nina's lives for many years. Ethel had her own authority in the family, as the oldest child, and so they had naturally fallen in with her request.

Iris was fond of her Aunt Ethel and Uncle Stan and did not mind at all when her father Sidney used to tell her she was fussy just like Ethel. Her parents might not have told her about the past, if she hadn't gone rummaging in the loft and found a box of papers and asked what they were. Even then, they never exactly discussed the case.

If Ethel was disappointingly ordinary and unglamorous, to Iris, she was at least kind and attentive, sharing her embroidery with her niece and sometimes inviting her to finish a piece she had started. Iris never heard her shout, and likewise remembered Uncle Stan as a proper gentleman, rather quiet, who always stayed behind if a group of them went to the pub.

When she tried to think of the house in Croydon, Iris remembered it as cosy and simple, if rather dark, in the way of old Victorian villas, as Iris imagined them. She could not precisely recall the brand of cigarettes that Ethel had smoked so heavily, but thought they might have been Du Mauriers, which were popular among female smokers in those days. Whenever there was an occasion, a family gathering, Iris could see that Ethel was particular about her appearance, looking just so with the hat and the pearls and sometimes a fur stole around her neck.

Ethel had suffered from bronchitis almost annually in later years, which was perhaps the inevitable consequence of her smoking. There was a story that, before her death in 1967, she had asked to be buried with a locket containing Crippen's photograph. The story had no source and seemed implausible, for whom would she have asked to carry out such a request? Her son Bob had no memory of a locket, but there had been one once, fifty-seven years earlier, according to the memoir of the journalist Philip Gibb, Ethel's ghost-writer. She had kept the watch, so she could have kept a locket as well. If she had always worn it, discreetly, she might just have been able to be buried with it discreetly too – her last private symbol of that 'sacred' love.

Iris had not gone to Aunt Ethel's funeral. She had been working, she had a child to look after, a husband, there was no time, she was too busy getting on with her life. And besides. She didn't like funerals. Full stop.

TWENTY-ONE

The writer Raymond Chandler was intrigued by the murder of Belle Elmore, but struggled to rationalise the actions of the perpetrator and generally seemed quite unable to make sense of Crippen or his crime. 'You can't help liking this guy somehow,' he wrote. 'He was one murderer who died like a gentleman.'

In the late 1940s and through the early 1950s Chandler appears to have been toying with the idea of writing at length about a real crime, as opposed to the complex fictional plots being unravelled by his private detective, Philip Marlowe. A friend, the writer and critic James Sandoe, was feeding him cases from the Notable Trials series and other sources. The two men discussed the cases in letters. Chandler complained at one point that Sandoe seemed to have misunderstood his request, to the effect that he had wanted a poisoning case in particular. He did not. He just wanted any good murder case of which a detailed account was available. 'I don't want any sordid cases except in the sense that all murders are a bit sordid. I prefer a case that can still be argued about . . . all the good ones I can think of are English.'

After reading *The Trial of H.H. Crippen*, Chandler wrote saying there were a couple of queer things about the case. He could not see why a man who would go to the enormous labour of de-boning and de-sexing and de-heading an entire corpse would not take the rather slight extra labour of disposing of the flesh in the same way, rather than burying it all.

The second thing was that Chandler could not understand Crippen's telling of his wife's death. Why? What had he gained? Why not let it stand that she had decamped and stay with that? He did not agree with those who thought that Crippen should have kept his nerve and stayed put after Dew's visit. Chandler was sure that, not finding Belle, Scotland Yard would eventually have 'come to the old digging routine'.

Still, he could not see why a man of so much coolness under fire should have made the unconscionable error of letting it be known that Elmore had left her jewels and clothes and furs behind. She was so obviously not the person to do that. 'Here was a man who apparently had the means and opportunity and even the temperament for a perfect crime, and he made all sorts of mistakes which usually are not the result of stupidity but of panic. But Crippen didn't seem to panic at all. He did many things which required a very cool head. For a man with a cool head and some ability to think he also did many things which simply didn't make sense.'

Chandler seems to have been trying to bring a novelist's logic and order to the circumstances of the case, losing sight of the messiness of real life, where people are not perfect murderers or cool killers and are apt to defy the stereotypes of fiction, such as mild-mannered little doctors who die like gentlemen on the scaffold.

In this respect, Chandler with his sympathy for Crippen was merely following most commentators, who appeared to take their cue from Filson Young and his lengthy introduction to the Notable Trials edition.

J.B. Priestley saw reflected in the case a growing taste for public drama – a fox and a hare being pursued halfway across a shrinking world by millions of baying, slavering hounds. He could not help wishing that Crippen had been able to slip away and start a new life somewhere with his devoted Ethel: 'He was fifty, only five feet and four inches in height, myopic, anything but handsome, yet Ethel, twenty-seven and five feet five, was ready to run away with him, even though it meant wearing boy's clothes. He must have had something that was not so much meat for the hangman.'

Likewise Dorothy L. Sayers, who really did believe that Crippen was the nice little man that people who knew him had told her he was. Murdering only under the overwhelming stress of circumstances, he had chosen a most merciful poison, which killed at once and without pain. (This, of course, was a completely false description of hyoscine.) 'His devotion to the girl he loved approached the heroic. It is ironical that his name should – owing to his method of disposing of the body – have become a byword for cold-blooded brutality; but the public is sensitive on certain points and will more readily forgive a man for inflicting the long-drawn agonies of arsenic on the living than for dismembering a senseless corpse.'

According to Filson Young, the murder had not long been contemplated and so there must have been a sudden trigger. He proposed three explanations, beginning with the case for the prosecution, that Crippen had wanted to get Belle out of the way so he could 'indulge his guilty passion' for Ethel. Young thought this might have been good enough for the jury but did not stand up to closer scrutiny since Crippen was already free, within the confines of his marriage, to maintain his relationship with Ethel and if he really only wanted to be with her he could have left Belle instead of killing her. And if he had been going to kill her for that reason, he would have done it earlier, before he had settled into some kind of routine with his wife and his mistress.

In his second hypothesis, Young was citing the criminal lawyer Sir Edward Marshall Hall who, having lost or refused the Crippen brief, apparently went around London dinner parties telling people how he would have secured Crippen's acquittal. In Young's version of the Hall defence, Belle was a woman of 'abnormal amative appetite' and, trying to keep up with his mistress too, Crippen was struggling with the double demand on account of his 'frail physique and advancing years'.

Knowing that hyoscine was sometimes used as a 'sexual depressant' in cases of 'acute nymphomania', he planned to administer a few drops to Belle, to quell her appetite, but he got the dose wrong and killed her by mistake. He was so frightened that he compounded his error by disposing of the body. Even Young was forced to acknowledge the element of comedy in this theory and seemed surprised that, as he said, Marshall Hall genuinely believed it too. Young did not accept it, on the grounds that he did not see how Mrs Crippen could have expressed her 'inordinate concupiscence' or asserted her conjugal rights, as all Crippen had to do was refuse her. And could he, a doctor, really have made such a colossal misjudgement with the dosage? (Although it's not quite the same thing, hyoscine hydrobromide is in use today as the active ingredient in a motion sickness pill, known as Kwells.)

Curiously, Marshall Hall's biographers found a variation on the theme, suggesting that the lawyer would have put forward the argument that the hyoscine was intended not to dampen Belle's sexual appetites but knock her out so that Crippen could bring Ethel into the house to have sex with her. Perhaps Hall could not decide between the two. He apparently claimed that Crippen had rejected the latter version on the grounds that it implicated Ethel. I doubt that Crippen ever even heard of it. Both ideas seem totally ridiculous, though you could imagine how an all-male jury of the age might have reacted with some sympathy, shortly before arriving at incredulity and a guilty verdict.

Travers Humphreys, in his memoirs, dismissed Hall's theories as not viable in law. Certainly they could not have justified a 'not guilty' defence. They would have required an admission that Crippen had killed Belle, albeit by accident – an admission he was clearly not prepared to make.

Young's favoured theory, which conveniently fitted his contemptuous, misogynistic view of Belle, rendered her as the cause of her own death, having provided the trigger by telling Crippen she planned to leave him. Young said that in January 1910 Belle had more than once told one of her friends that if Crippen didn't give up his association with Ethel she would leave him and take her money with her. She had long since worn out his affection for her, Young wrote, by her vanity, her extravagance and her shrewishness. He thought it possible that Ethel was discontented too: 'it would be remarkable if she were not'. Although Young hastened to add that there was no evidence Ethel had put any pressure of this nature on Crippen.

Young second-guessed Crippen, imagining that he thought things would be much worse if Belle went off and took all her things with her. No money for his business, and no jewellery to share with Ethel. Much better, then, that he murdered her. It is intriguinging to see how Young not only reversed the facts but, also, the traditional casting of 'good' wife and 'bad' mistress. Here, the grasping hussy was the wife, who compared unfavourably with the quiet, patient mistress. Perhaps this said as much, if not more, about Young as it did about Belle and Ethel.

In reality, there was no evidence I could find, other than Crippen's own unreliable testimony, that Belle had ever talked of leaving him. Ethel, on the other hand, according to her landlady Mrs Jackson, had made it plain to Crippen that she was unhappy with her position in his life and wanted her status resolved. That, I suspect, was the real motive for the murder: Ethel's urgent desire for the respectability of marriage.

Telling friends that she was engaged at her birthday in January, just after Crippen had collected the hyoscine, was tantamount to an admission that Ethel knew Belle would soon be out of the way. In this context her anxiety and depression, as described by Mrs Jackson, become the cause of the murder not the symptom of it.

Perhaps the approach of another birthday, her twenty-seventh, was a reminder to Ethel that she was still on the shelf. Her sister Adine was younger and had already been married for five years. Adine had given birth in proper circumstances. Ethel, at the very least, had already had one miscarriage, from the 'illegitimate' pregnancy of an illicit relationship. It was not guilty passion that Ethel wanted, but decency, which she must have desperately craved: marriage, legitimate babies and the improved social status of an elevation out of the lower middle classes. She wanted to stop being the mistress of somebody else's husband, and become the mistress of a house instead, as she briefly did, in the weeks before Inspector Dew came calling.

That was *her* vanity. Her extravagance, perhaps, was that Belle had to die for it.

It may well be that Crippen's subsequent account of his marriage to Belle and her frequent threats to leave him were either his invention or, as he well knew, just so much hot air from Belle. The reality may have been that the marriage suited them both, that each had found their space within it and Belle was not about to desert her source of freedom and funds for clothes and jewellery.

Crippen may have known that Belle would never leave him. He may also have realised or been told bluntly by her that, as a reborn, or newborn, Catholic she was unlikely to agree to a divorce. With Ethel pressing, he was trapped and could see no other way out. He must have wanted to be with Ethel too. Their love could well have been the consuming, driving force, leading inexorably to murder.

Inspector Dew came to believe that Crippen 'harboured an intense hatred' for Belle, and maybe he was right, but I imagine more of a simmering resentment between them. And I cannot forget all the evidence of Crippen's kindness towards his wife and the many displays of affection – the gifts, the solicitousness and so on, which others saw. No one can really know what goes on in a marriage but, even so, hatred is a devouring, ferocious state of mind that leaves little room for even the most occasional tender displays. No witness ever saw his hatred and I feel sure it would have been bound to seep out and be noticed, somehow.

Crippen must just have become careless about Belle, standing on the far side of the great emptiness that seems to have opened up between them. They had public parts to play, to maintain an appearance and retain the privacy of their unhappiness. But at home, just the two of them, it must have been pretty frosty and horrible for quite a while. Perhaps they sniped and bickered and gnawed away at each other, Belle becoming frustrated and loud and Crippen trying to shrink away from the confrontations, his silence only infuriating her even more, in the typical way that men and women sometimes relate. It was the kind of 'putting up with' that so many couples settle into. And only sometimes dream of committing murder to escape.

It is hard to see how, with £600 on deposit, Crippen had anything more than temporary money worries. He was not to know that the Charing Cross Bank was about to collapse and could surely have used the deposit as collateral for a loan, if he needed to. Even allowing for the possibility that some of the money was Belle's and not his – and there is no evidence that she ever brought more than small sums of money into the marriage – he must have had enough to maintain his way of life.

In this context, money does not make a plausible motive; at most a secondary consideration.

If it was not money, and it was neither lust nor hatred, then it must have been love that got Belle murdered. He might have cracked and killed her in a fit of rage, but then he would not have known to go out and buy the hyoscine two weeks beforehand. And you do not poison somebody in a moment of anger, you shoot them or hit them with a blunt object or even a sharp one, with anything, in fact, that comes to hand.

There has to have been a plan, and perhaps the supper was part of it. The junior Crown barrister, Ingleby Oddie, speculated in his memoirs that Crippen had planned to take advantage of the fact that his wife was 'very fat' and disguise the use of poison by passing her death off as natural causes, as heart failure. The supper would have provided evidence of her excesses, eating and drinking heartily, and when Crippen called a doctor in the early morning after the sudden death of his wife, no one would have been any the wiser. This falls down on the grounds that Belle, though overweight, does not seem to have been 'very fat' at all and, far from being in an unhealthy condition, was blooming and in the best of shape, as, ironically, the later examination of her organs would confirm.

All the same, Crippen does seem to have been determined to have the Martinettis round that night. That could be coincidental – it could have been at Belle's urging – but it is equally possible that he did plan to create the impression of a death by natural causes. Maybe he even administered the poison in a drink, or drinks, a little at a time, while the guests were still there, though in Mrs Martinetti's account it is Belle who does most of the fetching and carrying.

Alternatively, he may have already thought through the story he proposed to tell, and wanted to create the fiction of a 'final straw' during the dinner, to explain why Belle had finally left him: that his lack of attention to the ailing Mr Martinetti and the allegation that Belle had been angry with him about it afterwards had, in his story, been the catalyst for her departure.

If Crippen had planned to have a 'natural death', something had obviously gone wrong. It was possible that Belle had suffered one of the adverse side-effects of hyoscine and become highly aroused – hysterical – and there had been a struggle and Crippen had ended up using a different means to kill her. There was some support for this, in the cries and shots that some neighbours claimed they had heard. The clumps of hair that were found entwined in curlers could also have been evidence of a life or death struggle.

I asked a modern pathologist, Dr Richard Shepherd, to review the medical evidence in the case and offer some sober interpretation of what might have happened. He told me not to try and complicate the scenario and not to go looking for things that weren't there. There was inherent risk, he said, in trying to disguise a murder as death by natural causes. A doctor, of all people, would be alert to the possibility that any slight concern could lead to a post-mortem and the discovery of the poison. In his view, that risk of discovery was too great. Crippen had planned to kill her and dispose of the body, and that was what had happened.

In this way, it was still possible that he had needed to shoot

Belle to hasten her death and she could still have become conscious and cried out, beforehand.

Filson Young paid tribute to Crippen's skill and coolness in his attempts to conceal all traces of the crime. He very nearly succeeded, and Young suggested that this was technically admirable. The dissection and disposal, he said, must have been the work of days. One theory was that the dissection had been carried out in the bath and the bones and limbs burned in the kitchen grate, while the head was got rid of during Crippen's subsequent trip to Dieppe, 'dropped overboard in a handbag'.

This had first been suggested by MacNaghten, the Assistant Commissioner at Scotland Yard, who was apparently unaware that Crippen did not go to France for the first time until some seven weeks after the murder, which seems a long time to hang on to your wife's head.

In his unbounded praise for Crippen's clever murdering, you could tell that Filson Young was just as impressed with the stories he told afterwards describing how, 'with a certain completeness of artistic circumstances', Crippen had developed Belle's disappearance into her death in faraway California.

There was, of course, no puzzle, as Chandler had suggested there was, in why Crippen had told her friends that Belle was dead. He must have thought it would answer their continual expressions of surprise that she hadn't contacted them, and hoped it would finally end the constant querying of her whereabouts. It's possible that he had not initially intended to kill her off, but had only thought as far as announcing that she had gone abroad. He may not have anticipated so many questions and may not have fully appreciated his wife's reputation as a reliable correspondent. He might have thought she would simply be forgotten or, at least, not worried over by her friends.

On the other hand, he needed her death to become public knowledge in order to regularise and legitimise Ethel's place in his life. There is no evidence that they ever planned to get married, properly, but if they did, they could not fake a divorce between Crippen and Belle or risk accusations of bigamy, so Belle needed to be officially deceased.

Perhaps her eventual death was always part of the story he planned to tell, and the apparent masterstroke of his fake admission to Dew that she was still alive, really, and he had only pretended she was dead to prevent a scandal, was a position he had kept in reserve, in case it was needed.

But how then did he (or they) dissect and dispose of the remains?

Like Young, I thought it would have taken days too. A vile and laborious task which Crippen would have needed constant swigs of brandy to contemplate and complete. I thought perhaps the ashes in burning pails seen by neighbours and later collected by the dustmen were clues that he had burned Belle's body, piece by piece. I entered a debate about this with the writer and academic Julie English Early, who favoured and persuasively argued the theory that he had boiled the remains, gradually reducing them to an easily disposable mush.

The pathologist, Dr Shepherd, did not think either was likely. There had been attempts to burn bodies, he said, but they did not burn very easily or very completely and it was a long, slow process unless you had a crematorium oven that could achieve extremely high temperatures. Boiling was no good because it did not get rid of the bones. Dr Shepherd could not understand the crime scene, and the most puzzling factor of all was why there were no bones left and why – in an echo of Chandler – if he had disposed of so much he had not gone on and disposed of everything.

In Shepherd's experience, though a rare murderer would seek to retain a trophy souvenir of his killing, most of them would not choose to keep the body close by and, unless there was a particular psychological or practical reason for it, they would not choose to bury them at home, either. There was no apparent reason in this case and if Crippen had managed to complete the disposal or bury the remaining parts in another place, where in time they would have become unidentifiable, the chances of detection would have been greatly reduced and the police could have prodded and poked around in his home as much as they liked.

In these circumstances, Shepherd could only speculate that Crippen's original means of disposal, the place where he had put the rest of the remains, had suddenly stopped being available to him. Shepherd asked where the nearest stretch of water was and said that was the most likely way to dispose of the remains.

The Regent's Canal was just back down Camden Road, not much more than a mile from Hilldrop Crescent, and in those days it ran alongside the vast – and presumably quite deserted – railway depot behind King's Cross and St Pancras, beside the road that is now St Pancras Way.

Shepherd liked the sound of that canal, for Crippen's purposes.

When I told him that a fragment of brown paper had been found attached to one of the small pieces of skin in the remains, he said this could have been how the parts were packaged. Crippen could have strolled down to the canal and dropped them in. They would have sunk straight away, and never risen to the surface. Only whole corpses or torsos tend to rise back up, as the gases of decomposition fill the chest and abdomen and create buoyancy.

How much better than plastic bags or bin liners brown paper would have been, quickly rotting and allowing the parts inside to rot and be attacked and eaten by the fish.

Supposing, said Shepherd, Crippen had relied on this means and then been spooked in some way: a passing policeman hearing the splash and saying, 'Oi, what was that?' and Crippen saying, 'It was just some old rubbish,' and the policeman saying, 'Well, don't throw stuff into the canal again or you'll be nicked.' It could have been that, or something like it, that brought home to Crippen the risk of discovery and persuaded him against taking further chances outside and to put what was left in the cellar.

Shepherd said that he, as an experienced pathologist, could

dissect a body in an hour. He could not say what skill Crippen had but it seemed likely he had some former experience to draw on. If he had stripped all the bones out, that would have taken much, much longer, but perhaps the remains were misleading in this respect, suggesting that all the bones had been removed when in fact the bulk of the body could have been cut off in what he called the 'classical dismemberment', going through the joints, by head and limbs and then the torso cut into parts so that the remaining pieces of skin which ended up in the cellar were just extra pieces that he had cut away during the process. You did not need special surgical knives or scalpels for this. Just regular knives, well sharpened, would do. In those days it was common to have a knife sharpener in the kitchen.

Indeed, Shepherd favoured the kitchen as the scene of the dismemberment. A tiled floor, perhaps even with a drainage point, would make it easy to wash the floor down afterwards, while the otherwise obvious place, a bath, would be an awkward space in which to manoeuvre and try to cut up a corpse, and especially problematic for cleaning if it was not plumbed in, as many baths were not in 1910.

Shepherd could not understand why you would poison someone if you intended to shoot them. He thought perhaps the poison might not have been intended to kill Belle, but merely to make her unconscious so that she could be killed by other sure means, such as shooting or stabbing – though all the organs that were found in the remains were undamaged, so no deep wound could have been inflicted on the chest. Still, as Shepherd put it, Crippen could have 'slipped her a Mickey Finn' which either killed her or made her easier to kill.

If he had then wanted to complete the disposal before decomposition began, he had about twenty-four hours or thirty-six hours before the body would really begin to smell. Perhaps he had then kept the remains that were found in the cellar, either lightly buried or even just lying in the cellar until the smell was noticed and he then went out and bought the quicklime and tried to do a proper job of burial, which still turned out to be inadequate. He might have believed the quicklime would hasten the decomposition of the remains.

Shepherd had no explanation for the presence of the piece of skin bearing the scar. Why leave such a huge clue? Unless Crippen had thought it was commonplace and not specific enough to be identifying. It was not, after all, as Shepherd said, a clue in the way that, say, a tattoo with the words 'I Love Crippen' might have been.

The fragments of clothing were equally intriguing to Shepherd. What story did they tell? Had Belle been wearing the pyjama top when she died? Why not then the pyjama bottoms? Did this, plus the presence of a piece of laced underwear, imply the hope or promise of sexual activity? That would have been an ironic twist to the murder. But they might simply have been items to hand, that Crippen had used to carry body parts or mop up.

Shepherd could have no view on the possible involvement of Ethel, though he found it hard to imagine her being in the house on the night of 2 February, without noticing that a murder had been committed there and a body dismembered. That would have been quite a feat of prior disposal and clearing up, by Crippen.

Even Filson Young seemed to think Ethel could have been a party to the crime. Writing in 1920, he said that 'for obvious reasons' the collusion of an accomplice could not be discussed. He must have meant that such a discussion would be libellous, since Ethel had been acquitted at trial.

I suppose it's possible that she was so anxious to see Belle gone that she would have believed anything, and genuinely did blindly and unquestioningly accept Crippen's assurance that Belle had left him and gone to America without ever knowing the truth. I suppose all that is possible – it just seems unlikely.

She must have known, if not before or during, then soon afterwards. How else to explain her presence in the house, the tangle of lies she told about marriage and her account of when Crippen told her of Belle's death. She was lucky never to have been challenged on these points. She was lucky, I think, not to have faced trial for murder. Perhaps she benefited from shining so white in contrast to Belle. Almost from the start, Belle's character was being called to account while Ethel was being cast in Crippen's shadow.

And just how do you find the state of mind to kill and dismember your wife? And how do you live with it, afterwards? I believe you can see in Crippen some of the psychopathic arrogance that is common to the severest of disordered personalities. That quiet coolness in him, which Young and others find so admirable, suggests a towering superiority and narcissistic self-importance – a small man, inflated in his own imagination – that enabled Crippen to believe he was cleverer than all the others; could succeed where other killers had failed and outwit Belle's friends and the authorities by his ingenious and considered planning.

Think of Crippen showing the two officers around his home, knowing that they were walking where he had killed Belle; showing them the cellar, confident that they were not as clever as him and would never notice what was there. Think of him too, in bed with Ethel, in that house – in that very room, maybe – where the murder was committed. And think of Ethel beside him, and the horrors that might have gone through her mind, depending on what she knew.

Perhaps, like many murderers before him, Crippen had quickly made his psychological escape from the crime, finding a dissociated place of safety in which he could continue to live in the same house as the murder scene and what was left of Belle. The psychological escape would always be fragile and vulnerable to intrusive inquiries or even inconvenient reminders of what had happened.

When his self-protection began to collapse, with Dew's visit, he had no option but to make his real escape. How typical of that obsessively ordered, disordered mind that he should find the time to 'tidy his affairs' first, settling debts, writing letters, even a note for the servant. My guess is that his first instinct was to go alone on his last chance of evading justice. But he must have been torn between protecting Ethel by leaving her behind and protecting her by taking her along. Perhaps, for emotional and practical reasons, he needed to take her and she needed to go.

I am convinced that he would have killed himself at the end of the voyage. That too would be all of a pattern with the crime. There is a good chance he knew or guessed that the police would be waiting at Quebec. He would shortly be confronted with the enormity of what he'd done, and that would be too much to bear. There's the ultimate narcissistic act. Nothing noble in suicide, just a terrible potent mixture of selfishness and despair. Imagine Ethel, left alone to face the questions. He must have kidded himself that he would take all the guilt with him when he drowned.

Cheated of that by Dew's surprise early appearance, Crippen had no choice then but to rebuild his psychological barriers, perhaps almost achieving a delusional position that he really was not guilty, as is suggested by his final letters, when he was still fruitlessly challenging the case against him. No doubt he saw the trial as a test of his wits, his ability to answer the cross-examination and to sit in the dock staying calm, while Belle's flesh was handed round for scrutiny. His composure is extraordinary and pathological.

The evidence shows that, right up to the end, he was still looking for a way out, through suicide, which the prison authorities, even Churchill, implicitly understood and were determined to thwart.

All Crippen has by then is his visits and his letters: Ethel. She is slipping from him and he is fighting to keep her close with his sweet words of doomed romance, imploring her to retrieve his ashes (hadn't he asked the Governor if cremation and the release of his ashes were possible? Perhaps he didn't like to mention it, his hanging. Of course that would never be allowed) and take his name, and reminding her of their better moments together.

They are such powerful expressions of feeling, those letters of love, from such an apparently unexpressive source. Finally, he is stripped bare, his heart exposed, and there, in his own words, is the whole story of those tempered Edwardian passions and the famous tragedy they created.

TWENTY-TWO

November 1910

When I received your letter on Sunday eve I saw that you did not then know the bad news, and I prayed God to help you in the morning when you did learn it. I know what your agony will be, for I know your heart like mine will be broken. God help us indeed to be brave.

That is my constant prayer, now that the last refuge to which we had looked with some hope has fled. I am comforted at least in thinking that throughout all the years of our friendship, never have I passed one unkind word or given one reproachful look to her whom I have loved best in life, to whom I have given myself heart and soul, wholly and entirely, forever.

I think all our necessary points about business are settled, but there are one or two things I want to say. If by any possibility you can have my body, have it cremated and dispose of the ashes as you wish. I know you will be the only one to mourn for me, which I know will please you; but do not, dearest, think I expect you to put on mourning; that, dearest, I leave you to decide on. It may not be well for you to do it in going to Mrs H., and I know that not even the deepest of mourning will be more than a faint indication of your grief.

You have friends to help you. You have at least sufficient means to begin the battle of life not destitute nor helpless.

How shameful to be hounded in our last moments, so sacred to us, by newspaper men, and that they should continue to publish lies!

The Governor was so kind as to let me read yesterday
afternoon your story and my statement. I am, indeed, so
thankful to have been permitted to do so at the last. I
find, though, in some way they have omitted that part
entirely in which I criticised the Crown's evidence on
the scar and on the absence of a navel. My criticism on
this point was very important and I hope you can get it
put in next Sunday.

You will remember that the case for the Crown
depended on the identity which they tried to prove by
means of the so-called scar on the piece of flesh and
skin, 7in. by 6in. Now, on this piece of skin were found
two grooves, one as distinctly marked as the other. The
medical witnesses of the Crown made no assertion with
regard to this piece of skin until they were told that
Belle Elmore had had an operation.

Then they suddenly discovered one groove to be a
scar, although admitting the other groove to be caused
by a fold of the skin, which had been under great
pressure – notwithstanding the undoubted fact that one
groove was absolutely continuous with the other in a
curved line.

The medical witnesses for my defence brought forward
proof – to support their denial that the groove was a
scar – by demonstrating that there were certain
structures present in the so-called scar which could not
be present if the mark had resulted from an operation.
This proof showed so absolutely that the groove was not
the scar of an operation that the Crown could only
squirm out of their false position by bringing forward at
the last moment a theory that the presence of these
certain structures was to be accounted for by the
supposition that the edges of the skin had been turned
under and brought together in sewing up the wound of
the operation – a most unlikely thing to have been done
by skilled surgeons who specially avoid such an
occurrence in abdominal operations.

Another point advanced again at the last moment by the Crown when they saw their case weakening with regard to the so-called scar, was the fact that the groove was widest at its lowest point, just above the pubic bone.

This fact was emphasised by the Crown's witness as being distinctive of a stretched abdominal scar, but for the defence this was denied, the fact being that, anatomically considered, the tendinous or fibrous attachments of the abdomen are actually firmest at their attachments to the pubic bone, and if the groove had been a stretched scar its widest point would have been much higher up. Yet despite the fact having been annulled by my medical witnesses, the judge dwelt upon this point as of advantage for the Crown.

Finally, at Bow-street, the Crown's witness accounted for the entire absence of the navel by stating that it had been cut out during the operation; but when another Crown witness insisted that she had seen the navel on Belle Elmore's abdomen, any reference to this having been cut out was most carefully avoided at the Old Bailey.

Now, it is plain to everyone that if there exists a navel on Belle Elmore's abdomen, the fact that no navel was found on that piece of skin above the so-called scar is proof beyond any possible doubt that the remains found at Hilldrop Crescent were not those of Belle Elmore.

Yet the judge told the jury to accept the statement of the witness that she saw the scar, and to disregard her statement that she saw the navel.

I write these things in the hope that the unreliability of the case brought against me may be understood by thoughtful people.

But I want you not to go to any further trouble or expense in trying to get further evidence, beyond completing what correspondence you have with medical men here and with the hospital in Philadelphia.

I want my dear one to keep for her own use all that

can be realised by the sale of my estate. We can safely leave to the Hand of a just God the production later on, if necessary, of further evidence.

I hope so greatly that you have heard favourably from Mrs H., and that you will be comfortable, and made more cheerful, by the bright sunshine, and be free entirely from the newspaper men and their lying tales.

I feel sure my worries and troubles here will soon be ended, as I shall be tomorrow in God's hands and I have perfect faith He will let my spirit be with you always, and after this Earthly separation is finished will join our souls for ever.

The rest of this letter shall be sacred to you and me.

There will be no time for letters Wednesday morning.

ACKNOWLEDGEMENTS

Many thanks for their various contributions of information, support, advice, encouragement, tolerance and kindness to Bob Smith, Iris Crawford, Roger Palmer and Catherine Masterman, Leslie Andrews, James Patrick Crippen, Donna Logan, Dr Julie English Early, Dr Richard Shepherd, David Gainsborough Roberts, Robin Morgan and Cathy Galvin at the *Sunday Times Magazine*, Georgina Capel of Capel Land, Alan Samson at Orion, Margaret Monger, Sue Benson, Heather Wood, Susanna Lamb at Madame Tussaud's, John Ross (recently retired curator of the Crime Museum at Scotland Yard), the Governor Gareth Davies and staff of HMP Pentonville, Debbie Kirby at the Prison Service Press Office, staff of the Newspaper Library at Colindale, staff of the British Library at St Pancras, staff of the National Archives at Kew, staff at the Family Records Centre, David Ainsworth of the Wandsworth Local History Service at Battersea Library, staff of Camden Local Studies & Archive Centre at Holborn Library, staff of the Islington Local Studies Centre at Finsbury Library, staff of Lewisham Local Studies & Archives at Lewisham Library, staff of Croydon Local Studies & Archive Service at Croydon Central Library, staff of the London Metropolitan Archives, Kiran Rana and staff of Christie's South Kensington, staff of the Law Society information service, Christopher Dean and Jasmine Simeone of the Dorothy L. Sayers Society, Sarah-Jane Stagg of the British Pharmacological Society, Dr Jeffrey Aronson, staff of the Charities Commission, Brian Cathcart, Dorothy Wade, Steve Mason, Anthea Mason, Ashok Prashad, Allan Nazareth, Chris Williams, Tim Lott, Dominic Lloyd, Jamie Bruce, Ryan Emmanuel, Kamella Emmanuel, my patient children ('not now, I'm working') the Felix-Smiths: Mackenzie, Orealla, Kitty and Sitira, and their brilliant mother, my all-seeing, all-doing partner Petal Felix.

BIBLIOGRAPHY

Ackroyd, Peter, *London: the Biography* (Chatto & Windus, 2000)

Alverstone, Right Hon. Viscount, *Recollections of Bar & Bench* (Edward Arnold, 1914)

Baker, Richard Anthony, *Marie Lloyd* (Hale, 1990)

Bentley, Nicolas, *Edwardian Album* (Weidenfeld & Nicolson, 1974)

Birkenhead, the First Earl of, *Famous Trials* (Hutchinson, undated, circa 1938)

Birkenhead – *Frederick Edwin, Earl of Birkenhead* (Butterworth, 1933)

Birkenhead, the Earl of, *Law Life and Letters* (Hodder & Stoughton, 1927)

Bloom, Ursula, *The Girl Who Loved Crippen* (Hutchinson, 1955); *The Mightier Sword* (Robert Hale, 1966)

Bowker, A.E., *A Lifetime with the Law* (W.H. Allen, 1961)

Browne, Douglas G. & Tullett, E.V., *Bernard Spilsbury* (George G. Harrap, 1951)

Browne, Douglas G., *Sir Travers Humphreys* (George G. Harrap, 1960)

Constantine-Quinn, M., *Doctor Crippen* (Duckworth, 1935)

Cullen, Tom, *Crippen the Mild Murderer* (Penguin Books, 1988)

Dew, Walter, *I Caught Crippen* (Blackie & Son, 1938)

Early, Julie English, 'Technology, Modernity & "the Little Man": Crippen's Capture by Wireless' in *Victorian Studies*, Vol. 39 (1996); 'Keeping Ourselves to Ourselves: Violence in the Edwardian Suburb' in *Everyday Violence in Britain, 1850–1950* (Longman, 2000); 'A New Man for a New Century: Dr Crippen and the Principles of Masculinity' in

Disorder in the Court (Macmillan, 1999); 'The Woman Who Knew' (unpublished article)

Eddy, J.P., *Scarlet and Ermine* (William Kimber, 1960)

Ellis, J.C., *Black Fame* (Hutchinson, undated, circa 1929)

Ellis, John, *Diary of a Hangman* (Forum Press, 1996)

Farson, Daniel, *Marie Lloyd and Music Hall* (Tom Stacey, 1972)

Felstead, S.T., *Famous Criminals and their Trials* (George H. Doran, 1926)

Gardiner, Dorothy & Walker, Kathrine Sorley, *Raymond Chandler Speaking* (Hamish Hamilton, 1973)

Gibbs, Philip, *Adventures in Journalism* (William Heinemann, 1923); *The Pageant of the Years* (William Heinemnn, 1946)

Gilbert, Michael, *Doctor Crippen* (Odhams, 1953)

Goodman, Jonathan, *The Crippen File* (Allison & Busby, 1985)

Gordon, Richard, *A Question of Guilt* (Atheneum, 1981)

Grossmith, George & Weedon, *Diary of a Nobody* (J.W. Arrowsmith, 1892)

Herbert, Arthur, *All the Sinners* (John Long, 1931)

Hicks, Seymour, *Not Guilty M'Lord* (Cassell, 1939)

Honri, Peter, *Music Hall Warriors* (Greenwich Exchange, 1997)

Hooks, Nina Warner & Thomas, Gil, *Marshall Hall* (Arthur Barker, 1966)

Humphreys, Sir Travers, *A Book of Trials* (William Heinemann, 1953)

Jackson, Stanley, *The Life and Cases of Mr Justice Humphreys* (Odhams, 1957)

Keating, Peter, *The Haunted Study* (Fontana Press, 1991)

Le Neve, Ethel, *Her Life Story* (Daisy Bank Printing, 1910)

MacNaghten, Sir Melville, *Days of My Years* (Edward Arnold, 1914)

Marjoribanks, Edward, *The Life of Sir Edward Marshall Hall* (Gollancz, 1931)

Meaney, Joseph, *Scribble Street* (Sands, undated, circa 1945)

Moncrieff, A.R. Hope, *Victorian & Edwardian London* (Brockhampton Press, 1999)

Oddie, S. Ingleby, *Inquest* (Hutchinson, 1941)

O'Donnell, Bernard, *The Old Bailey and its Trials* (Clerke & Cockeran, 1950)

Parrish, J.M. & Crossland, John R., *The Fifty Most Amazing Crimes* (Odhams Press, 1936)

Pike, E. Royston, *Human Documents of the Age of the Forsytes* (George Allen & Unwin, 1969)

Priestley, J.B., *The Edwardians* (William Heinemann, 1970)

Pritchett, V.S., *A Cab at the Door* (Chatto & Windus, 1968)

Pope, W. Macqueen, *The Melodies Linger On* (W.H. Allen, 1950)

Roberts, C. Bechefor, *Lord Birkenhead* (Newnes, 1936)

Sims, George R. & others, *Edwardian London* (Village Press, 1990)

Taylor, Bernard & Knight, Stephen, *Perfect Murder* (Grafton Books, 1987)

Taylor, H.A., *Smith of Birkenhead* (Stanley Paul, 1931)

Vance, Leigh, *Doctor Crippen* (Brown, Watson, 1963)

Weinreb, Ben & Hibbert, Christopher, *The London Encyclopaedia* (Macmillan, 1983)

Williams, Emlyn, *Dr Crippen's Diary* (Robson Books, 1987)

Wood, Walter, *Survivors' Tales of Famous Crimes* (Cassell, 1916)

Yellon, Evan, *Surdus in Search of his Hearing* (The Celtic Press, 1906)

Young, Filson, *Trial of H.H. Crippen* (William Hodge, 1920)

NOTES ON SOURCES

ONE

'Circular 1027': HMP Pentonville archives.

'Executions had been . . . ': Author interviews with prison staff.

'Instructions to be observed': HMP Pentonville archives.

'Crippen's Corner . . .': Author interviews with prison staff.

'Crippen never spoke . . .': Ellis, John – *Diary of a Hangman*.

'Ellis was already fed up . . .': ibid.

'Ellis peered in . . .': ibid.

'Preventing suicide . . .': Correspondence in PCom 8/30, Prison Commissioners' files, National Archives.

'When he turned away . . .': Ellis, John – *Diary of a Hangman*.

'Letters addressed to Churchill . . .': Correspondence in PCom 8/30.

'After leaving the chapel . . .': Ellis, John – *Diary of a Hangman*.

'*Record of an Execution*': HMP Pentonville archives.

'Ellis had no time to dwell . . .': Ellis, John – *Diary of a Hangman*.

'Gentlemen . . . I have the honour to submit . . .': PCom 8/30.

'A short inquest . . .': *Daily Mail*, 24 November 1910.

'One Tuesday, in July 1910 . . .': Statement of Clara Martinetti, DPP 1/13, Director of Public Prosecutions: Case Papers, Old Series, National Archives.

TWO

'Clara answered the door . . .': ibid.

'Friends of the charity . . .': *Music Hall and Theatre Review*, 7 April 1910.

'According to Ethel Le Neve . . .': *Lloyd's Weekly News*, 6 November 1910.

'Melinda May was not one . . .': Wood, Walter – *Survivors' Tales of Famous Crimes*

'Melinda May had not planned . . .': ibid.

'Last September Belle had been honoured . . .': *Era*, 2 October 1909.

'In Ethel's version . . .': *Lloyd's Weekly News*, 6 November 1910.

'By her own account . . .': ibid.

'When he next called . . .': Trial evidence of Clara Martinetti in Young, Filson – *Trial of H.H. Crippen*.

'Paul asked what it was . . .': Statement of Paul Martinetti, DPP 1/13.

'By the time they met again . . .': Trial evidence of Clara Martinetti.

'He again saw the Martinettis . . .': ibid.

'Mrs Smythson asked . . .': Trial evidence of Louise Smythson.

'John Nash could not help . . .': Statement of John Nash, DPP 1/13.

'Perhaps poignantly . . .': Statement of Emily Jackson, DPP 1/13.

THREE

According to Crippen . . .': Trial evidence of Chief Inspector Walter Dew.

'In London, some years later . . .': Statement of Maud Burroughs, DPP 1/13.

'Later, when it was a matter . . .': Trial evidence of Theresa Hunn.

'In the old police files . . .': Letter in DPP 1/13.

'A brilliant, chattering bird . . .': Article by Adelene Harrison, *John Bull*, 10 December 1910.

'The year was either 1899 . . .': Trial evidence of Bruce Miller.

'In a statement to Chief Inspector Dew . . .': Statement of Bruce Miller, DPP 1/13.

'That great cesspool . . .': Doyle, Arthur Conan – A *Study in Scarlet*.

'Adelene Harrison says they were like . . .': Article by Adelene Harrison, *Daily Express*, 17 July 1910.

'There was a landlady in Bath . . .': Statement of Antonia Jackson, MEPO 3/148, files of Metropolitan Police, National Archives.

'Then there was the Palace Theatre . . .': Original poster owned by David Gainsborough Roberts.

'*The Era* in a later account . . .': *Era*, 23 July 1910.

'Crippen was followed to Drouet's . . .': *Daily Mail*, 30 July 1910 and Statement of William Long, DPP 1/13.

'The new owner was a character called Eddie Marr . . . : Statement of Eddie Marr, DPP 1/13.

'There had also been at least one death . . .': Cullen, Tom – *Crippen: the Mild Murderer*.

'In 1907 Crippen was cited . . .': *The Times*, 5 November 1907.

' . . . Crippen, who had started on £6 . . .': Statement of Eddie Marr, DPP 1/13.

'Unsurprisingly, when a genuine GP . . .': Statement of John Burroughs, DPP 1/13.

'It was to Maud . . .': Statement of Maud Burroughs, DPP 1/13.

'Following their marriage, Adelene . . .': Article by Adelene Harrison, *Daily Express*, 15 July 1910.

'Peter and Belle moved in . . .': Copy of rental agreement, DPP 1/13.

FOUR

' . . . he entered into a new business arrangement . . .': Statement of Gilbert Rylance, DPP 1/13.

'CURNOW: Well, doctor . . .': Statement of Marion Curnow, DPP 1/13.

'One morning around this time . . .': Statement of Fred Simmonds, DPP 1/13.

'A few weeks later, Crippen . . .': Statement of William Long, DPP 1/13.

'The Martinettis bumped into . . .': Statement of Paul Martinetti, DPP 1/13.

'Paul Martinetti was just about . . .': Obituary of Paul Martinetti, *The Times*, 30 December 1924.

'Here is a review from . . .': Review quoted in The Adelphi
Theatre, 1806–1900, 'A Calendar of Performances' at
www.emich.edu/public/english/adelphi–calendar.

'Paul called on Crippen . . .': Statement of Paul Martinetti,
DPP 1/13.

'When Crippen returned the visit': Statement of Clara
Martinetti, DPP 1/13.

'Ethel sent a series of postcards . . .': Statements of Adine
Brock and Lydia Rose, DPP 1/13.

FIVE

'Ethel would say later . . .': *Lloyd's Weekly News*, 6 November
1910.

'He took the name Le Neave . . .': *Answers*, 27 August 1910.

'He was always plain Neave in later life . . . : Author interview
with Iris Crawford, daughter of Sidney Neave.

'London Bridge! It is the apotheosis . . .': Ryan, P.F. William –
'Going To Business In London', article in *Edwardian
London*, Volume 1.

'A doctor . . .': Sims, George R. – 'Behind the Blinds', article
in *Edwardian London*, Volume 1.

'But J.B. Priestley . . .': Priestley, J.B. – *The Edwardians*.

'There is a press photograph . . .': *Weekly Dispatch*, 7 August
1910.

'Walter agreed with his wife . . .': *Answers*, 27 August 1910.

'Dr Rylance the dentist . . .': *Daily Mail*, 16 July 1910.

'Ethel's landlady . . .': Trial (of Le Neve) evidence of Emily
Jackson.

'. . . had more than twenty teeth removed . . .': *Answers*, 10
September 1910.

'. . . a hardy tomboy child . . .': *Lloyd's Weekly News*, 6
November 1910.

'. . . re-published as a book . . .': Le Neve, Ethel – *Her Life
Story*.

'Ethel later wrote that she was lonely . . .': *Lloyd's Weekly News*, 6 November 1910.

'Ethel at least told her sister Nina . . .': Statement of Adine Brock, DPP 1/13.

'Ethel did not seem to know . . .': Statement of Lydia Rose, DPP 1/13.

'There is, however, evidence of rooms he rented . . .': Statement of William Burch, DPP 1/13.

'The miscarriage . . .': Statement of Emily Jackson, DPP 1/13.

'. . . Ethel started walking out . . .': Statement of John Stonehouse, DPP 1/13.

'. . . William Long . . . became suspicious . . .': Statement of William Long, DPP 1/13.

'One earlier account of the case . . .': Cullen, Tom – *Crippen: the Mild Murderer*.

'. . . never a cross word between them . . .': Letter from Crippen to Le Neve, 22 November 1910.

'Ivy . . . always told her son . . .': Author interview with Roger Palmer.

'. . . there was ample evidence from Nina . . .': Statement of Adine Brock, DPP 1/13.

'. . . I would have wished our little one . . .': Letter from Crippen to Le Neve, 5 November 1910.

'A real piece of work . . .': Author interview with Julie English Early.

SIX

'He had written to Marr . . .': Statement of Eddie Marr, DPP 1/13.

'. . . at least one newspaper reported complaints . . .': *Lloyd's Weekly News*, 17 July 1910.

'Dear Sir, As I have received . . .': Letter in the archives of the Crime Museum at Scotland Yard.

'Rylance said he pestered him for months . . .': Statement of Gilbert Rylance, DPP 1/13.

'. . . Belle was worried about money that Christmas . . .': Article by Adelene Harrison, *John Bull*, 10 December 1910.

'In contrast to the lavish expenditure . . .': ibid.

'Crippen said they always had coffee in the mornings . . .': Trial evidence of H.H. Crippen.

'Some of Belle's other friends . . .': Statement of Melinda May, DPP 1/13.

'In one article, Adelene described . . .': Article by Adelene Harrison, *John Bull*, 10 December 1910

'In another article she had seen . . .': Article by Adelene Harrison, *Daily Express*, 15 July 1910.

'According to one of the Crippens' lodgers . . .': Correspondence in MEPO 2/10996, National Archives.

'He kept the letter Belle had written . . .': Letter in the archives of the Crime Museum at Scotland Yard.

'Later lodgers claimed to have witnessed . . .': Article in *Le Petit Parisien* quoted in *Lloyd's Weekly News*, 7 August 1910.

'In one book about the case . . .': Cullen, Tom – *Crippen: the Mild Murderer*.

'Harrison was a near neighbour during some . . .': Adelene Harrison quoted in Young, Filson – *Trial of H.H. Crippen*.

'The actor-manager Sir Seymour Hicks . . .': Hicks, Seymour – *Not Guilty M'Lord*.

'In January 1909 there was even a servant . . .': Statement of Rhoda Ray, DPP 1/13.

'Rhoda must have been there for the party . . .': Statement of Emily Cowderoy DPP 1/13.

'Moore had been one of the most popular vaudevillians . . .': *Era*, 2 October 1909.

'. . . Coon's Rest' . . .: Statement of Lil Nash, DPP 1/13.

'There was an apocryphal tale . . .': Farson, Daniel – *Marie Lloyd and Music Hall*.

'It was at Pony Moore's home . . .': Statement of Clara Martinetti, DPP 1/13.

'That summer Belle was invited . . .': ibid.

SEVEN

'The chemist who served him . . .': Statement of Charles Hetherington, DPP 1/13.

'... but the British Drug Wholesaler...': Statement of Charles Hill, DPP 1/13.

'... Belle complained of a headache...': Statement of Lil Nash, DPP 1/13.

'On 7 January she had gone...': Statement of Louie Davis, DPP 1/13.

'It must have been about three days after Crippen...': Statements of Lydia Rose and Lydia Rose senior, DPP 1/13.

'According to the full account she wrote down...': Statement of Clara Martinetti, DPP 1/13.

'When she thought it through afterwards...': Wood, Walter – *Survivors' Tales of Famous Crimes*.

'... two shots...': Statements of Lena Lyons and May Pole, DPP 1/13.

'Even the police hadn't bothered with Louisa Glackner...': *Islington Gazette*, 18 July 1910.

'Another neighbour, at 54 Brecknock...': Statement of Frederick Evans, DPP 1/13.

EIGHT

'Ethel usually arrived home from work...': Statements of Emily Jackson, DPP 1/13.

'Smith would claim this as a decisive victory...': Birkenhead – *Frederick Edwin, Earl of Birkenhead*; Birkenhead, the First Earl of – *Famous Trials*.

'Ethel gave another of Mrs Jackson's lodgers...': Statements of Emily Jackson, Caroline Rumbold, Lydia Rose and Lydia Rose Senior, DPP 1/13.

'Naturally, Ethel gave her sister...': Statement of Adine Brock, DPP 1/13.

'Even Ethel's mother...': Statement of Sgt William Hayman, MEPO 3/148.

'Elsmore gave rich descriptions of the clothes...': Statement of Caroline Elsmore, DPP 1/13.

'An actress, Kathleen York...': Statement of Kathleen York, MEPO 3/148.

'Ethel moved out of 80 Constantine Road . . .': Statements of Emily Jackson, DPP 1/13.

'Several neighbours noted all the burning . . .': Statements of Frederick Evans, Elizabeth Burtwell, Elizabeth Cox, DPP 1/13.

'The binmen went to 39 . . .': Statement of William Curtis, DPP 1/13.

'Right at the end of February . . .': Statement of Adine Brock, DPP 1/13.

'Walter was openly annoyed . . .': Statement of Walter Neave, DPP 1/13.

NINE

'Crippen told his partner Dr Rylance . . .': Statement of Gilbert Rylance, DPP 1/13.

'It certainly seems that the Ladies Guild . . .': Statements of Clara Martinetti and Louise Smythson, DPP 1/13; their trial evidence in Young, Filson – *Trial of H.H. Crippen*.

'Mrs Smythson wrote to a trade paper . . .': *Performer*, 21 July 1910.

'In one of the studies of the case . . .': Cullen, Tom – *Crippen: the Mild Murderer*

'The Guild could not let the matter rest . . .': Statement of Clara Martinetti, DPP 1/13; her trial evidence in Young, Filson – *Trial of H.H. Crippen*.

'The ship's name was passed on to a man . . .': Statement of Michael Bernstein, DPP 1/13.

'That week's edition of *Music Hall and Theatre Review* . . .': *Music Hall and Theatre Review*, 1 April 1910.

'One Wednesday afternoon, Crippen walked in . . .': Statement of Melinda May, DPP 1/13.

'Ethel was busy playing house . . .': Statements of Adine Brock and Walter Neave, DPP 1/13.

'She produced Valentine LeCoq . . .': Statement of Valentine LeCoq, DPP 1/13.

'My dear Ma . . .': Ethel's letters to Emily Jackson, DPP 1/13.

'John Nash would later describe . . .': Statement of John Nash, DPP 1/13.

TEN
'It must have been while Dew was busy with Ethel . . .': Statement of Marion Curnow DPP 1/13; her trial evidence in Young, Filson – *The Trial of H.H. Crippen.*
'Gilbert Rylance asked Crippen . . .': Statement of Gilbert Rylance, DPP 1/13.
'The true story was that Crippen had called Long . . .': Statements of William Long, DPP 1/13.
'Ethel had taken a taxi to Tottenham . . .': Statement of Adine Brock, DPP 1/13.
'Mrs Long asked Valentine . . .': Statement of Flora Long, DPP 1/13.
'Sergeant Mitchell did not give evidence at the trial . . .': Statement of Arthur Mitchell, DPP 1/13.

ELEVEN
'Even the undertaker noticed the smell . . .': Statement of Albert Leverton, DPP 1/13.
'Robinson would later be obliged to admit . . .': Statement of Arthur Robinson, DPP 1/13.
'In the ensuing days the suspects would be reported in all corners . . .': *Daily Mail, The Times* and other newspapers, July 1910.

TWELVE
'Dew would later send a long handwritten letter . . .': Dew's letter in MEPO 3/148.
'In the end it was not the lack of baggage . . .': Statement of Henry Kendall, DPP 1/13.
'Why I should have furnished the Officer . . .': Statement of Francis Barclay, DPP 1/13.
'Each ship has on its upper decks . . .': *Daily Mail*, 30 July 1910.

'I thought that she would be wondering what had become of me . . .': *Lloyd's Weekly News*, 13 November 1910.

'Dew believed Crippen really had intended to kill himself . . .': Dew, Walter – *I Caught Crippen*.

'Ethel later recalled . . .': *Lloyd's Weekly News*, 13 November 1910.

THIRTEEN

'Reduced to writing about themselves . . .': *Toronto Daily Star*, 30 July 1910.

'No wonder then that Dew was mobbed . . .': Dew's letter in MEPO 3/148.

'Crippen would later say he had a powder . . .': Crippen's letter to Le Neve, 28 October 1910.

'I had her goddaughter, my little girl, in my arms . . .': *Lloyd's Weekly News*, 28 August 1910.

'The *Daily Mirror* said no more dramatic story . . .': *Daily Mirror*, 30 August 1910.

'Later a hostile crowd of around 500 people . . .': *The Times*, 30 August 1910.

'. . . held with a unique guard of two additional warders . . .': Correspondence files in PCom 8/30.

'*The Times* could not help complaining in a leader . . .': *The Times*, 2 September 1910.

'Arthur Robinson the mortuary keeper . . .': *The Times*, 13 September 1910.

'Halfway through the hearing Ethel went over to Arthur Newton . . .': *The Times*, 10 September 1910.

'The ruse was discovered when the clerk told prison warders . . .': Correspondence files in PCom 8/30.

'Newton must also have been raising funds for himself . . .': *The Times*, 21 September 1910.

'Now that the case was going ahead, the police . . .': Pinkerton's correspondence in DPP 1/13.

'Early on, apparently, Muir became extremely dissatisfied . . .': Felstead, S.T. – *Famous Criminals and Their Trials*.

'Travers Humprhys felt the same way too . . .': Humphreys, Sir Travers – *A Book of Trials*.

'All along, it had been planned to try Crippen and Ethel together . . .': Memo in DPP 1/13.

'Travers Humphreys, in one of his numerous memoirs . . .': Humphreys, Sir Travers – *A Book of Trials*.

'According to Hall's clerk . . .': Bowker, A.E. – *A Lifetime with the Law*.

FOURTEEN

'In 1910 the Central Criminal Court . . .': O'Donnell, Bernard – *The Old Bailey and Its Trials*.

All trial evidence from Young, Filson – *The Trial of H.H. Crippen*.

'Victor and his brother were taken by their father . . .': Pritchett, V.S. – *A Cab at the Door*.

'Many years later, Spilsbury would disclose . . .': Browne, Douglas G. & Tullett, E.V. – *Bernard Spilsbury*.

FIFTEEN

'Crippen's composure was frightening . . .': Oddie, S. Ingleby – *Inquest*.

'The Lord Chief Justice wrote to the Home Secretary . . .': Letter in HO 144/1719/195492, Home Office files, National Archives.

'The governor of Brixton, having lost his prisoner . . .': Correspondence in PCom 8/30.

'. . . the turpitude sweeping through modern British society . . .': *The Times*, 24 October 1910.

'The commentary had not gone far enough . . .': *The Times*, 26 October 1910.

'Richard Muir later said privately . . .': Felstead, S.T. – *Famous Criminals and Their Trials*.

'Once again, Churchill was personally involved . . .': Correspondence files in PCom 8/30.

'Eddy made several trips to Pentonville . . .': Eddy, J.P. – *Scarlet and Ermine*.

'Gibbs's memoirs described how Ethel...': Gibbs, Philip – *Adventures in Journalism*.

'Earlier that week, the governor had withheld...': Correspondence files in PCom 8/30.

'Ethel must have been referring to her...': *Lloyd's Weekly News*, 27 November 1910.

'When she wrote to Crippen a day or so later....': Crippen's letter to Ethel, 31 October 1910.

'Crippen had been told he could write no more than once a day...': Correspondence files in PCom 8/30.

'In an account of the appeal...': *Daily Mail*, 7 November 1910.

SEVENTEEN

'The actor Seymour Hicks...': Hicks, Seymour – *Not Guilty M'Lord*.

'That Monday a man appeared before Cambridge...': *The Times*, 8 November 1910.

'The Lord Chief Justice must have been asked his views...': Correspondence in PCom 8/30.

'With next Wednesday's execution now only...': *The Times*, 18 November 1910.

'When she took it to Pentonville...': Correspondence files in PCom 8/30.

'Newton went to see Crippen that Monday...': *The Times*, 21 June 1911.

EIGHTEEN

'The most eloquent campaigner...': *The Times*, 8 December 1910.

'I started to believe she had never been to Canada at all...': Author interview with Stanley Robert Smith.

'One relative – a niece of Ethel's...': Author interview with Iris Crawford.

'Ivy, the daughter of Nina...': Author interview with Roger Palmer.

'In fact, the files prove that Crippen had asked . . .': Correspondence in PCom 8/30.

'There was some support for this from the Ladies Guild . . .': Wood, Walter – *Survivors' Tales of Famous Crimes*.

'The value of Belle's estate was boosted . . .': *The Times*, 15 September 1911.

'Perhaps because the will had been settled, fresh rumours arose . . .': *Toronto Daily Star*, 15 February and 26 April 1911.

'To the best of my knowledge, this was the last . . .': *Toronto Daily Star*, 27 June 1932.

'John Nash, the husband and manager of Lil Hawthorne . . .': Correspondence files in MEPO 3/148.

NINETEEN

'Iris, who turned eighty in 2005 . . .': Author interview with Iris Crawford.

'Rex kept the letters he exchanged with Ethel . . .': Letters in the collection of David Gainsborough Roberts.

'The Music Hall Ladies Guild enjoyed Gracie Fields's patronage . . .': Archives of the Charity Commission.

'During the night of 8 September 1940 . . .': Archives of Islington Local Studies Centre.

'In 1969 a plan to put a plaque on the wall . . .': *The Times*, 17 November 1969.

TWENTY

'Bob and Nina, Ethel's children . . .': Author interviews with Stanley Robert Smith and Iris Crawford.

TWENTY-ONE

'The writer Raymond Chandler . . .': Gardiner, Dorothy & Walker, Kathrine Sorley – *Raymond Chandler Speaking*.

'J.B. Priestley saw reflected in the case . . .': Priestley, J.B. – *The Edwardians*.

'Likewise Dorothy L. Sayers . . .': *Sunday Times*, 7 October 1934.

'According to Filson Young . . .': Young, Filson – *The Trial of H.H. Crippen*.

'Curiously, Hall's biographers . . .': Hooks, Nina Warner & Thomas, Gil – *Marshall Hall*.

'Travers Humphreys in his memoirs . . .': Humphreys, Sir Travers – *A Book of Trials*.

'Inspector Dew came to believe that Crippen . . .': Dew, Walter – *I Caught Crippen*.

'There has to have been a plan and perhaps the supper . . .': Oddie, S. Ingleby – *Inquest*.

'There was an inherent risk, he said . . .': Author interview with Dr Richard Shepherd.

'This had first been suggested by MacNaghten . . .': MacNaghten, Melville – *Days of My Years*.

INDEX

wireless message reports
  whereabouts of, 156–7, 164
arrested, 176, 177, 178
in Quebec, 178–9
travels from Quebec to
  Liverpool, 179–80
arrives in London, 181
at Bow Street, 181–2, 184, 185
father asks to see, 182–3
in Holloway, 183
murder charge withdrawn,
  184
decision taken not to try with
  HHC, 188–9
named at HHC's trial, 197, 206,
  209, 212, 213
trial, 104–5, 189–90, 218–23
not guilty verdict, 223
possibility of complicity in
  murder, 111, 219, 221, 222,
  283, 294–5, 302–3
visits HHC in Pentonville, 223,
  224, 245
life story ghost-written, 224–6
HHC's letters from Pentonville
  to, 63–4, 226–36, 239–42,
  243–4, 246–7, 249–50, 252,
  306–9
and Lady Somerset, 228–9
photographed in man's suit, 243
and failure of HHC's appeal,
  243
life story begins serialisation,
  243
model in Madame Tussaud's,
  246
prepares article to be published
  in HHC's name, 248
and publication of HHC's
  farewell message, 253
referred to in farewell message,
  254–6
HHC's final telegram to, 6
life after HHC's execution, 111,
  259–69, 270–6, 277–81,
  282–3, 288–9
keeps the past secret from
  family, 283, 286–8
family photograph, 286

death, 281–2
and reasons for BE's murder,
  292, 293–4, 294–5, 298–9
LeCoq, Eudoxie, 120
LeCoq, Valentine, 120, 129, 132,
  134, 135, 140, 141, 143
Leicester Square: Empire, 37
Leukaemia Research Fund, 281
Leverton, Albert, 148, 149, 192
Lewis & Burrows (chemists), 91,
  92
Lewisham, 282
Lincoln, C.C., 29
Liverpool, 3, 4, 156, 157, 158,
  179, 181, 258
Liverpool Street Station, 138
Llangranog, 155
Lloyd, Edward, 224
Lloyd, Marie, 28, 88
Lloyd's Weekly News, 15, 224, 228,
  230, 234, 243, 246, 247, 248,
  252, 253–6, 266
London, 29, 32–3, 35–6, 38–9, 50,
  55, 59, 88, 155, 161, 165,
  174, 181, 187, 260
  cabs in, 97
Munyon's office in, 13, 35–6
music halls in, 17
rush hour, 56–7
scene of BE's murder *see* Hilldrop
  Crescent, No. 39, Camden
suburbia, 57–8
see also names of locations in
  London
London Hospital, 201, 204
London Pavilion, 88
Long, Mrs Flora, 140, 141, 143
Long, William, 37, 43–4, 48–9,
  51, 52, 68, 76, 112, 135–6,
  140, 141, 143–4
Long Acre, 251
Lord Chief Justice *see* Alverstone,
  Lord, Lord Chief Justice
Los Angeles, 32, 35, 112, 118, 252
Los Angeles Examiner, 153
Lulot Street, Highgate, London,
  277
Lyons, Mr, 99–100
Lyons, Mrs Lena, 99–100